The Miami Herald

REPORT

The Miami Herald
REPORT

DEMOCRACY
HELD HOSTAGE

MARTIN MERZER

AND THE STAFF OF *THE MIAMI HERALD*

St. Martin's Press ⚓ New York

www.stmartins.com

ISBN 0-312-28452-7

First Edition: June 2001

10 9 8 7 6 5 4 3 2 1

CONTENTS

(Photographs follow page 154)

ACKNOWLEDGMENTS

This book is the dividend of an enormous investment of energy and expertise, talent and toil by the staff of the *Miami Herald*. The effort began during the run-up to the election of 2000, and it intensified on Election Day, and it expanded and deepened during the thirty-six-day interregnum between the vote and the outcome. And then, when many newspaper staffs packed up and went home, the finest instincts of journalism trumped the natural instincts that demanded rest, and the staff of this newspaper redoubled its labor. It shouldered tedious and rigorous investigations and a statewide, county-by-county ballot review and finally the additional demands of this book.

No finer, more dedicated group of professionals exists anywhere in journalism, and it has been an honor to work with my colleagues at the *Miami Herald* on this project.

That said, some people merit particular gratitude. Among them: *Miami Herald* publisher Alberto Ibargüen, who found and provided the resources that fueled this enterprise and never wavered, even when the expense accounts began arriving; Tony Ridder, chairman of the *Herald's* parent company, Knight Ridder, who made those resources available; Executive Editor Martin Baron, whose steady hand directed the newspaper through truly uncharted waters, whose sharp editing skills and penetrating intellect informs every chapter of this book, and whose friendship is deeply appreciated; and Managing Editor/News Mark Seibel and Assistant Managing Editor/Metro Judy Miller, who day after day commanded the ground troops, dispatching an ever-larger army of reporters and, eventually, accountants, while simultaneously conceiving and editing election, post-election, and non-election stories.

Dozens of reporters provided material for this book, and some deserve special recognition. *Herald* Political Editor Mark Silva contributed the foundation for the political profile of Florida and, often without being asked, generously offered his fine reporting and counsel to other chapters of the book. Elinor J. Brecher, Tyler Bridges, Daniel de Vise, Amy Driscoll, Meg Laughlin, Beth Reinhard, Andrea Robinson, and Jay Weaver also played substantial roles in the reporting and writing of this book, devoting many hours of work to the effort, often on their own time. Their talent and professionalism were crucial to the success of this project.

This book also benefited from the probing labor of the *Herald*'s investigative reporting team led by Judy Miller: Tom Dubocq, Manny Garcia, Ronnie Greene, David Kidwell, and Joseph Tanfani. The *Herald*'s Geoff Dougherty, a computer-assisted reporting expert, developed and refined techniques to process and distill the data generated by the ballot review and other reporting efforts. *Herald* research editor Elisabeth L. Donovan and reporter Daniel A. Grech rate special mention.

Also, mention must be made of the reporters who spent long days reviewing ballot after ballot in the farthest reaches of the state: Steve Bousquet, Paul Brinkley-Rogers, Lesley Clark, Tina Cummings, Anabelle de Gale, Lisa Fuss, Jasmine Kripalani, Larry Lebowitz, Phil Long, Shari Rudavsky, Charles Savage, and Andres Viglucci. Their efforts were expertly coordinated by Lila Arzua.

On a personal note, I owe a great debt of gratitude to my wife, Marion, and daughter, Allie, for their love, encouragement, and understanding during this protracted election project and also through many years of assignments that too often seemed too important to pass up.

I would also like to thank Ronald Goldfarb, who conceived this project and opened the door for all of us; Flint Craig, who represented the *Herald* so ably; and Surie Rudoff, who read the manuscript with a careful eye and a caring, enthusiastic manner. Special thanks must go to Matthew Shear and his staff at St. Martin's Press. Publishing a book on a rapid production schedule is one thing—publishing one that is being constantly updated with new material is quite another, and the people at St. Martin's proved themselves both tolerant and flexible.

Foremost on that list is Joe Cleemann, who once must have done something quite terrible. Otherwise, how could one explain his assignment to not only edit this book but also shepherd it and its writer through the intricacies of such an endeavor, and in record time too? I profoundly appreciate his help and guidance, and now his friendship.

—MARTIN MERZER

Miami, Florida
March 2001

1

"I Came Out of the Ballot Box Totally Confused"

They've hit a rhythm now.

Front. Pause. Back. Pause.

Next.

Front. Pause. Back. Pause.

Next.

Like a dealer at a blackjack table, Miami-Dade County elections worker Jesus Arrechea is ready with another ballot. He holds it up for inspection by a two person team. One is a reporter for the *Miami Herald*; the other, an independent accountant.

Following a now routine pattern, Arrechea shows the ballot front side first. He holds it steady with two hands. Then he flips it over for a look at the more revealing back side. He angles it ever so slightly, and now it leans at a precise position they have arrived at through laborious trial and error, a posture that allows light to catch the smallest of dimples. The team jots notations on special forms. The ballot joins others in a pile.

Already, Arrechea has another ready for inspection.

Scan, flip. Scan, put it down. All performed at high speed, mostly in utter silence. They toil to achieve a balance between speed and accuracy. They cannot relax. They must not be lulled into inattention. It is intense, tedious work.

They are detectives, these three people and dozens more around the state, searching for dimples and hanging chads, pinpricks and clean punches, seeking clues and clarity, striving to divine the intent of thousands of citizens, determined to unravel a mystery unlike any other: Who really collected the most votes in Florida's presidential election of 2000? Would the outcome have been different if the nation's highest court had not terminated a recount?

Pinpricks, dangling tabs of cardboard, pen marks.

The intent was often obvious; it was the execution that so frequently failed. On November 7, 2000, the most basic privilege and responsibility of American citizenship—voting—proved unrewarding for about 174,000 Floridians and countless residents of other states. Thwarted by antiquated technology whose defects had long been recognized by experts but concealed from voters, undermined by indifferent or incompetent election workers, hindered by their own inexperience or haste, many people exercised the right to vote, but their ballots—often cast emphatically, unambiguously, but also imperfectly—did not count. Some other citizens wouldn't even get a chance, despite their best efforts.

Normally this would provoke scant notice or comment. Most Americans gave little thought to their electoral system. They voted and they assumed that their vote was counted. If not, what difference did it really make? Most elections were won by large margins. A lost vote here or there? No big deal.

In fact, few Americans knew it, but most of their electoral systems were designed to accommodate voter apathy rather than voter enthusiasm. These systems were based on the premise that turnout would always be low, margins of difference would always be high, and the exact vote count would never really matter.

"Every time we have an election, we basically say a little prayer," said Sanford Minkoff, county attorney in Florida's Lake County. "It has nothing to do with our partisan interests. No matter who wins or loses, we pray that it's by a very wide margin."

But in 2000, in the presidential election between Republican George W. Bush and Democrat Al Gore, all three assumptions proved mistaken and the nation endured thirty-seven days of unprecedented electoral drama.

Motivated by the closeness of the race, if not the personalities and policies of the candidates, Floridians turned out in relatively high numbers—70 percent of a rapidly growing electorate, and many were rookies or were otherwise inexperienced with the mechanics of democracy.

Voters spoiled ballots in scores of ways that rendered them unreadable by the machines that were supposed to count them. At times you had to admire voters' creativity. Among the many bizarre examples found by the *Herald*: A Tampa resident used clear nail polish to paste a tab back into an absentee ballot. Other voters used tape. Some scrawled unfathomable notes on their ballots. To some extent the arguments made by Republicans during the various recounts were justified: many ballots indicated no clear vote for president.

But at the same time, counting machines discarded thousands of ballots that—upon closer inspection—revealed the intent of voters and their determination to have their voices heard. In Bay County, one voter wrote only this on the bottom of the ballot, and in large letters too: "I forgot my glasses and can not see this please put Bush down for my vote." Unfortunately, no state law required Florida election supervisors to promptly examine ballots like these by hand and attempt to redeem them. If that had occurred, the result of the election might have been different.

The official margin of difference was agonizingly tight in many states, but was especially so in Florida. There, in a state that became vital to both candidates, the presidential election was ultimately decided by an official margin of 537 votes—0.0091 percent of the 5.9 million votes cast.

So the exact vote count proved critically important—and the deficiencies of a system mirrored by most others in the nation were finally exposed.

"There was failure in voter technology and failure in training the voters in technology and a failure in administration," said Ion Sancho, supervisor of elections in Leon County, which includes the state capital, Tallahassee. "The state doesn't spend money telling folks how to vote. This is a state that spends thirty-five million dollars to tell people how to play Lotto."

As a result, the United States, the world's most luminous icon of democracy, suddenly resembled a banana republic. Many thousands of people—citizens who heeded calls to participate in participatory democracy—were disenfranchised. Democrats felt robbed of the presidency. Republicans felt robbed of legitimacy. Millions of Americans worried that the dysfunctional electoral system could strike again, and much closer to home, and they were right.

And the presidency of George W. Bush commenced under a cloud of doubt, shadowed by several tangled questions: What happened in Florida? What went wrong there? Who actually attracted the most votes in the decisive state in the closest presidential election in 124 years?

It is important to note at the outset that this may not be the same as asking who won Florida. That answer is now definitive and firm. Five weeks of political gamesmanship and unrestrained legal combat ended with Bush winning Florida and thus the presidency. The U.S. Supreme Court essentially made that decision, the result was ratified by Congress, and Bush was inaugurated on January 20. History will show that Gore won the popular balloting by 540,000 votes nationwide, but Bush triumphed in the all-important Electoral College, where he held 271 votes, one more than the minimum required for victory. And that was that.

But many people still wondered: If the U.S. Supreme Court had not halted a recount ordered by the Florida Supreme Court and already frantically under way, what would the ballots have shown?

The *Miami Herald,* which overturned a corrupted city election in 1998 and won a Pulitzer Prize for its investigation of voter fraud, sought an answer. It believed that the 2000 electoral debacle in Florida merited intense scrutiny, and it had already embarked on a comprehensive, impartial investigation to determine what went wrong and how the system could be improved.

Among the *Herald*'s findings, explored in detail later in this book:

• Florida election officials knew for decades that punch-card balloting was so obsolete and unreliable that thousands of votes were routinely discarded. Counties that modernized their systems enjoyed marked improvements in accuracy, but most larger counties ignored repeated warnings and retained punch-card systems that often silenced or misled voters.

Typically, around the country, 2 percent of votes in presidential elections don't count—because voters either spoil their ballots somehow or, more rarely, make no selection in that race. In fact, a loss rate of 2 percent had become the unspoken but accepted standard for most election supervisors. That means that in the election of 2000, 2 million American voters would have been disenfranchised—and that would have been considered perfectly satisfactory.

And it was getting worse. In Florida's presidential election of 1992, 2.3 percent of all ballots could not be counted. In 1996 that rose to 2.5 percent. In 2000 it jumped again, this time to 3 percent. About 174,000 ballots were tossed out statewide—largely because residents of twenty-four Florida counties, including many of the most populous, still used punch-card systems. So did other voting districts across America, which were home to one-third of all voters.

"People had no idea that so many people could screw up a ballot," said Jim Smith, a former Florida secretary of state, two-time candidate for governor, and cochairman of a new state task force on electoral reform. "For whatever reason, there has always been an acceptance of a fairly large error rate in elections. But when you have the situation we did, where the error rate all of a sudden exceeded the margin we had in our election, and you have a world with the technology we have, people are saying, 'We are not going to accept that.' "

• Optical scan systems—in which voters make marks in lottery-card-type ovals or connect the ends of arrows—are not foolproof either. The *Herald* found that discard rates were relatively minimal in precincts where electronic machines immediately scan ballots and alert people to spoiled votes so they can correct them. But those precinct scanners are critically important. Optical scan systems in counties that count votes in a central location and thus lack the error-notification feature had discard rates *higher* than those in punch-card counties.

• In an unguarded moment, Republican Florida Secretary of State Katherine Harris, the state's chief elections official, who was reviled by Democrats and praised by Republicans for her actions during the post-election chaos, revealed that she saw herself in Biblical terms. In response to an e-mail from a supporter who praised her as a protector of the unborn, Harris wrote in an e-mail obtained by the *Herald*: "This was the exact conversation and prayer that I shared with my sister last night. I re-read a book about Esther. She has always been the specific character in the Bible that I have admired."

In addition, the examination of e-mail showed that Harris's aides could not contain their partisan zeal, even as they worked in an office that was supposed to be politically neutral.

Months after the election, Harris took her case to network television audiences, but she also absorbed punishing new criticism. After she rejected responsibility for the botched election, the U.S. Civil Rights Commission scolded her for marooning county election supervisors. "I feel as if I'm on this merry-go-round called denial," commissioner Victoria Wilson told Harris during a hearing. "Supervisors were desperate for your help, and you abandoned them. They wanted money, they wanted guidance. Voters ended up having to pay the price."

• Voters in Palm Beach County were 100 times more likely than those elsewhere in South Florida to spoil their ballots by voting for both Al Gore and Pat Buchanan. In addition, that county was the only one in Florida to use a knock-off version of the already questionable Votomatic punch-card machine. Many people had trouble properly casting votes on those cheaper machines.

Theresa LePore, the Palm Beach County election supervisor who authorized use of that machine, who helped design and who ultimately approved the controversial butterfly ballot that cost Gore thousands of votes, required police protection at one time and ended up losing twenty-two pounds as a result of her trial by media.

• Statewide, ballots in majority-black precincts were discarded at a rate three times higher than that in nonblack precincts. In rural Gadsden County, Florida's only predominantly black county, an astonishing 12.4 percent of all ballots were thrown out.

Angered by the policies of Florida Gov. Jeb Bush, brother of the Republican candidate, the NAACP, other black organizations, and union leaders had sponsored massive drives to register new voters. But no one had shown these often elderly, poorly educated citizens how to cast votes, resulting in shocking numbers of ruined ballots.

In addition, voters in large urban counties and some small, poverty-stricken counties—both with relatively large concentrations of minorities—were far more likely than voters in other counties to use the problematic punch-card ballots. And a *Herald* investigation found that thirteen of twenty voting machines in the two Miami-Dade precincts with the highest rates of discarded ballots—both in predominantly black neighborhoods—did not record votes for some candidates during a test vote minutes before the polls opened.

• While legal voters were disenfranchised, thousands of illegal voters from the Florida Panhandle to the Florida Keys were freely given ballots to punch. Most of the illegal ballots came from people who were not registered to vote. Others were cast by people who lived in one county but voted in another or by felons who had lost their right to vote. One vote came from a person declared mentally incompetent by the courts. Another was cast under the name of someone who died thirteen months before Election Day.

"It's very troubling," said Kurt Browning, Pasco County supervisor of elections, whose office identified 65 bad votes. "What this does is chip away at the credibility of our whole elections system."

• Balloting problems were not exclusive to Florida. About 123,000 punch-card ballots were discarded as invalid in Chicago and suburban Cook County, Illinois, far more than in 1996 or 1992. In the past twenty years, punch-card and other voting systems have been questioned in Illinois, Ohio, Massachusetts, New Hampshire, Missouri, Colorado, Pennsylvania, Washington, Indiana, Texas, and elsewhere.

"If you sent lawyers into any jurisdiction in America, no matter what voting system is being used, they could find something to pick apart if it were a close election," said Doug Lewis, executive director of the Election Center, a nonprofit, nonpartisan group in Houston that monitors voter registration and election administration.

Now, as part of its overall investigation, the *Herald* was determined to complete the truncated statewide review of undervotes—ballots on which counting machines could not detect a vote for president. The newspaper did not intend to overturn the election or undermine the legitimacy of George W. Bush's presidency. When the effort began, no one knew if the results would widen, narrow, or reverse Bush's 537-vote margin. The newspaper did intend to fully obey its usual and enduring mandate—to gather information, to publish that information, and to provide readers with the opportunity to assess that information as they saw fit.

In the end, the *Herald* found this:

If all of the undervotes had been inspected by election supervisors as ordered by the Florida Supreme Court, Bush almost certainly would have won anyway. In fact, the examination of all 64,248 ballots in the state showed that—depending on the standard employed to assess the ballots' legitimacy—Bush's official 537-vote lead over Gore might have grown if the recount had not been halted by the U.S. Supreme Court.

But the review sponsored by the *Herald,* its parent company, Knight Ridder, and *USA Today* also produced a fascinating irony: Though Bush supporters insisted on restrictive standards, his final margin would have diminished as the standard grew more restrictive. Under the least restrictive standard, which would count every dimple, pinprick, or hanging chad, Bush's lead would have tripled. Under the most restrictive standard, which would count only cleanly punched ballots, Bush's margin of victory would have disappeared, replaced by a Gore lead of 3 votes. That lead is so tiny that it leaves the outcome in doubt, and that standard was highly unlikely to have been imposed. Among two dozen states that impose standards on manual recounts of undervotes, only one—Indiana—insists on cleanly punched chads.

Think of that as scenario number 1, which re-creates the precise terms of the Florida Supreme Court order. This is the real-world scenario, and under it, the *Herald*'s results from some counties had to be replaced with the results of earlier, official recounts conducted by those counties. The reason? Those counties completed undervote recounts so promptly—in some cases even before the Florida Supreme Court issued its ,rder on December 8—that the justices would have accepted their results. Even if the *Herald*'s results differed, and differ they did in sixty-six of the sixty-seven counties, the official results are the most relevant for those particular counties.

But also consider scenario number 2, which disregards those official recounts and instead adds the unofficial statewide result of the *Herald*'s undervote review to the last official statewide machine count (plus absentee ballots). In other words, if the *Herald*'s undervote reviewers were somehow deputized by the state and their findings were considered definitive in every county, what would have happened?

In that case, which is purely hypothetical, Gore wins Florida if undervotes are tallied under relatively permissive standards, but if more restrictive standards are applied, the Republican strategy actually does pay off and Bush wins the White House.

So who really collected the most votes in Florida's presidential election of 2000?

If one counts every marked undervote in every county as an indication of voter intent, the winner by a small margin is Gore.

But would the outcome of the election have been different if the nation's highest court had not terminated the recount of undervotes?

No.

The *Herald*'s review also raised substantial questions about official recounts conducted by canvassing boards in predominantly Democratic Broward and Palm Beach Counties. The review found that hundreds of ballots were discarded in those counties even though they contained marks that seemed identical to marks on ballots that were officially tallied. Why this happened is not entirely clear, but the factors might have included: (1) frequent objections from partisan observers during the counties' official recounts, (2) the scores of people enlisted by the counties to conduct these recounts without a common standard, (3) inconsistent decisions by canvassing boards, and (4) sheer fatigue.

The *Herald*'s review also identified a void in state law that allowed thousands of salvageable undervotes and overvotes (ballots rejected because they contained more than one presidential vote) to go to waste. These votes could have been recovered if election officials were required to examine all ballots not tabulated by machine. But state law is unclear on the matter, and most county canvassing boards did not conduct such examinations.

Each of those anomalies disenfranchised voters—and may have cost Gore the presidency.

On the other hand, the *Herald*'s analysis showed that if Harris, the secretary of state, had allowed the four counties targeted by Gore to complete their manual recounts before she certified the election results, Bush most likely would have won the presidency outright—without the weeks of indecision and political warfare and without the issue of a statewide recount ever arising.

Gore would have netted no more than 49 votes if a manual recount of Miami-Dade's ballots had been completed, according to the *Herald*'s review. That would have been 140 too few to overcome Bush's lead, even when joined with Gore gains in Volusia, Palm Beach, and Broward Counties—the three other counties where Gore requested manual recounts.

The review took *Herald* reporters and representatives of a national accounting firm, BDO Seidman, LLP, to all sixty-seven counties in Florida.

They worked on the nineteenth floor of the Miami-Dade County Hall on Miami's tumultuous Flagler Street. They worked in a tiny white concrete-block bungalow in the farming and ranching town of Okeechobee. They worked in Room 129 of the dimly lighted county courthouse in Crawfordville, a crossroads town in North Florida's Apalachicola National Forest. They worked in the fortresslike jailhouse of Bay County in Florida's Panhandle. They worked in the grand jury room of the Union County courthouse on Main Street in Lake Butler and were escorted by a trustee from a nearby prison. And they worked in every county in between.

Some examinations required weeks; others just hours. Some election supervisors were accommodating, even hospitable. Union County's Babs Montpetit offered her visitors coffee and Krispy Kreme doughnuts. Others were less welcoming. Palm Beach County's Theresa LePore required ballot reviewers from the *Herald* and other organizations to work from 10:00 A.M. to 3:00 P.M. without a lunch break and with just a single daily bathroom break of five minutes. But all election supervisors were required by law to cooperate. Florida's Sunshine Law projects light into all corners of government, a fact that many people around the world learned during those thirty-seven days in November and December.

In Miami-Dade, the state's most populous county, with 897,000 registered voters, *Herald* reporter Amy Driscoll and BDO Seidman employee John Cox logged eighty hours in the elections office, where worker Jesus Arrechea showed them ballot after ballot. After ballot. After ballot. A total of 10,644 undervotes.

"We became a team, the three of us," Driscoll said. "Together, our eyes became increasingly bloodshot with each passing day, our necks aching more and more as we craned to see each dimple, each pinprick. Cox compared the task to a very long car trip. We stretched our legs, massaged our cramping necks and muscles through waves of sleepiness. It made me appreciate my own power of concentration."

Around the state, the two-person teams found that thousands of undervotes were precisely that—ballots on which people recorded no presidential vote whatsoever. These voters simply passed on that race, choosing instead to cast votes in other contests on the ballot.

But the teams also found many votes for president that were not counted—instances where voter intent seemed clear but the voter proved unable to properly express that intent. Though no common *standard* exists for gauging the legitimacy of such votes, if common *sense* had been applied, thousands of additional votes would have been counted.

The *Herald* found many people partially bored holes in punch-card ballots, leaving behind the now-famous hanging chads. In some cases, chads dangled by nearly microscopic threads of pulp. In others, chads had apparently fallen off more recently because of handling. Those votes were not read by machine originally, but they represented near misses then and would be recorded as votes now in a machine or manual recount.

At one point, during an examination of ballots in Central Florida's Marion County, ballot observers unaffiliated with the *Herald*'s team debated how many corners of a chad were detached on a disputed ballot. Suddenly the chad broke free and fell to the table. A brief silence. Finally, one observer said: "Now it's cleanly punched," and the others laughed.

The *Herald* found that thousands of people circled, underlined, or otherwise mismarked their selections instead of punching through ballots or coloring in the bubbles or arrows of optical scan ballots. Many of these votes would have been salvageable if only someone had seen them in time. In some cases, voters botched their first selection of the day—the presidential race—but improved their skills as they worked through the lengthy ballots.

The *Herald*'s teams also inspected about 110,000 overvotes. These are ballots that were not counted by machine because more than one selection for president was made. Yet here too voter intent could often be deduced.

In rural Wakulla County in Florida's Panhandle, for instance, some voters punched holes for Bush and his running mate, Dick Cheney, or Gore and his running mate, Joe Lieberman. Only one punch was necessary and allowable in each case. The second punch created an overvote and caused vote counting machines to discard these ballots.

"If we were counting by hand, these would have counted," Wakulla County Supervisor of Elections Sherida Crum said.

Around the state, some voters made their selections on punch-card or optical scan ballots and also used the write-in category to repeat the name of their candidates, apparently believing that this represented a more emphatic vote. Machines rejected these ballots as overvotes, but the intent was obvious. In most counties, manual recounts would have added these ballots to the totals.

What propelled the newspaper to these places, what fueled its hunt, was an election between Bush, the Republican governor of Texas, and Gore, the Democratic vice president, that crumbled under the weight of forces most participants could hardly have imagined. Obsolete equipment. Well-intentioned reforms that welcomed a record number of candidates but produced crowded, confusing ballots. Aggressive voter registration drives unaccompanied by voter education projects. The sheer size of the turnout and the limitations of a patchwork electoral system employed only once or twice a year and designed to handle far fewer people.

And yet none of that would have mattered if not for a confluence of unusual circumstances that created the environment for this mess.

For instance, Ralph Nader harvested 97,488 votes in Florida, nearly all of them from fields cultivated by Gore. If 1 of every 150 such voters had switched to Gore, Gore would be president today.

The Elián González affair also cost Gore thousands of votes. Many Cuban-Americans still resented the Clinton administration's handling of that little boy's plight and his eventual return to the Communist regime of Cuba's Fidel Castro.

The controversial, confusing butterfly ballot in Palm Beach County siphoned many additional votes from Gore. Does anyone really believe that the largely Jewish or black populations of that county intended to vote for conservative Reform Party candidate Pat Buchanan at rates far higher than the rest of the state? Even Buchanan didn't believe it. "I came out of the ballot box totally confused," said Lillian Gaines, sixty-seven, of West Palm Beach, one of hundreds of people in Palm Beach County who complained they were led astray by the poorly designed punch-card ballot and might have voted for Buchanan rather than Gore. "I don't know whether I have thrown away my vote and voted for Buchanan. I would drop dead immediately."

All of those forces collided to nearly wreck the presidential election of 2000.

No single villain emerged, no apparent conspiracy bubbled to the surface. At the same time, precious little nobility shimmered into view.

Harris, the secretary of state, appeared to many Democrats as too eager to seek refuge in the strictest possible interpretation of laws that in this case aided her Republican Party and the candidate for whom she had campaigned. On the other hand, the Republican election supervisors in Martin and Seminole Counties seemed flexible indeed, allowing GOP workers to "correct" nearly 3,000 applications for absentee ballots.

Though outnumbered in state and many county governments, Democrats also pressed for every advantage. When it came time to challenge the election, they insisted that every vote must count, but they did not demand a recount of every vote. Instead they sought manual recounts only of undervotes and only in four large, predominantly Democratic counties.

In nearly every corner of the state, in nearly every scene of the story, partisanship reigned supreme and self-interest triumphed over altruism, and this was not new. Many believed it was a brew that was slowly poisoning American democracy.

And yet, and yet, the nation survived. Aside from some pushing and shoving, some yelling and chanting, tranquillity prevailed. No tanks rolled and not a drop of blood spilled. Many feared that America's image was tarnished abroad, but how could that be? The nation was rocked by this discord, but in the end, only briefly. The system, odd and unwieldy, often slow and frustrating, worked.

"We stuck with the rule of law," said Robert P. George, a professor of politics at Princeton. "A lot of people had been worried, when push came to shove, whether the American public would accept a winner of the electoral vote who had lost the popular vote. But no respected leader stood up and said, 'We shouldn't allow a constitutional anachronism to undermine the will of the people.' "

So, a nation more absorbed in cell phones and other new gadgets than in ballot machines and the rusting gears of its electoral system got the sloppy election it deserved. And a citizenry that demands instant everything, and has been conditioned to learn the outcome of elections long before many polls close, was compelled to reach into its shallow reservoir of patience.

At first it seemed exhilarating. At 7:50 P.M. EST on Election Night, the networks projected Gore as the winner of Florida and therefore the likely winner of the presidency.

Jeb Bush, the state's first-time Republican governor, was having dinner with his brother, George W., and their parents in Austin, Texas. For months, Jeb had been telling his brother not to worry about Florida. A loss was unthinkable. It would mean he'd have to face his family around the Thanksgiving dinner table at Kennebunkport, Maine, and acknowledge that his failure had cost his brother the presidency.

Now it looked bad, and Jeb was shaken. Still, he didn't quite believe the networks. It seemed too early for such a definitive prediction. "Please let me confirm it," Jeb told his brother.

His instincts were sound. At 10:00 P.M. EST, the networks began rescinding the calls, and Americans knew something special was happening.

For weeks, analysts had predicted that Florida would play a crucial role in the election. Despite Jeb Bush's efforts, Democrats kept making inroads—and their candidates devoted vast amounts of time to Florida. Gore spent the early morning hours of Election Day in the state, visiting Miami-Dade's South Beach just after midnight and Tampa's voters before dawn. Lieberman appeared in the state so often that he joked he should apply for residency.

Even these main players could not guess how vital the state would turn out to be. As Election Night dragged into the next day, as the suspense multiplied, America stayed up well past its bedtime. At 2:00 A.M. EST, 22 percent of the nation was still watching television, still in search of a new leader.

Finally, at 2:18 A.M. EST, the network proclaimed Bush the winner in Florida and the nation's forty-third president. At 2:30 A.M. EST, Gore called Bush and conceded. Many newspapers, including the *Herald,* started press runs saying that Bush had won, but it was not over yet.

At around 3:30 A.M. EST, with Bush's lead evaporating, Gore retracted the concession and the networks grew nervous again. "That would be something, if the networks managed to blow it twice in one night," NBC's Tom Brokaw said on the air.

Jeb Bush sat hunched over a laptop computer, trying to download the latest returns. He watched incredulously as his brother's lead kept shrinking. Relatives and friends clustered around him. "People were looking at me and saying, 'What's going to happen?' My answer was, 'I'm not sure.'"

At 4:00 A.M. EST, they found out. The networks rescinded their prediction of a Bush victory, and the long post-election ordeal began.

Soon the late night comedians weighed in. The nation was evenly divided, and in Florida the election was a statistical tie. Which was not to say that either candidate generated widespread devotion.

David Letterman of CBS: "So let me see if I have this right. Al Gore isn't our next president, and George W. Bush isn't our next president. Can't we just keep it that way?"

For Gore, it never should have come to this anyway. If he had won his home state of Tennessee or President Bill Clinton's home state of Arkansas, Florida's 25 electoral votes would have been largely meaningless.

But that did not happen, and so the presidential election of 2000 distilled itself into the confines of one state, and revealed what a strange, perplexing place it can be.

2

FLORIDA:
THE STATE OF THE UNION

Looking back, it seemed inevitable.

Florida's twenty-five electoral votes sparkled like jewels, dazzling both parties and entrancing both mainstream presidential candidates. Either Bush or Gore could have won the election without Florida, but each candidate's most promising formula for success—his most achievable bracelet of states—included this treasure. And each had reason to believe he could seize it.

→ When Bush gazed at Florida, he saw a state controlled by Republicans. His brother possessed the keys to the governor's mansion. His party held both houses of the legislature. His supporters were on the brink of capturing a majority in the Cabinet, the six-member executive board that largely runs the state. Republican candidates for president had carried the state all but three times since 1952.

→ When Gore gazed at Florida, he saw a state with a Democratic plurality of registered voters. He saw a state with large concentrations of elderly, black, Hispanic, and Jewish voters, all natural constituents of his party. He saw a state with a strong economy that many people attributed to eight years of a Democratic presidency. He saw a state captured just four years earlier by Bill Clinton.

Yet when independent analysts gazed at the state, they saw trouble for both parties. They knew that the one-time Democratic bastion had been attracting growing numbers of Republicans and independents. And they knew that many old-line Democrats— once known locally as "yellow-dog Democrats" because they'd sooner vote for a dog than a Republican—were now crossing party lines in rebellion against the liberalism of their party.

That so many experts could see things so differently and that 6 million Florida voters could end up so equally split is explained in large part by one sweeping factor: rapid and intense growth has transformed the place into a rainbow of ages, races, and religions, with no dominant group. It is a microcosm of what the rest of the nation soon will become, as America itself grows more diverse, more old—and more crowded. Florida's growth has been simply phenomenal. Now the nation's fourth most populous state, it exploded from 2.7 million people in 1950 to 15.9 million by Election Day 2000. In the last decade alone, its population swelled by 23 percent.

This place of perpetual summer and low taxes still harbors many deep-rooted, conservative Floridians who proudly call themselves "crackers." But it also serves as a refuge for immigrants who have fled the oppression of Fidel Castro's Cuba and the economic tyrannies of other lands, and they spice the brew with their energy and their customs. And it remains a haven for retirees, who contribute their IRA accounts, their own cultural preferences, and, of course, the "early bird" dinner special.

Nearly one of every five residents is over sixty-five years old. More than 15 percent are black, another 17 percent Hispanic. More than half the residents of Miami-Dade County, the state's most populous, speak a language other than English at home, most often Spanish but also Creole, Jamaican Patois, French, Portuguese, Chinese, and many others.

Florida simmers with tension, more a cauldron of special interests than a melting pot of shared interests. Racial disparities. Immigration disputes. Crowded classrooms. Social Security concerns. Environmental and growth issues. Even vestiges of Cold War anxieties. Florida has it all. "You've got racial and ethnic diversity and age diversity across Florida," said Susan MacManus, a political scientist at the University of South Florida. "It's the most diverse, most competitive big state in the country."

The result: a state in which partisan advantage shifts from election to election, and where close elections are becoming more common. It is this deeply split personality that punched the hold button on the presidential election of 2000 and thrust the nation into five weeks of suspended animation.

Taken as a whole, Florida is a geographically southern but demographically homogenized state that was desperately needed by two technically southern but completely homogenized candidates. At the same time, when examined more closely, it is a state with distinct regions and affinities, and few bridges between them. This contributes to a sense that Florida really is two—or even three or more—very different states. It is often said that the farther north you go in Florida, the more south you get.

Conservative, laid-back residents of North Florida's Panhandle, a hilly and still forested land of small towns, glistening beaches, and bustling military bases, often seem offended by those loud, passionate, distinctly urban residents of crowded South Florida, which encompasses the counties of Miami-Dade, Broward, and Palm Beach, and the Florida Keys. The cities of Miami, Fort Lauderdale, and West Palm Beach dominate this region.

Residents of North Florida are mostly white and mostly rural. The place is more evocative of the Old South than the new Sunbelt, the Georgia and Alabama borders blurred by the soft accents of the old-timers. South Florida is anything but rural, and the accents are anything but soft. To North Floridians, the people of South Florida seem almost undisciplined. "They have no loyalty to the state of Florida," claimed James Witt, a professor of government at the University of West Florida in the Panhandle. "They don't understand the [connection] we have to the military. People in the military come back and retire here. You've got more stability in this area. It's not like Miami, where everything is a hassle all the time."

At Mr. P's sandwich shop in downtown Pensacola, waitresses joke that they live in L.A.—Lower Alabama. It is only a few miles to the Alabama border from anywhere in the western Panhandle, but more than five hundred miles and a cultural light-year to Miami. At one point during the post-election ordeal, Democratic lawyers swooped into Pensacola to challenge overseas military ballots everyone suspected would favor Bush. The locals did not cotton to that. "If you guys are here to try to steal an election, you'll have a lot more luck in Palm Beach County," local Republican Dale Perkins told them. When he pronounced those last three words, he emphasized every syllable. Palm. Beach. Coun. Tee.

But fewer than one-fifth of all Floridians live in the northern tier of counties. Most prefer to occupy the coastal cities and suburbs spread like beads of a necklace around South and Central Florida. And South Florida, blessed by its proximity to the trade centers of Latin America, has become the state's economic engine, along with Central Florida's bustling tourism industry. South Floridians often think of North Floridians as museum pieces—remnants of an age long past—when they bother to think of them at all. "There's no respect for North Florida from South Florida," said Ron Book, a lobbyist from Miami. "They can't get themselves north of Orlando. I think people ought to get out in their automobiles and travel this state, all sixty-seven counties."

What a panorama they would see, what contrasts they would draw, and what a difference all of this would represent from the early days, when Florida was little more than a handful of rustic settlements scattered along a wagon trail that reached from the Atlantic Ocean across the northern third of a vast and mostly uninhabited frontier. Woodsmen made turpentine from the tar of pine trees. Early entrepreneurs experimented with pineapple plantations in remote, tropical reaches of the peninsula. Hurricanes defeated early attempts to carve communities at the southern end of the untamed state. At the beginning of the twentieth century, railroads were still under construction down the Atlantic and Gulf Coasts, finally opening ports at Miami and Tampa. The last rail link, connecting Homestead with the southernmost tip of Florida at Key West, was not even begun until 1905.

Florida's extraordinary growth was engineered by politicians and developers who bridged rivers and filled in swampland and bays, and rolled out a come-one, come-all invitation. It was fueled by opportunity, that quintessentially American pioneer spirit—and it was turbocharged by a steadfast aversion to taxes: Florida's Constitution has barred a personal income tax since the 1920s, and the state imposes low property taxes on homeowners. Florida's 59 million annual tourists pay much of the state's bills, and Floridians thank them for it. But it took more than low taxes and cheap land to lure new Floridians. It took air-conditioning—like the railroads before it, one of the single greatest catalysts of Florida's rapid expansion.

The northern corridor that stretches from Jacksonville to Pensacola remains an unofficial preserve of the old way, harboring some of Florida's least settled land. State Road 90 courses through picturesque towns such as Monticello, where antebellum mansions have been restored, and Madison, a center of tobacco production. In this land of live oak and pine, Tallahassee was the way station for settlers and Indians before them, the territorial and then the state capital.

And for much of its history, Tallahassee was a stronghold of the Democrats, the dominant party in government until the mid-

1990s. The state's political foundation had been laid by those "yellow-dog Democrats" of old North Florida, "pork-chop" politicians who wielded an inordinate amount of power well into the 1950s. This was a conservative strain of Democrats, yet some were open to the social change that swept the South after World War II. Florida relinquished racial segregation more easily than its neighboring southern states, though integration drove wedges through the party.

In the 1950s, Democratic Gov. LeRoy Collins helped smooth the state's path toward school integration, at considerable cost to his own political future. Collins became the first director of President Lyndon Johnson's Community Relations Service, an agency established under the Civil Rights Act of 1964. But back home, his advocacy of equal rights cost him election to the U.S. Senate in 1968. He won his party's nomination, but lost the race. George Wallace, the Alabama governor and archetypal segregationist of the South, carried 28.5 percent of Florida's presidential vote that year. Republican Richard Nixon prevailed with just 40 percent in a three-way race; Hubert Humphrey won 31 percent.

Still, the schools were not desegregated until the 1970s. And not until Florida abandoned a hierarchy that assured white rule—electing state representatives and state senators in groups instead of individually—were minorities able to gain access to the Legislature. With the drawing of smaller, single-member legislative districts in the early 1980s, blacks and Hispanics started winning proportional seats in the Legislature. But even by 2000, severely gerrymandered districts were required to ensure election of black representatives to Congress. One such district roamed oddly from Jacksonville to Orlando to amass black precincts.

By the last quarter of the twentieth century, the Democratic Party's hegemony in Florida politics had begun to erode. In 1970 Democrats held a 114 to 53 advantage in the two houses of the Legislature, but slippage was already evident. In 1980 the edge fell to 108 to 52. In 1990 it was 97 to 63. In 1994 the State Senate turned Republican; in 1996, the House. That year, Republicans grabbed an 84 to 76 advantage and Florida became the first southern state with both legislative houses controlled by the GOP since Reconstruction. In 2001 Republicans hold a commanding 103 to 57 advantage in the Legislature.

When Jeb Bush was elected Florida governor in 1998, he was only the third Republican to achieve that office in the century. Like most modern Floridians, Bush is a transplant, having moved from Texas in 1980 to help his father, George Bush, then campaigning as the vice presidential candidate on Ronald Reagan's ticket. He settled in the Miami area and made his fortune in real estate development.

The two Republican governors before Bush were ousted after only one term in office, but Bush won his first term with a 10-percentage-point advantage over his Democratic rival, and he remains popular in opinion polling. In 2000, with Bush's popularity running high and the Legislature firmly in the grip of Republicans, voters also handed a majority of Cabinet seats to the GOP, giving the party across-the-board control of the state for the first time. It was a stunning turnaround.

Other factors are also at work to change the shape and voice of the state.

Long before 2000, Cuban-American immigrants emerged as the dominant political force in Miami-Dade County, their anti-Castro politics linked to the Republican Party since President John Kennedy's perceived betrayal of the exiles who invaded Cuba at the Bay of Pigs. Castro's takeover of Cuba had triggered an influx of refugees to South Florida in the 1960s, and that was followed by another mass exodus from Mariel, Cuba, in 1980. Mel Martinez, an attorney and chairman of the Orange County Commission, tapped by George W. Bush as secretary of Housing and Urban Development, came to Florida as a young refugee aboard one of the "Peter Pan" flights that rushed children out of Cuba. After the 1989 death of Alabama-born Claude Pepper—the Democratic Party's mainstay in South Florida—he was replaced in Congress by a Cuban-born Republican, Rep. Ileana Ros-Lehtinen of Miami, whose enduring popularity made her a powerful asset during the campaigns of both Jeb and George W. Bush.

Nevertheless, in another example of the state's complexity, the overall region of South Florida served as the Democratic Party's statewide base. Before his death, Pepper, a Dixie-tongued orator who championed causes dear to the aging newcomers, had become the exemplar of the new Florida Democrat. His own career had spanned much of Florida's twentieth century. Starting as a legislator in North Florida, he had won election to the U.S. Senate in 1936. From 1963 to 1989, he served in the House from South Florida, emerging as an advocate of social services for the elderly.

Indeed, a steady migration of Democratic retirees from the Northeast, people of modest means who left Brooklyn for Broward County, Manhattan for Miami Beach, added a liberal balance to Florida's old-line Democrats. Soon the state reported the largest proportion of senior citizens in the nation. Service industries grew to support them, and they needed workers (as did the tourism industry), so many of the children and grandchildren of these older people joined the parade south. South Florida's population boomed, and the Democratic Party's power center shifted toward it. Retirees have settled in condominiums so densely crowded that entire voting precincts are contained within single high-rises, precincts so reliably Democratic they might as well be called yellow-dog.

Miami-Dade, Broward, and Palm Beach Counties now account for nearly one third of the state's Democratic voters. The margins of victory that Democratic candidates claimed in Broward alone—often two to one—are sometimes sufficient to support their election statewide. Broward's Democrats helped then-Gov. Lawton Chiles, a self-styled cracker and among the last of the old

Florida Democrats, fend off Jeb Bush's first gubernatorial bid in 1994. That was the year Bush's older brother, George W., was first elected governor of Texas. The turn of events, one Bush's election and the other's defeat, served as one predictor for which of the former president's sons would be poised to seek the presidency in 2000.

By the day of that disputed election, Democrats still outnumbered Republicans in Florida by 3.7 million to 3.4 million. But neither party held an outright majority in voter registration, 8.5 million all told. Voters who registered independently of either party—about 15 percent of the total—had denied Democrats majority status for nearly a decade. And these party-free voters have become a pivotal force in most statewide elections. Sometimes they support Democrats. More often they support Republicans.

How did the Sunshine State's power structure turn so Republican?

The same low-tax lure that nourished the retirement mecca of South Florida—the state remains one of a handful without a personal income tax—is now drawing Republican retirees from the Midwest, and they have settled on the Gulf Coast. Virtually all local offices in that part of the state are held by Republicans. In Sarasota, for instance, conservative and affluent retirees who followed Interstate 75 down from Michigan and Ohio helped elect Republicans to forty-one of the county's forty-two elected offices. "Only the tax collector is a Democrat, and that's an appropriate job," said Tramm Hudson, a banker and veteran GOP activist from the dependably Republican county. He seemed amused by the notion.

Around the military bases of the western Panhandle, including the massive Eglin Air Force Base near Pensacola, Republican retirees are responsible for the political takeover of a region long known as the Redneck Riviera. Even W. D. Childers, a onetime

State Senate president and the "banty rooster" of Pensacola, fore-saw the turning tide, switching parties during the final years of his three decades in office.

The arrival of the Cuban and other Latin American refugees—one in ten Florida voters was Hispanic by 2000—also benefited the Republicans. (At the same time, however, newly arriving vot-ers of Puerto Rican descent, drawn by Orlando's thriving service industry, have turned Orange County narrowly Democratic.)

And an influx of younger workers throughout the state, set-tling in suburbs around Florida's urban centers—Miami Springs near Miami, Weston near Fort Lauderdale, and similar areas around Tampa, Orlando, and Jacksonville—form a fertile field for the Republican Party's perennial seedlings: promises of prosperity and low taxation.

"More freedom, less taxes" was the streamlined and successful campaign appeal of Connie Mack in 1988. The Republican grand-son of a baseball legend was elected to the U.S. Senate on little more than a name and a promise to keep government out of peo-ple's lives. Indeed, the Legislature had not raised state taxes since 1994, when the Republican takeover of the State Senate effectively blocked Chiles's attempts to boost spending and overhaul a tax structure that, in 2001, still depends largely on the 6 percent state sales tax. That tax, responsible for three-quarters of the state's tax revenue, is largely paid by the tourists who flow through Central Florida's theme parks and South Florida's cruise-ship ports.

To a large extent, a Libertarian philosophy pervades politics in Florida—most residents, for instance, are pro-choice on abortion. In 1989 Florida's Supreme Court relied upon a unique Privacy Amendment in Florida's Constitution to rule that the state could not limit a woman's right to choose abortion. That prevented the Republican-run Legislature, and Bush, from enforcing new re-strictions on abortion. Courts in Florida also overturned legisla-tive attempts to require parental consent for, or even notification by, teenagers seeking abortions, and reversed a ban on "partial-birth" abortions.

While legislative district after legislative district has turned Republican—fifteen of Florida's twenty-three congressional seats are held by Republicans in 2001—voters maintain a sense of independence. One-fifth of Florida's voters tell pollsters they have no interest in either political party, and many Democrats and Republicans are easily peeled from their party if the opposition offers a stronger candidate. At the same time Republican Mack was elected and reelected to the Senate, former Gov. Bob Graham, a Democrat from Miami Lakes, maintained a Senate seat he first won in 1986. When Mack retired in 2000, voters replaced him with a Democrat, Bill Nelson, a former congressman from Melbourne and the "Space Coast" who had flown aboard the space shuttle.

This swing-voting tendency of Florida's independent electorate is most evident in the central corridor of Florida, which stretches from Tampa on the Gulf Coast to Daytona Beach on the Atlantic. The main artery of that fast-growing region, Interstate 4, also courses through the tourist mecca of Orlando, representing the modern-day version of the wagon trail that once connected the modest towns of northern Florida.

In presidential elections, the conservative instincts of Florida's voters prevail. Yet the most recent margins of victory are not overwhelming. George Bush defeated Bill Clinton by only 100,000 votes in 1992, and Clinton beat Republican Bob Dole in 1996 by 300,000 votes. (Chiles's defeat of Jeb Bush in 1994 was the closest governor's race of all time, only 64,000 votes between them.)

So, both parties knew they had a chance in 2000. While Bush was focused on a divisive fight within his own party with Arizona Sen. John McCain, Gore focused early on winning Florida—despite the entrenched organization of Bush's brother. Gore's allies reasoned that a thriving economy, his stance on public education, his devotion to preserving Social Security, his desire to expand Medicare, and his pro-choice politics gave him an edge among older voters, minorities, and women.

Much of the campaign's television war—in a state dominated by eleven media markets—focused on the fight over Social Security and Medicare, Bush and Gore casting each other as threats to the elderly. The Democrats also attempted to capitalize on the state's stressed environment, placing ads that portrayed Texas oilman Bush as a threat to offshore waters and the Everglades. From the start, Bush ran strong among men, Gore among women.

Although opinion polls reflected a dead heat during the final months of the campaign, no one could predict the tight vote margin that held this contest in limbo for thirty-six days after Election Day. Both Bush and Gore campaigned most intensely throughout the I-4 corridor, with clear results for both candidates: Gore narrowly carried Orange County, home of Orlando's tourist attractions and booming suburbs filled with younger working couples, a normally Republican fortress. His opponent carried Hillsborough, home of Tampa's more Democratic-leaning voters. Bush's success in that hard-fought area was a portent—Hillsborough has voted as Florida has in every presidential race since 1964.

In an election that close, almost any factor could have provided the winning edge: Bush's successful appeal to surburbanites in Tampa was as significant as the Cuban-American community's anger at Clinton over the handling of Elián González, a development that deprived Gore of many votes Clinton secured across Hispanic districts in 1996. Bush also ran stronger among elderly voters than Democrats had expected. Gore's appeal for Medicare coverage of prescription drugs failed to secure Florida's sixty-five-and-older vote for him.

On the other hand, an exceptionally strong turnout by women and black voters buoyed Gore. According to exit polls, about 15 percent of Florida's presidential vote was cast by black voters—

compared with only 10 percent in the last presidential election. Many black voters flocked to the polls in bitter response to Jeb Bush's efforts to dismantle affirmative action. The extraordinary get-out-the-vote drive mounted by the Democratic Party and black leaders not only produced those numbers but also inflamed emotions after the election. Later, an accounting of black votes lost in Florida's flawed ballot count and allegations that some black voters were intimidated spawned an investigation by the U.S. Commission on Civil Rights. Suddenly the new century's first election in Florida was being debated in terms reminiscent of the Civil Rights movement of the 1960s. This new Florida confronted the old Florida face to face in the state's closest race ever.

But back at the start, with Election Day approaching, Florida's balloting supervisors girded for action. Pollsters said the national race was too close to call, itself a first in recent memory. Analysts said Florida would be vital to each side, another first. The supervisors noted that requests for absentee ballots had been unusually vigorous.

They knew turnout would be heavy.

They thought they were ready.

They were not.

3

MADAME BUTTERFLY

The story of Theresa LePore's recent life resides in two plastic mail bins at the election supervisor's office in West Palm Beach. She was just an ordinary person in a nondescript job, but she helped design, finally approved, and ultimately was responsible for Palm Beach County's infamous and consequential butterfly ballot. She was caught in the maelstrom, and now she is part of history. "If you want to be happy, look in that one," LePore says, indicating the box marked "good comments and ideas." She averts her blue-green eyes from the box marked "complaints," as if it contains snakes. "Look there," she says, "if you want to get depressed."

Then she disappears into her private office, where her teddy bears emerge from drifts of paperwork, like survivors of an avalanche. For two months LePore became the target of rage and ridicule, of eighteen lawsuits and countless threats of recall, of endless insulting jokes. She was demonized as "Madame Butterfly." She ended up with police protection. She lost twenty-two pounds.

From the "good comments" bin, these words of support from

the Rev. Charles Klassen at the First Baptist Church of Louisburg, Kansas: "I believe that your pain in this can far exceed the pain of our Vice President. . . . I am here to tell you that . . . George Bush is President-elect today because God willed it, not because of a ballot."

In the other bin, most complaints are businesslike critiques of the voting process, but a few, like the letter accompanied by tiny paper tabs from "The Chad Pyles Family, 2000 Dimple Way, Orlando," hiss with sarcasm. And there are worse ones. Someone crossed out the "Hey there" and "Hi there" in a Mickey Mouse Christmas card, leaving "Ho there" above a handwritten note: "You lovin [sic] Jeb Bush crooked bitch."

Six weeks after the election, LePore appeared on ABC's *Good Morning America,* looking fragile and exhausted. Her eyes have a natural downward cast at the corners, shading even her smiles with melancholy. But she wasn't smiling when host Diane Sawyer asked her to describe her life since the election in a single word. "Hell," said Theresa LePore.

Throughout the state of Florida, LePore and other election supervisors wrestled with a vexing new complication during the run-up to the 2000 election—a problem caused by an obscure, well-meaning tax collector in Sarasota. Ten presidential candidates had to be squeezed onto the ballot, more than twice as many as in 1996. It is a statistical near-certainty that LePore's solution to this problem altered the outcome of the 2000 election. She is a Democrat, but her facing-page butterfly ballot confused thousands of people and apparently cost Gore thousands of votes, cracking open the White House door just enough for Bush to slip through. A *Herald* analysis found that voters in Palm Beach County were 100 times more likely than those elsewhere in South Florida to spoil their ballots by picking both Gore and Reform Party candidate Pat Buchanan. The two candidates' names appeared across from each other on LePore's unconventional presidential ballot, and in her heavily Democratic county, more than 5,000 voters punched holes for both of them. In addition, Buchanan rolled up more than 3,000 votes in Palm Beach County, far more than he received in any other county in Florida. Afterward, Buchanan conceded that many of those people undoubtedly voted for him by mistake.

Even before that debacle became evident, LePore and other election supervisors already had to face the usual chaos that accompanies a big contest like the 2000 election. Preparing for an election is a lot like planning a wedding: months of work go into an event that lasts just hours. For Election Day, an entire infrastructure is constructed from scratch. Machines must be prepared, programmed, delivered, installed, and tested. Workers must be recruited and trained. Ballots must be designed, customized for each precinct, printed, and distributed.

Further complicating matters, much of the work must be accomplished late in the game. People can register to vote until twenty-nine days before the election. Primary runoffs are held just one month earlier. Many polling places will not accept election machinery until the day before the election itself. "It's all very difficult," said Jane Carroll, veteran supervisor of elections in Fort Lauderdale and the rest of Broward County, who retired shortly after the 2000 election. "It takes a lot of organization." In the two months before the October 10 registration deadline, 31,178 people joined the voter rolls in Broward, a 27 percent increase over the number of last-minute new voters in 1996.

The experiences of LePore and her staff in Palm Beach County are also instructive. She leads a $2.7 million operation with twenty-eight employees, overseeing 531 precincts and an estimated 655,000 voters. One top aide, Tony Enos, has worked for the supervisor's office since 1982. As voting systems manager, he runs the 18,000-square-foot Riviera Beach warehouse where the county stores its 5,200 punch-card machines. Enos and others spend much of the year cleaning machines, lubricating parts, repairing torn side curtains. "Some come back pretty banged up [from a day of voting]," he said. "We have four or five that we scavenge for parts." And more than five hundred ballot collection boxes must be maintained. Before the 2000 election, Enos's staff painted every one.

A week before the election, they began delivering the fourteen-pound machines and ballot boxes to schools, churches, fire stations, and other polling places. Driving three twenty-four-foot moving trucks, they started at the far ends of the county—Jupiter in the north, Boca Raton in the south—and worked back toward West Palm Beach, so that if problems surfaced in distant places, they would have time to deal with them. But some facility managers wouldn't take the equipment until just before Election Day because they didn't want the responsibility, and that added another layer of complexity. "It's a mind-boggling task," LePore said.

At the same time, election supervisors throughout the state wrestled with a perennial problem—the hiring and training of temporary poll workers. LePore needed four thousand, and many of them were brand-new, hired to replace those fired after the March 2000 local election. "The good, the bad, and the ugly," LePore said, referring to those she'd let go. "All around the state we were joking—and I don't know what was going on—that all the workers took stupid pills. The dumbest mistakes.

"One clerk was nowhere to be found and hadn't turned her ballots in at ten P.M. We were getting ready to call the sheriff in. We called the house, and her husband didn't know. She and the person riding with her—because they're not supposed to ride alone—decided to stop and visit her daughter and lost track of time. She came in crying a week later and couldn't understand why I fired her." Soon, during the presidential election, this temporary, inexperienced, and—and in some cases—incompetent statewide workforce would prove unable to stem a flood of illegal voters.

But now, with Election Day fast approaching, more complications piled up. "Two days before Election Day, you're bombarded with phone calls," said Jackie Winchester, LePore's predecessor and longtime mentor. "The press realizes they have all these different races to cover, so they put all these reporters on them who have never covered an election and don't know anything, and they're trying to get clued in. A tremendous amount of time is taken up with that, when you're really busy trying to put out any fires. And the absentee ballots in the last few days are a huge hassle because they pour in by the thousands and every one has to be entered in the computer before it can be opened. They're the tail that wags the dog."

Winchester ran elections in Palm Beach County for twenty-three years. She says that every time, just before the polls opened, "I always prayed." Because one never knows what's going to happen. A precinct clerk might arbitrarily decide that an untrained, partisan poll watcher can work the registration checkoff table. Computers might crash. Bordering precincts might get voting machines meant for each other. An always unknown number of voters must be guided to correct voting stations, ballot booths, and collection boxes and then to the exits to make room for the next wave of voters.

All of this for just twelve hours, after which the entire system is demolished. All of this under the general supervision of state law and for a citizenry ever less tolerant of delay and inefficiency. "It's a sad commentary when you are electing a president and you can't be bothered to stand in line," Carroll said. "Some of these same people stand in line for the early-bird special."

Enter the new complication, inspired by that tax collector from Sarasota County, a reformer named Barbara Ford-Coates, another unintentional draftee in the ranks of those who inadvertently changed the course of the 2000 election. In 1997, then-Gov. Lawton Chiles appointed her one of thirty-seven members of the Constitution Revision Commission, which meets every twenty years to propose changes to the state constitution. Ford-Coates championed an election reform package that, among many other things, made it easier for obscure presidential candidates to get on the ballot. "It was a real back-burner issue," said Jon Mills, dean of the University of Florida's law school and another member of the commission.

At the time, Florida had some of the toughest rules in the nation for recognizing minor parties. Common Cause and many newspapers supported the reform, which was endorsed by voters in 1998. The result: The state ballot, which listed four presidential hopefuls in 1996, listed ten in 2000. No state offered more candidates, and only three—Rhode Island, Vermont, and Washington—offered as many. Among the hopefuls in Florida were Howard Phillips, who received 1,371 votes for his no-income-tax Constitution Party, and Monica Moorehead, who gained 1,804 votes for the socialistic Workers World Party. Another candidate logged 622 votes statewide. Another, just 562.

Yet by law, all had to be on the ballot. And election supervisors had to figure out how to accommodate them without confusing voters. Some supervisors reduced the size of the print, squeezing all ten candidates (and their ten running mates) onto one page. Some broke the list into two parts and printed it on two pages. And one, LePore, found a more creative solution. But no answer seemed perfect, and the large number of presidential candidates—many of them unfamiliar—baffled many voters. More than 110,000 Floridians selected more than one presidential candidate, instantly disqualifying their vote in that race.

Attempting to deal with the unprecedented number of candidates, Duval County Supervisor of Elections John Stafford, whose jurisdiction includes Jacksonville, divided the presidential lineup into two pages. The bottom of the first page said, "Turn page for continued list of candidates for president and vice president." Voters were also instructed to "Vote appropriate pages." But the sample ballot published two days earlier in the area's largest newspaper listed all presidential candidates on a single page and told voters to "Vote all pages." State law requires that "sample ballots shall be in the form of the official ballot as it will appear at that polling place on Election Day."

So, if voters went to the polls with the understanding that they should vote on every page—because the long-standing instructions had become common knowledge or because they were widely distributed on the sample ballot—their plans conflicted with the ballot actually on the punch-card machines. Some might have turned the first presidential page and found another page filled with names so unfamiliar they weren't recognized as presidential candidates. This must be a different contest, these voters might have thought.

In any event, many voters admitted afterward that they were confused by the ballot. Helen Garland, who runs a Duval County business providing in-home care for adults, said she knows she wasted her vote. After voting for Gore, Garland turned the page and punched a hole on the second page of presidential candidates. "I was like, 'Why are there people back here?' I was confused, so I just punched out a name. I thought I had to vote for somebody," Garland said. "My vote was one of those thrown in the trash. I should have asked [a poll worker]. I should have voted only for people that I knew. I am not happy about it."

In total, almost 22,000 voters in Jacksonville and the rest of Duval County—a disproportionate number of them in predominantly black areas where Gore overwhelmingly defeated Bush—cast spoiled "overvote" ballots. Robert Phillips, director of operations for the Duval elections office, said that voters should not have been confused. The bold-faced type prompted them to turn the page, and the corresponding number and order of candidates were the same on both the sample and actual ballots, he said. Stafford said he regretted the large number of overvotes, but "the voter has to take some responsibility."

In Broward County, Carroll found a simpler solution: She simply decreased the size of the print, squeezing all twenty names on the same page. But in Palm Beach County, LePore rejected that idea. Many of her voters were elderly. Their eyesight was poor. Some other way would have to be found.

Before November 7, 2000, Theresa Ann LePore, then forty-five, was an obscure career bureaucrat, which is just the way she liked it. "I'm a very private person," she said, repeating a cliché that is so often disingenuous among those in public life. But little about her life was public until election day. Why would it be? Hers was a singularly glamourless position. But that changed, and circumstances thrust her into the spotlight. Television cameras tracked her every move during the vote recounts, and millions of viewers came to recognize her as that sad-faced, wounded, drained figure rarely heard from but always in view.

Now her ill-gotten fame mortifies her. Strangers ask for her autograph. She needs two hours to get through the grocery store. "It's embarrassing when people come up and talk to me." She has cried behind closed doors at home and at her office. She has cried on national television and during newspaper interviews. She hates when that happens: "It's a sign of weakness."

Media reports persisted in calling LePore a "staunch Democrat," and a "lifelong Democrat." She is neither. If she's a staunch anything, it's Catholic. Politically, she seems without ideology. Former colleagues, as well as relatives and Palm Beach County officials of both major parties, claim they've never heard LePore advocate a political position since she joined the supervisor's office as a summer file clerk two days before she turned sixteen. She initially registered as a Republican. That's what her father was at the time, having run unsuccessfully as a Democrat for the Palm Beach City Commission in 1964. She changed to independent after joining the supervisor's office. When Independent became a registered party, she switched to unaffiliated.

"When I had to run [in 1996], I chose Democratic because the incumbent was Democratic and the majority of the county's voters are Democratic," she said. She may change yet again, back to unaffiliated. But events, she said soon after the election, "are just too fresh for me to make any decisions."

Her rise to power began in 1973, when Gov. Reubin Askew appointed Jackie Winchester to replace the previous county election supervisor, who had died. LePore was already serving as Winchester's secretary and was elevated to assistant in 1978. She handled voter registrations and eventually began dealing with the media during elections. When Winchester, then sixty-six, retired in 1996, LePore ran for her job and won easily. In 2000 she was unopposed in both the primary and general elections.

LePore says she has always enjoyed her job so much that, while she was a student, she shelved the notion of going to law school, preferring to pursue a career at the supervisor's office. "I like the contact with the public and doing a part of democracy that helps people elect the people who make the laws," she said. She viewed the work as "a way of giving back to the community. It gives me a sense of accomplishment that I'm helping people do something important to society." Though the events of 2000 caused her pain and some fleeting doubt about her career choice, two months after the election she was still able to say: "I like the elections business. I love my job."

U nder normal circumstances, LePore spends much of her time on administrative matters, in addition to attending political club meetings, civic gatherings, and school programs. She extracts particular satisfaction from prepping the youngest voters of tomorrow with educational coloring books.

But after the 2000 primaries, the other end of the age spectrum began to concern her. LePore worried that many of the county's older residents might have trouble reading type small enough to cram all ten presidential candidates and their running mates on a single page. She also had to leave space for write-ins. Three different times, she and her staff tried to squeeze all of that on one page. It just didn't seem to work.

"We never had that many to put on one ballot page, so we started looking at different configurations to see what would work best," she said. "We could fit them on one page, but the print was pretty small. We'd never had ten candidates before, and we had nothing to compare it to."

So LePore decided to split the names onto two pages, technically a facing-page ballot, something that Palm Beach County had never used, according to Winchester. LePore asked Tony Enos, her voting systems manager, to develop a prototype. Enos sat at his computer in the warehouse, booted up a program called BPS System, inserted the candidates' names, and gave it a try.

"We talked on the phone," Enos said. "It's not that detailed. You just get the names and lay them out on a page. It produces a design." Enos did this two or three times before LePore settled on the layout she liked. Then he printed it out and took it to her office for approval. "It's a process that takes place at each election," he said. "You don't think much about it."

The ballot opened like a book, with larger type on both sides. Arrows from the candidates' names pointed to circles which, when stabbed by a small, sharply pointed stylus, were supposed to punch through. This created a hole next to the name of the voter's preferred candidate. All the punch holes ran down the central spine. Voters were supposed to follow the arrow from their choice to the corresponding hole. The first name on the left corresponded to the first hole, the first name on the right to the second hole, the second hole on the left to the third hole, and so on. George W. Bush and Richard Cheney occupied the top spot on the left butterfly "wing," with Al Gore and Joseph Lieberman just underneath. Reform Party conservative Pat Buchanan was listed opposite Bush, on the right "wing," appropriately enough. It sounds simple. It was not as simple as it sounded.

But LePore approved the design, and Enos printed about five thousand ballot pages for the voting machines. "You print them on heavy index paper," he said. "There's a crimper that crimps little metal hinges on the bottom so it can go into the booklet. They're being produced about the same time as the sample ballots are being sent out" to voters. "The turnaround is only a few weeks, so everything's happening all at once. And the absentee ballots are going out." If voters object to their sample booklets, "there isn't much you can do about it at that point," he said. The election is right around the corner.

LePore anticipated no problems. This design, she thought, ought to make things easier for her voters. She sent it to all 159 candidates on the ballot, the presidential campaign offices, and local party officials. No one complained then, nor did anyone send up red flags when all 655,000 registered voters received sample ballot booklets in the mail. Interestingly, the state once had a mechanism that could catch ballot problems, but no more. "For many years, ballots had to be sent to the state Division of Elections in Tallahassee for approval, by state statute," Winchester said. "But they didn't know anything about ballot layout. Because of the tight schedules between primaries and the general, it created a problem with tight turnaround time, so they deleted the law."

So LePore was on her own. "We just put together what we thought was best," she said.

But within minutes after the polls opened on November 7, it became clear that the butterfly ballot was a disaster. Voters could not follow the arrows to the proper holes. They punched the second hole down, thinking it corresponded to the Democrats— Gore's was the second name on the left. But that second hole was assigned to Buchanan, so they ended up voting for *him* instead. Sometimes they voted for both, or for neither if they failed to punch cleanly. In Miami-Dade and Broward Counties, where the butterfly ballot was not in use, 184 of the 1.2 million ballots cast were for the Gore-Buchanan combination. In Palm Beach County, 5,264 of nearly 500,000 votes cast were for Buchanan and Gore, making it the most common type of overvote. Susan Mac-Manus, a political science professor at the University of South Florida, said the difference between Palm Beach County and its neighbors is easy to explain. "That was the butterfly ballot and the ballot format itself," she said.

Within a few months, LePore's ballot had become nearly synonymous with bad design. Copper Giloth, an associate art professor at the University of Massachusetts at Amherst, featured it on posters promoting a course on information design. The posters asked: "Can design change history?" Giloth's answer: "In this case, bad design did change history. It is very easy to see how people became confused." She said many voters might have been led astray by lines that were supposed to separate the candidates but actually pointed to punch holes.

When the polls closed that evening, Buchanan, the oft-perceived anti-Semite, had piled up an astounding number of votes—3,407 was the official tally—in a county heavily populated by the constituency least likely to have supported him: elderly Jews. "Yasser Arafat could have gotten more votes here," said Sigalit Flicker. She is the Israeli-born daughter of a Holocaust survivor, and when she realized she'd given her vote to a man who praised Hitler, she screamed. She lost sleep. And it turned out, she was very much not alone.

LePore is a hometown West Palm Beach girl, the eldest of eight. Her parents were transplanted working-class Pennsylvanians who moved to Palm Beach County in the 1950s. "I helped out around the house—cleaning, cooking, laundry. When my parents said to do something, I didn't ask questions." She aspired to little more than a decent job and a loving husband. If she has an obvious vice, it is jewelry. A half-dozen gold bracelets adorn each wrist. Her marquise engagement diamond rests atop a hefty gold dome festooned with baguettes. "You can never have too much jewelry," she said. Before the election, putting down a seventeen-year-old golden retriever with cancer "was the hardest thing I ever had to do." It is something that a very private person might say.

LePore attended elementary school and daily Mass at St. Juliana Church in West Palm Beach. She graduated first from the parochial Cardinal Newman High School, then Palm Beach Junior College—now a community college—where she majored in political science. She attended Florida Atlantic University, a branch of the state university system, but left before earning a degree. Exploiting her father's political connections, she obtained a position at the election supervisor's office in 1971. "I'd already gone through the 'women things' you were supposed to do back then—typing and shorthand. It was basically file clerking, but I liked the job."

Her father, Joseph LePore, was an art student from New Castle, Pennsylvania, who owned a neighborhood tavern, then drove a city bus. He headed Local 1267 of the bus drivers' union and was a Democratic Executive Committee member before switching parties. The army declared him 100 percent disabled because of a World War II combat injury that caused nerve damage to one arm. "He was always having surgery," LePore recalled. "He had to wear this big metal brace. It was either that or have his arm cut off, and he wouldn't do that. Then he had heart problems and got a pacemaker." He died in 1983. Her mother, also Theresa, worked as a waitress, and helped out at the election supervisor's office. She died in 1993.

Theresa LePore: "I can remember as a kid going to the polling places with my mom and dad in the neighborhood, at a little church, then at a middle school after that. My dad was involved in politics—though I don't consider myself in politics."

There was always enough money for the essentials, but LePore was on her own for the extras. In fact, after their third child, her parents started sending their kids to public school because parochial school was too expensive, according to Theresa's brother Allen, who owns a window screen company in West Palm Beach. She bought her first car with money she had earned. The 1965 blue Mustang had been deteriorating in an empty lot. She paid $25. "Myself and the guys in the neighborhood and my dad totally refurbished it. It was the neatest thing."

In 1989 tragedy struck the family. One of Theresa's brothers, Marine Sgt. Paul E. LePore, was killed near Tallahassee. He was twenty-six. It was a gunshot accident, Theresa LePore said. "Anything that happens to any of you, when you have that many kids together, affects us all. But my mother was a strong woman: Italian Catholic. When things happen, you go to church. You pray."

And so, when it seemed the whole world was furious at her for her ballot design, Theresa LePore also went to church—her childhood church, St. Juliana, although St. Ann's sits across the street from her office. "If I can't go, I really feel guilty," she said. "I'm very traditional. If I had my way, we'd be back to Latin. My husband kids me about how 'old school' I am. You're allowed to take communion in your hand, but I can't do it."

There's little else in her life but her husband, her dogs, and a job that pays $108,000 a year. "My sister eats, sleeps, and drinks the election office," Allen LePore said. "When all this started, she was in another world and totally hurt."

She's married to her second husband, Michael G. Lally. They bonded over softball and dogs. Neither had, or wanted, children. And they're tall: she, five-foot-nine, he, six-foot-two. That's the main reason a mutual friend fixed them up for a blind date to a comedy club. "She thought we'd look good together," said LePore. They married in 1993 and live in Lake Clarke Shores, a tiny residential city of midsized houses and communal tennis courts.

In the aftermath of the election, she said, Michael didn't ask many questions. "He knows that I'm a really private person and when I'm ready to talk, I'll talk. He's just there for when I do say something." Did she ever wake him up at 3:00 A.M. to say she was ready to talk about her experiences and new notoriety? She thinks that is a ridiculous question. "Very boring," she said of the inquiry.

From 1984 to 1989, LePore was the third wife of George L. Hudspeth Jr., then a powerful union organizer and Democratic activist involved in publicly funded construction projects. They met at the election supervisor's office. "She was a good-looking woman and still is," said Hudspeth, now national sales director for Northern Trust Bank. While they were together, LePore was involved in two "horrific" traffic accidents, he said, one that "messed up her neck and back," another that "put her head through the side windshield. That messed her up for a long time."

Hudspeth thinks that anyone looking to blame his ex-wife for the election mess is looking in the wrong direction. "There's no doubt in my mind that she didn't do anything wrong on purpose. I know her makeup and how she was raised: strict Catholic. She is just not dishonest. But it's politics as usual, and you can't take that stuff personally."

The juiciest rumor about LePore ran dry as soon as it surfaced. On December 1, the *Wall Street Journal* carried the tantalizing snippet that LePore had once been a flight attendant on former Saudi Arabian arms dealer Adnan Khashoggi's palatial private jet. On December 4, *Slate Magazine*'s chatterbox column, calling the *Journal* item "gratifyingly noir," followed up: " 'Madame Butterfly' Theresa LePore wasn't always an embattled Palm Beach ballots chief. In the 1980s, she moonlighted as a flight attendant on private planes owned by Saudi weapons dealer Adnan Khashoggi, a middleman in Reagan administration arms sales to Iran."

LePore was stunned that this bit of past-life trivia had surfaced. She explained that in the late 1970s and early 1980s she had worked part-time as a ramp attendant at the West Palm Beach airport, where she waved planes to their gates. She was in her early twenties at the time. She said she never worked for Khashoggi. "It was outdoors on the weekend, and it was fun. [Khashoggi] used to come in all the time," because he vacationed in Palm Beach. "I started dating one of his pilots." The romantic liaison took LePore to exotic locales in Europe and Africa. She insists that her conversations with Khashoggi never extended beyond mere pleasantries.

But it will be a long time until she can laugh at the rumors or at any of this, she said. She remembers the way angry people swarmed in her office lobby three days after the election. She'd been upstairs in the office of a close friend, County Attorney Denise Dytrych, and was spotted leaving an elevator, bracketed by officers. "Everyone's pulling at me and yelling, 'There she is!' and booing. It just . . . I got very scared. I didn't know what to expect."

When she managed to return home during the weeks after the election—which was seldom and at odd hours—she found reporters camped at her house. "I live in a small town with its own police department watching the house, and they tried to chase them off every chance they could," she said. "Neighbors were getting phone calls from reporters to see what kind of person I was. One neighbor spoke Spanish . . . so the reporter gave her a piece of paper and asked her to write it down. Stuff like that. My other neighbor, *Inside Edition* kept calling. She usually checks caller ID, but one time she picked up the phone and she said, 'I just moved here,' and they said, 'No you didn't. We checked the tax rolls. You've been there ten years.' That got her really upset. It's uncalled for."

Onrushing events also carried an avalanche of e-mails, faxes, and letters to LePore's office. While many were pointed critiques of the voting process, they soon grew increasingly ugly and personal, especially after LePore at one point cast the tie-breaking vote to stop a recount. From an anonymous correspondent, on

November 16: "Dear Theresa LePore: I empathized with you for a time, but so far you have helped design the flawed ballot, you voted not once but twice to stop the recount the people of Florida want. Are the Republicans paying you?"

None of this will deter her from running again, she insisted. She figures she'll be able to raise enough money, maybe even from other Democrats. "I'm sure there's some who don't hate me," she said ruefully. "I have a lot of good friends on both sides." Asked nearly two months after the election to describe the last thing that made her happy, she ponders for a moment. "Really, really happy? Probably when I was elected vice president of the state association [of election supervisors] last summer, by my peers. In my personal life? It's been so long. I just can't think."

As for guilt, she doesn't harbor any, she said. "But hindsight's twenty-twenty, and maybe I should have, um, you're always second-guessing, and you can't in this business because what's done is done. But perhaps I could have taken the ballot out and let people look at it, really been proactive in that, other than just mailing it out to everybody. I felt I did what I needed to do as far as outreach goes—going into the community and talking to them trying to get out the vote. Going to the kids in the schools." At the same time, she concedes, "Probably we won't use the facing-page ballot."

Months after the election, she was still trying to find her bearings, often with the help of her staffers and coworkers. Charmaine Kelly, LePore's deputy, often tried to comfort her boss. "She is so dedicated and gave so much of her life to this office and is very proud of the position she holds. It was very heartbreaking to the entire staff. We're in this together."

LePore: "I'm a very private person and I don't like getting into confrontations. I will avoid it at all costs. My defense mechanism is to be quiet, keep my head down, and keep going. I just figure that they'll get it out of their system, scream and holler, rant and rave as much as they want. Not that I don't care what they're saying. I've found if you try to defend yourself and make comments, it only makes it worse."

Who have her real friends been? She pauses when asked this, and she twists her engagement ring. Her eyes redden. Her voice wavers. "My husband. My family. My staff. They are very supportive." Does she feel betrayed by anyone she thought was a friend? "All I'm going to say is when you go through a difficult time, you find out who your true friends are. I'll leave it at that. I do my job, and I wouldn't let that affect me in the way I treat them in my professional capacity." Still, even from her real friends she has endured some gentle hazing. "We had some friends over Christmas, and I was putting out crackers and cheese. One package had butterfly crackers. They were all teasing me. I said, 'Shut up and eat 'em.' "

When she did try to explain her actions, LePore drove a stake through her own heart. She said that while she understood how the ballot design might have been confusing, voters needed to take some responsibility for their own mistakes. It was the last thing most people wanted to hear. What they wanted was an apology, a heartfelt, guilt-ridden mea culpa. But not directed toward the party professionals and the candidates, insisted Peyton McArthur, Palm Beach County Democratic Party executive director. "She doesn't have to be sorry to me," he said. "She needs to be sorry to those people who think they were denied their vote."

What hurt LePore, according to McArthur, "was her attitude, when she blamed it on the voters. Some of these people—eighty-five years old—have been waiting to vote for a Jewish vice president their entire life, and she's going to tell them they're stupid? You never do that."

Winchester, long a supporter of the woman who was her protégé, recalibrated her view after the botched election and is now an outspoken critic. She said LePore, though diligent and fair, is a workaholic who tries to do too much herself. "That's a big problem for her," Winchester said. "She's always been that way. She thinks she can do anything better than anyone else. She doesn't trust other people. But when you have a huge responsibility like that, you need to get good people in." McArthur agrees. "She got into this mess because she has a weakness," he said. "She doesn't delegate. She was molded in that job and doesn't have the ability to deviate in how to do things differently than she's been doing them for twenty-five years." LePore rejects that criticism. "I was responsible to see that things were done," she said. "I delegated what I needed to."

In any event, there's one other thing that miffs Winchester. "Theresa never asked my advice—not even once. I did that job for twenty-three years." Winchester's front-door welcome mat is a butterfly. It appears fairly new.

LePore and another brother, Joe, developed fundamental personal differences over the years and sometimes don't see each other for months at a time, though both live in the same county. Still, he fully supports her. A born-again Christian, he sees divine intervention in the election. "If you believe in God, you believe that it's God's will and God is in control, and he allowed this circumstance to bring Bush into office. Who are we to dispute that?"

His sister, he said with pride, "was an instrument. God will be over her." President George W. Bush, he said, "owes it to my sister to pat her on the back and say, 'You did a good job.'"

4

KNOWN DEFECTS, LOST VOTES

But ballot design was just part of the problem. Most Floridi-ans—and about one-third of all Americans—exercise their right to vote on machinery that was designed nearly half a century ago and is based on technology introduced in 1890. Manufacturers of punch-card ballot machines soon recognized the contraptions' faults. Inventors repeatedly sought to correct defects. Election su-pervisors in Florida and around the country knew for decades that box loads of votes were being lost in every election. But they slowly came to accept this as inevitable—and acceptable: a loss rate of 2 percent eventually became the standard for many elec-tion supervisors. Two percent of the national presidential vote in 2000 would equal about 2 million votes—more than the total electorate of Miami-Dade, Broward, and Palm Beach counties.

"It happens," said Theresa LePore, that beleaguered election supervisor of Palm Beach County. "You can talk to any punch-card county and you are going to have undervotes and overvotes. And I'm sure if you checked any other state in the nation, you'd find the same thing. It was not really an issue in the past. We knew it was there." What she did not know was that many of her machines were particularly vulnerable. Her county is the only one in Florida to use a cheaper "knock-off" version of the punch-card machine. A *Herald* investigation found that many of these machines were crippled by worn and defective parts, and that they had produced the highest numbers of lost votes. No one felt compelled to share the details of this situation with voters. So a presidential election came into question, and the lawsuits, challenging not only the election but also the punch-card system itself, began flying.

"The question you have to ask is, 'Why did elections supervisors continue with punch cards?' " Roy Saltman said in an interview. Many years earlier, he wrote the second of two scathing reports on the subject for the National Bureau of Standards, a unit of the U.S. Department of Commerce. "All the evidence said there was a serious problem." His report was distributed to elections offices around the country in 1988. In that same year, the machines were implicated in a disputed statewide election in Florida.

Democratic U.S. Senate candidate Buddy MacKay, who ultimately lost by 33,612 votes out of more than 4 million cast, still believes he truly won that race but that his victory evaporated along with thousands of uncounted votes. During that same election, one in twelve Miami-Dade voters cast a ballot on which the machine did not find a valid presidential vote.

Soon thereafter, Howard Kleinberg, editor of the now-defunct *Miami News,* wrote words that would prove prophetic: "We cannot accept the excuse that there is no better way to tabulate votes; there has to be. Voters should not and cannot be disenfranchised because the current system of vote counting has a built-in glitch, to wit: If the chad is left attached to the ballot, it may cover the hole again in the recount and not count as a vote cast.

"This is not what the Founding Fathers and subsequent Supreme Court decisions have called for. Everyone's vote is to be counted. Do voters have to stand before the ballot box plucking their ballots as one would pluck a chicken, for fear their vote may not count? Since computer punch-card systems are used more and more nationwide, it's a national problem. How many races across the country were determined by pinheads of paper clinging to the ballot?

"There needs to be a national investigation, perhaps by the Congress or a presidential commission—if not the Federal Bureau of Investigation. To paraphrase: If it is broke, then fix it!"

It was broke. No one fixed it. And twelve years later, when control of the White House would depend on those same error-prone machines, this phrase suddenly appeared on everyone's lips: hanging chads. Manufacturers blamed election supervisors, saying they failed to properly educate voters. Election supervisors blamed voters, saying they hastily or otherwise improperly cast their ballots. And voters had no idea that special education or expertise was required to punch a hole in a card and cast a vote.

The punch-card system's roots reach back more than a century. The Votomatic machine, the most commonly used device (the name is also used generically to describe its several clones), depends on punch-card technology invented by Herman Hollerith—a Census Bureau employee searching for a better way to count the nation's population—in 1890. In part, Hollerith based his system on that used for railroad tickets, which conductors punched with identifying characteristics of passengers, such as hair and eye color, to prevent ticket fraud. Hollerith went on to start a company that, in 1924, took the name International Business Machines. IBM adopted the 3- by 7-inch card, with a standard hole layout, that remains in use today. A computer code, named for Hollerith, was developed to interpret hole patterns on the cards, and, throughout the twentieth century, IBM punch cards were employed for a variety of business purposes.

In 1964 that technology finally reached the voting booth. Joseph P. Harris, a professor of political science, had long contemplated a system less expensive, less massive, and—foremost in his mind—less vulnerable to fraud than the huge mechanical lever machines then in place in many large cities. Harris often quoted New York City's infamously corrupt Boss Tweed: "The ballots made no result. The counters made the result." He argued that a better way of counting votes had to be found. Finally, in 1964, teaching at the University of California at Berkeley, he hit on the idea of using punch cards as ballot forms, and he won a patent for what he called the Votomatic. The patent boasted that, by design, "complete punching out of the [chad] is insured." Sensing new business opportunities, IBM bought patent rights to the Votomatic the following year.

Though improved over the years by various manufacturers, this voting system has always featured the same fundamental design: A ballot card with pre-scored holes is inserted into a hollow mechanical holder. A hinged booklet is attached to that holder. As voters turn pages of the booklet, various rows of the punch cards become exposed. Voters use the stylus to punch through a hole that corresponds to their preferred candidate. The tabs of paper left behind are called chads. Later, machines that can read punched holes by detecting light that passes through them tabulate the ballots. That information is then tabulated by a computer.

According to several lawsuits filed after the 2000 election, the system's most commonly cited flaw involves the now notorious chads. Chads sometimes do not detach properly when holes in the computer card are not lined up with the slots in the T-strips—underlying soft rubber surfaces with chambers designed to remove the chad from the card. "Such misalignment occurs frequently, and, when it does, voters—unaware of the misalignment—proceed with their voting attempt," the class-action suits maintain. The problem can also occur when the stylus fails to penetrate the T-strips because they are not supple enough. And, it can occur when the T-strips become worn. And, it can occur when chads accumulate in the T-strips' chambers.

The resulting problem: a hanging chad, attached to the card at one, two, or three corners. Or a pregnant chad, penetrated by the stylus but attached at all four corners. Or a dimpled chad, indented by the stylus but with no penetration. Pregnant and dimpled chads go unread by the machine's card reader because it fails to detect enough light through the pre-scored hole. The same flaw often happens with a hanging chad because it tends to fall back into place in the pre-scored hole. In instances where the hanging chad falls off during the ballot tabulation, it can become stuck in the card-reading machine, blocking light and causing the machine to count votes inaccurately. At the same time, the free-moving chad can become lodged in other holes in the same card or those of another voter's card, covering a punched hole. That leads to more errors.

By the 1980s, the computer disk had eclipsed punch cards in almost all business applications—and experts were by then famil-iar with the machines' myriad defects. Yet to this day, Votomatics and their clones are still deployed in most states on Election Day.

Voters first encountered the Votomatic in significant numbers during the November 1964 presidential election between Lyndon Johnson and Barry Goldwater. Among the first areas that en-dorsed the new system: Fulton and DeKalb Counties in Georgia, San Joaquin and Monterey Counties in California, and Lane County, Oregon. IBM aggressively marketed the Votomatic across the nation, but the system's shortcomings soon became evident.

In 1966 the company lobbied the town of Braintree, south of Boston, to test the Votomatic during an actual election. It did not go well: the card-counting machine jammed, requiring a partial hand recount. Unbowed, IBM persuaded the Massachusetts Leg-islature to sanction the delivery of ballots from precincts to a central tabulation site. Previously, ballots were counted at the pre-cinct level.

Even in those early years, the Votomatic's Achilles' heel was becoming exposed: It was susceptible to two of the most serious problems that could afflict any mechanical voting system—overvotes and undervotes. Overvotes occur when people choose more than one candidate in a race. That mistake is easy to make on a Votomatic, which allows voters to punch any number of holes. Undervotes occur when people do not select any candidate in a race—or their selection is not recorded. And unrecorded votes have plagued punch-card machines throughout their history. Experts discovered that chads often did not separate cleanly from ballot cards. That undermined the entire system.

In the fall of 1968, with the nation preparing for another presidential election, Ira G. Laws applied for a patent to help correct the problem. Laws thought a better stylus would help. From his patent application: "In some instances, after the stylus is inserted through a selected pre-scored area on the card and is then withdrawn, the chip or card position within the selected pre-scored area was merely folded downwardly on the card along an edge but still remained attached to the ballot. This often resulted in an inaccurate counting and tabulation of the vote when the cards were later processed or counted in a vote-tabulating machine."

Laws was working at the time for Seismograph Service Corp., which made machines closely related to the Votomatic. Thirty-two years later, he told the *Herald* that the machines' defects were easy to recognize. "Anyone who worked on these things noticed that every once in a while at least some of the holes will not punch cleanly," he said. "It wasn't uncommon at all. It's not the fault of the voters that the chad does not punch out occasionally. I think it's just inherent in the device. We didn't think we had eliminated the hanging chad problem, but we thought we had made an improvement."

Soon after Laws filed his patent application, the Votomatic

suffered another embarrassment. Due to a programming error, votes in Missoula County, Montana, were switched: Republican Richard Nixon lost in GOP strongholds, and Democrat Hubert Humphrey lost in Democratic areas. In 1969, IBM leaders realized that the company was saddled with a public relations disaster, and the company essentially abandoned the business, licensing five other companies to produce and sell the Votomatic and variations of the machine. The most successful of these would be Computer Election Systems of Berkeley, California, founded by former IBM employees.

Throughout the 1970s, Votomatics widely replaced the old closet-sized, lever-operated voting systems. The advantages seemed clear: Several Votomatics, smaller and less expensive than lever machines, could be placed at each precinct, shortening the delays encountered by voters. In addition, they were less susceptible to fraud than the lever machines. But there was an associated cost that frequently surfaced—they were also more susceptible to the inaccurate recording and counting of votes—and a pattern soon became clear.

In Los Angeles, for instance, 0.5 percent of all ballots during a 1970 gubernatorial primary could not be read during the initial machine count. When ballot inspectors fanned uncounted stacks of cards, clouds of chads fell out. Later that year, Detroit used the machines for the first time, in a primary election. The result: hanging chads, misplaced punches, and jammed card readers. The city tried again during the general election and confronted another epidemic of problems. Detroit subsequently dropped the Votomatic system. In 1971 West Virginia looked into buying the Votomatic from Computer Election Systems but rejected the system because of the risk of overvoting. That phenomenon, which plagued Florida's 2000 presidential election, is nearly impossible on other automated voting systems.

In 1975, only eleven years after IBM introduced the Votomatic, a report from the National Bureau of Standards sharply criticized the machines' performance. In the first of its two reports, the bureau exposed what was becoming a nationwide problem: hanging chads and jammed card readers. "In an election, the system is to be used by voters of varying abilities," the report reads. "The concept of the vote-tallying system must be that it is there to serve the voters, and the system must be geared so that the overwhelming majority of voters, approaching 100 percent, can use it to record their votes as they intend."

But the Votomatic remained in use and continued to chip away at the accuracy of elections. The outcome of a 1976 Los Angeles legislative election was reversed twice—once by machine recount and again by hand recount. In a scene now familiar to anyone who monitored events in Florida, inspectors held up every ballot to the light to examine the holes. Hanging and bulging chads accounted for the reversals.

Florida's Miami-Dade County bought its $1.7 million Votomatic system from Computer Election Systems two years later, in 1978. What cinched the deal: the company's promise that the machines would not create hanging chads. But that same year, a defeated candidate for Miami Beach City Council, Robert "Big Daddy" Napp, claimed that the system failed to count 710 votes, which could have changed the outcome. The candidate had no recourse to state election laws, since they offered relief only if vote fraud could be established.

In 1980 Computer Election Systems tried to interest Pennsylvania in the Votomatic. One state examiner offered this impression: "Antique, obsolete, unreliable technology packed with a systems approach that was even more unreliable." Another examiner agreed—yet officials certified the machines for use in Pennsylvania anyway. That year, Votomatic card readers broke down in election after election, from Arkansas to Michigan, from Indiana to Utah.

Still, the hanging, dangling chads remained the main problem. In 1981 another inventor thought he had a solution. John Ahmann, who worked for IBM and Computer Election Systems, offered what he called a better design. He identified the chad problem as "one of the main detractors of punch card voting." He proposed a number of changes to better align the permanent punch holes and the cards that are positioned below them. In his patent application, he also noted that chads removed from punch cards could accumulate under the surface, making it difficult for voters to press the stylus through the hole. He said: "The surface of the punch board has become so clogged with [chads] as to prevent a clean-punching operation. Incompletely punched cards can cause serious errors to occur in data processing [while] utilizing such cards." Ahmann virtually repeated that statement when he testified in Tallahassee during Gore's attempt to contest the presidential election. Republican lawyers called him as a witness—to verify that chads could be dislodged from ballots during recounts—but he ended up stating that in a close election, supervisors are often well advised to recount ballots by hand, testimony that tended to favor Gore's case.

Regardless of all efforts to fix the machines, Votomatics and their clones remained at the core of many electoral disputes. Florida. Ohio. Texas. Illinois. Georgia. Missouri. Virginia. All reported trouble, and it went on for decades. In the early 1990s, three Ohio political science professors published a study of the machines. Participants observed mock campaign commercials and voted on one of three systems: paper and pencil, punch cards, or an ATM-like touch-screen device. Published in the *Western Political Quarterly*, the study found that people using punch cards were more likely to cast undervotes and overvotes. It concluded: "Punch-card voting systems present a technological barrier to voting which results in reducing the number of votes cast in a field race or in overvoting, which invalidates the entire ballot. . . . The technological disenfranchisement concomitant with the use of the punch-card system causes millions of votes to be lost in field race elections across the nation each election cycle. Clearly this is an unsatisfactory situation for supporters of representative democracy."

New Hampshire and Massachusetts eventually banned the machines because they distorted election results there. No matter. Punch-card systems remained in place elsewhere because they were cheap and relatively easy to maintain, but problems surfaced on a regular basis, and no state should have been more familiar with those problems than Florida. There, election supervisors continued to use punch-card ballots despite evidence that they botched thousands of votes in state races and could throw into doubt the outcome of any close contest. Candidates in close races had complained about overvotes and undervotes as far back as the 1970s. In addition, a survey of Florida's twelve most populous counties shows that in 1992 and 1996 elections, the earliest for which complete data are available, presidential votes on more than 20 of every 1,000 ballots were not counted because ballots were either double-punched, unpunched, or incompletely punched.

As was the case elsewhere, punch-card ballot machines became widespread in Florida during the 1970s, as did the problems. Candidates complained—even after the design changes the manufacturers made to eliminate problems. Canvassing boards and courts frequently dismissed the complaints, citing issues such as the cost and impracticality of hand counts.

In 1984 David Anderson, a candidate for Palm Beach County property appraiser, filed suit over, among other things, hanging chads. He lost that legal battle—on what Anderson says was a technicality—but he now feels vindicated. "All of a sudden to say 'Oh, we're so surprised by these problems!'—they're not surprised," Anderson said. "Those Votomatics should have been changed a long time ago." In 1991 taxpayer activist Al Hogan lost a seat on the Oakland Park City Council in Broward County by 3 votes. He appealed to the canvassing board for a recount but lost, even though the board acknowledged that hanging chads might have cost him votes. Hogan still believes hanging chads undid his candidacy. "I always felt it was that way," he said. "I'm just about positive I won. I didn't think it was fair all the way through."

Buddy MacKay, who believes his 1988 Senate candidacy became a casualty of punch-card voting, says it is unthinkable that so many Florida counties still use punch-card ballots. "This was the technology used at the University of Florida when I was there, and that was before the Earth cooled," he said. "If anybody ever focuses on it, it's an outrage."

Election supervisors in most large counties said they either did not recognize the ruined ballots as a significant issue or believed that no other voting method was significantly more accurate. Miami-Dade Supervisor of Elections David Leahy: "Until we got to this election, no one ever looked at undervotes or overvotes. I didn't think of them." Later, asked about a number of undervote and overvote complaints brought by candidates in Miami-Dade, he said: "I've always been concerned about hanging chads. It's always been a flaw in the system." Later still, he said he had no clue that the margin of error in punch-card balloting would become a factor in Florida's presidential vote. "Had I known, we wouldn't have stayed with it," he said.

In fact, election supervisors have long viewed the rejection of thousands of ballots as a natural part of elections, not as an ominous warning sign. Some supervisors and some Republicans argue that the proportion of uncounted ballots in the 2000 presidential election was not unacceptable. "I don't get it," said Joan Brock, deputy supervisor of elections in Pinellas County. "Not everyone votes for president, and it wouldn't surprise me to see that two percent of them didn't want to vote for president." A closer look at voting records, however, suggests that very few people go to the polls in presidential elections without intending to vote for president, and that thousands of would-be votes every election are nullified by unread punch-card ballots—adding considerably to the resulting undervotes.

Consider, for example, the experience of Brevard County, which includes Melbourne, Cocoa Beach, and Titusville and is the largest Florida county that has used both punch cards and optical scan—or fill-in-the-oval—ballots. In 1996, the last presidential election tallied on punch cards, 26 of every 1,000 voters failed to cast a valid presidential vote. That is 2.6 percent of the vote—close to the 2 percent that seems to have become the comfort level for election supervisors. But in 2000, after the switch to fill-in-the-oval ballots, the proportion fell to fewer than 2 of every 1,000 presidential ballots cast. That is less than 0.2 percent of the vote. "We knew we had voters out there who were being disenfranchised because of overvotes and undervotes," said Gayle Graham, assistant supervisor of elections in Brevard. "So we switched. Using a pencil to mark a ballot is just so much simpler. It's like filling in a lottery ticket."

Moving from punch-card ballots to fill-in-the-oval ballots in Daytona Beach and the rest of Volusia County also led to a steep drop in rejected ballots. With punch cards, 26 of every 1,000 voters failed to cast valid presidential votes; after the switch, that number fell to just 3 of every 1,000.

Optical scan systems work better for two reasons, election supervisors in those counties said. First, using a pencil to fill in ovals on a ballot comes naturally to most people. They've done something similar on SAT tests and lottery tickets. Few people ever punch cards with a stylus, aside from when they vote. Second, the fill-in-the-ovals method often has counting machines in every precinct that immediately kick back ballots to voters who overvote, so they can immediately make corrections. "Voters find the optical scan ballots much easier to use," said Deanie Lowe, supervisor of elections in Volusia. "They are much more user-friendly." But the improved accuracy with optical scan systems comes only when scanning equipment is present at each precinct and botched ballots can be corrected by voters. A *Herald* survey found that the system's accuracy suffers considerably when scans are performed at a central location.

Hillsborough County Supervisor of Elections Pam Iorio said: "Whether it's punch-card or optical scan . . . what you're accepting going on in elections is, there's a certain amount of voter error." She said that optical scan devices, at about $6,000 per precinct, offer only a marginal improvement in accuracy for millions of dollars in expense.

Still, the future of the punch-card machine now seems dim. A high-profile Washington, D.C., law firm targeted what it said was the election's main culprit—the Votomatics and their descendants. Cohen, Milstein, Hausfeld & Toll is known for its public interest work, and representatives said they do not trust state election officials and legislators to spend the tens or even hundreds of millions of dollars necessary to replace faulty 1960s-era technology.

Representing a class of frustrated voters, the firm sued the state of Florida and its largest counties, demanding that they stop using punch-card machines because the system allegedly "disenfranchises large numbers of voters in election after election." The suit claims that counting errors caused by the machines violate voters' constitutional rights of equal protection under the law. Named as defendants in the suit, filed in state circuit court in Tallahassee, were Secretary of State Katherine Harris, Attorney General Bob Butterworth, and many counties that use punch-card machines.

No companies actually manufacture the Votomatic and similar machines anymore, though a handful specialize in replacement parts and computer support systems. But the same law firm sued four companies that provide computer hardware and software and other services that support the machines in twenty-eight states. They are: Election Systems & Software, Inc., of Omaha, Nebraska; Sequoia Pacific Systems, of Hayward, California; Fidlar Doubleday, Inc., of Rock Island, Illinois; and Melbourne Technical Services, Inc., of West Melbourne, Florida. In that suit, filed in Saint Clair County, Illinois, the firm accused the companies—on behalf of its clients—of engaging in unfair and deceptive trade practices because they sell computer products for a voting system that allegedly fails to count ballots accurately. The companies also face allegations of violating the equal protection provision of the Constitution.

According to Attorney Michael Hausfeld, a senior partner in the firm, Florida's recount exposed defects that elections experts kept secret for decades. "It's pretty clear no one guarantees a perfect election," Hausfeld said. "But there is a flaw in the Votomatic, and it is denying people their most fundamental right to vote and that their vote be counted. It was our belief that if we take care of elevating the voting process in the first place, there will be a better count and there won't be a need to create standards for recounting ballots."

Hausfeld handles many public interest cases for free and has filed this case on the same basis. He is known for using the courts as agents of social or corporate change. He represented Holocaust victims who claimed that Swiss banks had confiscated their assets, and won a $1.25 billion settlement. He also sued the German government and companies that used Jewish slave labor during the Holocaust, and won a $5.2 billion settlement. His firm led a major racial discrimination case against Texaco, Inc., and won $176 million for black employees.

He feels very strongly about the voting issue. "While every other information system in the United States has been adapted to the extraordinary capabilities of modern computers, the precious voting right of millions of Americans is contingent upon the proper functioning of a system that dates to the stone age of computers," both of his suits claim. "Worse, the adaptation of that system to voting usage has resulted in numerous and severe defects. The Votomatic system contains a host of well-known defects that routinely frustrate the intentions of voters, disenfranchise large numbers of voters, and severely undermine the democratic process."

One of the class representatives, Mary Ellen Peyton of Miami, said she felt it was her civic duty to join the suit. "If the system had worked, I wouldn't have a problem," said Peyton, fifty-eight, a Democrat who voted for Al Gore. "But I don't think the system worked."

On the other side, a representative of one of the software companies named as a defendant said the Votomatic was being unfairly blamed. Michael Limas, chief operating officer of Election Systems & Software, said the suits miss the point. Regardless of the voting technology, he said, election officials must maintain the equipment and train poll workers and voters in its proper use. His company also provides software for other voting systems. "Administrators have to be able to manage all of these things well," he said. "It's a wrong solution if the punch-card [machine] is eliminated but no attention is paid to how an election is run."

The suits point primarily to the chad as the reason for botched elections, but they also point to other defects in the Votomatic. The printing of card inserts must be precise, so that arrows on the booklet page that point to candidate names line up with the proper holes. Variations in the quality of the computer-card stock or the pre-scored holes can magnify the chad problem. Humidity or human perspiration can swell the cards, causing card-reading machines to spit them out unread. Also, the machines frequently take in more than one ballot at a time, leading to miscounts. And they often jam.

Hausfeld said he hopes to force counties around the country to buy modern voting technology, such as optical scan or touch-screen systems. That, he said, would lead to nearly perfect election results—making ballot recounts unnecessary.

Election supervisors in Florida's large counties offer various reasons for sticking with punch cards, at least through 2000. LePore, the supervisor of elections in Palm Beach County, thought that past undervote problems had been solved in 1996 when the county bought new styluses: "We thought they were fixed and didn't look anymore," she said.

But she had a unique problem: Palm Beach is the only county in Florida that uses Data-Punch voting machines, cheaper clones of the Votomatic, and her county had one of the highest undercount percentages in the state in 2000. Voters were almost three times as likely to cast an undervote on a Data-Punch machine as on a Votomatic (which are also used in parts of the county). A *Herald* review of more than 250 voting machines in Palm Beach County clearly showed that the undervote problem there had more to do with bad equipment than voters. LePore's machines were peppered with worn-out, outdated, and ineffective parts— wimpy plastic springs, battered templates, rubber T-strips more than twenty years old. Two months after the election, *Herald* reporter David Kidwell—aware of the machines' faults—went to the warehouse where they were stored and tried voting on some of them. His ballots ended up showing significant numbers of dimpled chads—votes that would not count. LePore inherited the problem when she took office in 1996, but her staff assured her that the machines had been fixed. "The styluses were breaking and they were replaced," she said. Now, she says the county will scrap the Data-Punch machines.

Some election supervisors continue to blame voters for most of the difficulties associated with punch-card ballots. "When used properly, it's not a bad system," said David Leahy, the Miami-Dade supervisor of elections. "The problem we have with the system is it's prone to voter error. People aren't familiar with the device and don't vote properly. Or they don't inspect their ballots and remove the [hanging] chads." Still, he said, the problems that plagued the 2000 elections will have to be addressed. "From this experience we're going to look to see if we can find a better system for this county," Leahy said.

Katherine Harris, the embattled secretary of state, also blames voters for much of the problem. "The issues were not with our system," she said. "The issue was the closeness of the election. When someone doesn't follow the instructions or remove the chad, that becomes an issue." Still, she agrees that changes must be made. "It is a matter of perception that our systems were so poor. One-third of our nation uses the punch card. What we will work on is trying to get more technologically advanced. What I care most about is making certain that the will of the voter is self-evident."

Only one election officer working in any of Florida's largest counties seemed to have recognized the serious shortcomings of punch-card ballots and sought new voting equipment, not that it did her or her voters any good. Broward Supervisor of Elections Jane Carroll, elected in 1968 and considered a national expert, criticized punch cards as antiquated, confusing, and inaccurate.

Beginning in 1993, she tried to replace the system she had purchased in 1974. But the predominantly Democratic County Commission, which monitored the Republican supervisor's budget, kept turning her down. Commissioners said they feared that manufacturers would develop better equipment, leaving the county with expensive and outdated technology. Their stance drew a snide rebuke from Carroll. "If the theory of waiting to see what will come along in the future had been employed, we would still be on a manual registration system and hand counting paper ballots brought in by horse-drawn carriages," she wrote in a 1993 memo.

Earlier that year, the state had "decertified" the computer that counted ballots in Broward because it did not meet state standards. Carroll hastened to replace it before March 1994 elections in fifteen Broward cities. She personally lobbied commissioners to approve a $2.9 million contract with Global Election Systems for an optical scanning system. "I sent my staff all over the country," she said. "They found this was the best one."

County Finance Director Phil Allen thought otherwise. He strongly advised commissioners against skipping competitive bidding and awarding the contract. He also questioned Global's ability to live up to the deal. "It is clearly a start-up company experiencing the need for capital," Allen wrote of the company, which was founded in 1991. Today, the company manufactures optical scan and touch-screen machines used by more than 850 municipalities in North America. Still, Allen maintains that the commission made the right decision at the time. "We would have been their largest installation, and we had concerns about the timeliness of delivery and about the company's ability to provide ongoing maintenance support," he said. "The supervisor of elections never said the equipment we had would not provide an accurate vote. She only said [the new equipment] would speed things up."

The majority of commissioners agreed with Allen. They decided to spend $117,757 on new computers and software for the punch-card system. Looking back at that decision, Carroll blames politics. She says she had the votes lined up until a competitor of Global Elections System hired lobbyists to influence commissioners. "Literally overnight, support evaporated," Carroll said. "I think it was definitely the lobbying." Broward Commissioner Lori Parrish now regrets her opposition to new equipment. "All of us are kicking ourselves in the rear end," Parrish said.

Carroll launched another campaign for new voting technology in 1996. The county convened a committee, which heard presentations from three manufacturers of optical scanning equipment, including Global Election Systems. But after a state computer analyst warned that all three systems had potential flaws, that modernization effort also failed. Four years later, when dimpled and hanging chads turned Broward's election into a national joke, Carroll felt vindicated. "If we had a marking pen [optical scan] system, we would not be quibbling about whether a voter meant to make a mark," she said. "We're quibbling about chads, about a pinprick that could change a ballot."

Carroll retired recently, and she believes that her Democratic successor will have better luck persuading the commission to spend the money. "We'd look pretty stupid if we said no," said Commissioner Kristin Jacobs, who was elected in 1998. "The likelihood of this historic event ever repeating itself is slim, but it really highlights the need of engaging in a more accurate method of counting the will of the people."

Around the nation, other local governments are moving toward similar conclusions, thrust in that direction by their own, less publicized problems with punch cards in 2000—and by the lawsuits. Florida's election meltdown pushed nearly everything else off the front pages, but state officials elsewhere endured a plethora of Election Day problems, including punch-card ballot malfunctions.

In Chicago and the rest of Cook County, 123,000 of the 2 million presidential ballots—6 percent—were spoiled, twice the error rate of the 1992 and 1996 elections. Like many cities, Chicago experienced a surge in voter registration just before Election Day, and city leaders believe that some of those new voters, taking their first crack at a punch card, lost their way among 456 punch holes on a long and complicated ballot.

Cook County election officials purchased their PBC 2100 voting system for $25 million in 1999. They first used the system in

every precinct in the November 2000 election. A close cousin of
the Votomatic, the PBC (Precinct Ballot Counter) uses the same
punch-card technology Chicago has employed since 1976. But it
is the first and only punch-card system in Illinois that enables
election workers to tabulate ballot results at every precinct. The
results are transmitted to the election headquarters in downtown
Chicago over cellular airwaves, allowing for quick returns. The
system has a feature that can reject overvotes, undervotes, and
ballots that don't bear the required signature of a poll judge. Election experts say such technology greatly reduces voter error and
can put a punch-card system on the same legal footing as newer
voting technology that allows errant voters a second chance.

Which sounds perfect, except that state law forbids local lawmakers to use the second-chance feature without the consent of
the state Legislature. Chicago leaders didn't have that permission,
though they had been seeking it for two years. Some observers,
including the Rev. Jesse Jackson, accused Republican lawmakers
of intentionally blocking the technology to thwart voters in
Democratic-leaning Chicago. Cook County Clerk David Orr, who
initially downplayed ballot problems, eventually joined the chorus
calling for answers. "The bottom line is, I am very angry, and so
are many thousands of Cook County voters, that the legislators
just haven't let us turn on the switch," Orr said. "And that is quite
literally what happened."

And so the stage was set, and not just in Florida. Turnout
was expected to be heavy. Ballot forms were crowded and in some
cases confusing. Much of the machinery was old and flawed.
The mechanics of democracy were stressed to near the breaking
point.

"Usually, in close elections, nobody paid attention to the
problem [of punch-card voting], because it tended to happen in
races for minor offices," said Kimball Brace, president of Washington, D.C.–based Election Data Services, a consulting firm.

"Well, we just had this election for a small office called the president of United States. And it was close, very close.

"The fact that this problem was uncovered in such a prominent race doesn't mean the problem wasn't there before this election. It was always there."

And soon, everyone would know it.

HOW AMERICA VOTES

Survey by the political consulting firm Election Data Services, 1998

Type of Voting Equipment Used	Number of Counties	%	Number of Precincts	%	Est. 1998 Population	%	Registered Voters	%
PUNCH CARD								
CES	48	1.53	1,675	0.87	2,345,723	0.87	1,254,846	0.81
PBC Counters	9	0.29	2,645	1.37	126,649	0.05	65,080	0.04
Punch Card*	460	14.65	44,215	22.98	54,560,615	20.23	31,499,680	20.43
Vote Recorder	18	0.57	1,039	0.54	3,322,794	1.23	1,742,706	1.13
Votomatic	43	1.37	14,763	7.67	27,031,718	10.02	13,212,065	8.57
Totals	578	18.41	64,337	33.44	87,387,499	32.40	47,774,377	30.98
OPTICAL SCAN								
Accuvote	106	3.38	4,009	2.08	7,331,610	2.72	4,122,503	2.67
Air Mac Tech	10	0.32	142	0.07	292,948	0.11	188,504	0.12
American Information System	127	4.04	4,125	2.14	4,898,663	1.82	2,950,803	1.91
CES—Optech	9	0.29	468	0.24	1,299,217	0.48	731,064	0.47
Mark-A-Vote	11	0.35	4,207	2.19	4,470,628	1.66	2,153,947	1.40
Optical Scan*	729	23.22	26,195	13.61	37,923,156	14.06	22,292,879	14.46
Optech III-PE	141	4.49	3,582	1.86	6,054,406	2.24	3,694,542	2.40
Mark-Sense								
Optech II	10	0.32	247	0.13	598,432	0.22	362,332	0.23
Optech 3P Eagle	37	1.18	2,656	1.38	7,079,855	2.63	3,661,559	2.37
Mark Sense	37	1.18	1,858	0.97	3,514,426	1.30	1,971,244	1.28
Totals	1,217	38.76	47,489	24.68	73,463,341	27.24	42,129,377	27.32

LEVER MACHINE							
AVM	223	7.10	23,130	12.02	30,916,038	11.46	18,425,620	11.95
IES Shoup	185	5.89	15,992	8.31	15,155,162	5.62	8,466,084	5.49
RF Shoup	16	0.51	189	0.10	310,374	0.12	163,669	0.11
Voting Machines*	6	0.19	487	0.25	610,815	0.23	399,612	0.26
AVM—Printomatics	50	1.59	2,109	1.10	1,981,519	0.73	1,168,210	0.76
Totals	480	15.29	41,907	21.78	48,973,908	18.16	28,623,195	18.56
ELECTRONIC							
Electronic Voting*	13	0.41	1,541	0.80	2,556,814	0.95	1,588,308	1.03
Microvote	33	1.05	1,382	0.72	2,794,693	1.04	1,871,914	1.21
Sequoia Pacific AVC Advantage	24	0.76	3,342	1.74	4,870,764	1.81	2,764,099	1.79
Shouptronics	118	3.76	4,303	2.24	7,854,599	2.91	4,562,990	2.96
Votronic	5	0.16	104	0.05	260,144	0.10	152,577	0.10
Direct Recording Electronic (DRE)	64	2.04	3,361	1.75	5,578,020	2.07	3,140,672	2.04
Totals	257	8.18	14,033	7.29	23,915,034	8.87	14,080,560	9.13
Datavote**	57	1.82	7,690	4.00	10,872,450	4.03	5,151,928	3.34
Paper Ballots	410	13.06	5,551	2.88	3,750,397	1.39	2,427,669	1.57
Mixed (more than one system)	141	4.49	11,412	5.93	21,324,009	7.91	14,033,374	9.10
TOTALS	3,140		192,419		269,686,638		154,220,480	

* Many respondents did not list the brand name of their voting system.
** Datavote is a punch-card system that includes candidates' names on ballots and allows voters to file multiple cards.
Source: Election Data Services (www.electiondataservices.com)

5

SOMETHING BAD
IS HAPPENING OUT THERE

It is 2:30 P.M., Tuesday, November 7, 2000. Election Day. Democratic politicians—a congressman, two state legislators, one county commissioner—surround Palm Beach County Supervisor of Elections Theresa LePore. The politicians are frantic, and their constituents are furious. They say the presidential election is being botched—maybe even stolen—right in front of their eyes.

LePore's phones ring incessantly as thousands of people get nothing but busy signals. All over the county, voters are having trouble deciphering the ballot. Even those who thought they voted correctly are hearing horror stories from friends and relatives, and now they are worried too. Did they really vote for the candidate of their choice? They do not know. They will never know. And waves of voters are still rolling to the polls, which will be open another six and a half hours. Soon the after-work crowd will line up. Do something, the politicians say. Do something, the callers say.

LePore pulls out a piece of yellow paper and scribbles a message on it—"ATTENTION ALL POLL WORKERS: Please remind ALL voters coming in that they are to vote only for one presidential candidate and that they are to punch the hole next to the arrow next to the number next to the candidate they wish to vote for."

OK, the politicians say, that might work. When can you fax it to voting stations? LePore says she can't. The stations don't have fax machines. The politicians say, so call them. LePore says she can't. The phones are too jammed up. Instead she tells employees to read the script to any poll worker who happens to call in and to deliver it by hand if anyone happens to visit a precinct. Less than half of the county's 531 precincts receive the message before 4 P.M. Some never receive it.

Crowds and confusion. Bad ballot design and defective equipment. It was a recipe for a flawed election, and a bad election is what Florida got. The state's 5.9 million voters ruined at least 174,000 presidential ballots—some by voting for more than one candidate, some by failing to cast any vote that could be read by a ballot-counting machine. That is a failure rate of nearly 3 percent—half again the 2 percent level that had become commonly accepted by election officials around the country.

Thousands of people in Palm Beach County and possibly elsewhere, confused by ballot designs or subverted by ballots that became misaligned in machines, voted for candidates they did not intend to choose. Within four days of the election, 7,000 Palm Beach County voters filed affidavits with Democratic Party lawyers. All suspected that they had miscast their votes.

Tony Fransetta, president of the Florida State Council of Senior Citizens, drove his wife, Lena, home after they voted at Precinct 159J in Palm Beach County's Wellington area at 8:50 A.M. On the way she exclaimed, "Oh my God, I think I voted wrong." He returned to his office and found a phone message from a friend, Jewel Littenberg. She said she also believed she had punched the wrong hole. He spoke to a worker at the county's

Democratic headquarters, asking if the office had received any complaints. "She said they were overwhelmed with them."

Democratic State Senator Ron Klein, one of the politicians who implored LePore to confront the problem that afternoon, said his fifteen-year-old son accompanied him to his precinct in Boca Raton at 7:10 A.M. It was intended as a learning experience, Klein said, and it turned out that they both learned something. The teenager thought he noticed a strange alignment of names on the ballot. Klein said his son told him it looked as if someone might mistakenly select Buchanan rather than Gore. "I looked at my ballot," Klein said, "and I noticed the misalignment."

He put the ballot in the box and began what he thought would be a routine visit to other precincts to see how the vote was going. "By ten o'clock," he said, "I ran into people who were crying. There were many of them. I called the Palm Beach County Gore campaign offices at ten-thirty and told them what was going on. Then I drove from Boca to see LePore at two-thirty, and when I got there she turned to me and said, 'I know there's a problem.' "

F lorida wasn't the only state that endured problems on Election Day. Around the nation, election workers chalked up much of the trouble to the sheer volume of voters, many of them casting ballots for the first time. Nevertheless, irregularities did appear in many states.

In Wisconsin, the Republicans cried foul. They claimed that a Democratic activist offered homeless people cigarettes to vote for Gore and that 174 students at Marquette University voted twice. One Marquette freshman gave the story credence, bragging to ABC News that he voted four times. He later recanted. Such stories mattered in a state where the margin separating Gore and Bush was 6,099 votes out of more than 2.5 million cast, but Milwaukee County District Attorney E. Michael McCann found no evidence of double voting. The cigarettes-for-votes case remains under investigation.

In New Mexico, where Gore and Bush were barely 10,000 votes apart, a computer glitch forced a delayed count of 67,000 absentee ballots that hadn't been recorded accurately on Election Day. The final tally gave New Mexico to Gore—by 366 votes—more than a week after the election. New Mexico had the closest result outside Florida and was the second-to-last state to declare a winner.

The most vexing problem around the nation concerned the sheer size of the electorate. Nationwide, 51 percent of eligible voters turned up at the polls. They caught poll workers off guard; just four years earlier, turnout had dipped to 49 percent, the lowest level in seventy years. And of course the population had grown since 1996. Chicago saw a surge in voter registration just before Election Day, which helped generate those 123,000 ruined ballots and complaints from Democratic politicians. In New York City alone, 76,700 citizens registered to vote on the last possible day. In Georgia, 150,000 people joined voter rolls in the ten days before November 7.

In Saint Louis, telephone lines became so clogged on Election Day that poll workers found it nearly impossible to verify voters' eligibility, a problem mirrored across the nation. With no one to tell them otherwise, poll workers in Saint Louis allowed 135 unregistered people to cast ballots. An unknown number of registered voters were turned away. Some poorly bound voter lists fell apart, leaving workers unable to find voters' names.

Election workers in Saint Louis weren't prepared for the throngs. Voters waited for hours in lines that stretched out polling place doors. Democrats, fearful of losing votes, persuaded a local judge to order the polls to stay open until 10 P.M. Missouri Republicans quickly appealed, and an appeals court panel reversed the order at 7:45 P.M. But the city elections board didn't close the polls until half an hour later. Some polling places remained open until the lines had cleared, and the last vote wasn't cast until 8:45 P.M. Other poll workers left their posts at 7 P.M., defying the first court order. A subsequent investigation found that fewer than 100 people had voted after 7:00 P.M., not enough to change the outcome of any major election.

Judges denied similar requests to extend voting hours in Detroit and other voter-clogged cities. Democrats in Portland, Maine, made a failed bid to keep the polls open after a clerical error purged as many as 3,000 people from voter rolls in that heavily Democratic city.

Thousands of New York City voters who called the Board of Elections' much-celebrated help line on Election Day were told that all circuits were busy. Voters across the boroughs waited in long lines. Poll workers at several precincts in Brooklyn briefly turned people away when voting machines failed and paper replacement ballots ran out. Angry New Yorkers spilled out of the polls spewing obscenities.

In Georgia, where old-fashioned lever voting machines remain the most common system for casting ballots, the rate of presidential undervotes and overvotes on Election Day reached 3.5 percent, nearly double the national average. Almost 1 of every 30 ballots—94,000 in all—showed no valid vote for president. Georgia election officials blamed machine malfunction and human error—two problems now associated most closely with Florida.

Back in Palm Beach County, a *Herald* investigation found that many of LePore's poll workers had learned of serious mechanical problems before the polls opened but did nothing to resolve them. By state law, poll workers are required to confirm the accuracy of ballot books on all machines just before precincts open, and that procedure often includes a mechanical test of the machines themselves. But many machines in Palm Beach County—and some in Miami-Dade County—failed those mechanical tests. They remained in service anyway, apparently preventing some voters from casting proper ballots.

In punch-card counties, it usually works like this: One poll worker reads aloud names and referendum items on the ballot, while another punches the number corresponding to each name or item. Then the person who punched the card makes certain that each hole is completely punched and that each punch is properly aligned with the number of each name or item on the ballot. That worker initials the card and adds the machine's serial number. If the worker detects a problem, the machine must be taken off-line and replaced with another.

But the *Herald* found a distinct correlation between bad test ballots—conducted by poll workers before 7:00 A.M. on November 7—and precincts that registered alarmingly high undervotes later in the day. In Palm Beach County, for instance, reporters inspected test ballots from 462 machines: 96 of those test ballots— nearly 21 percent—showed failures. Many had hanging or dimpled chads. Others had half-moon indentations on the lower border of a chad, indicating that the stylus had not hit the chad squarely, instead touching the bottom perforation, a sign that the ballot was misaligned in the machine. Some test ballots were completely mangled—not a single proper vote on them. Yet poll workers apparently kept those machines in service. LePore and her aides received no calls on Election Day about bad test ballots or faulty voting machines.

The analysis also showed that the test-ballot failure rate was far higher for the "knock-off" Data-Punch machines than for brand-name Votomatic machines and that the undervote rate was also far higher on Data-Punch machines. Palm Beach County precincts that had at least one Data-Punch machine had an undervote rate three times higher than those that didn't. Countywide, brand-name Votomatics were used by 75 percent of the voters, and 1.6 percent of them cast undervotes; Data-Punches were used by 25 percent of the voters, and 4.4 percent of them cast undervotes. The *Herald* found that the Data-Punch machines were plagued by worn out parts, including plastic springs that had been discontinued years earlier by their manufacturer because they were associated with spoiled votes.

Another indication of the problem: In the fifteen precincts that registered the highest number of undervotes, all but 16 of the 242 machines in use were Data-Punches. Of the 186 test ballots already reviewed in ten of those precincts, 21 failed, showing hanging or dimpled chads. No machines were taken out of service.

Shown many of these failed test ballots, LePore shook her head and bemoaned the behavior of her poll workers. "What am I supposed to do?" she said. "They are told over and over again how to check these things. Look at this, it's written right there on the top of the test ballot."

Her county was not alone in this. Another review by the *Herald* showed that thirteen of the twenty voting machines in the two Miami-Dade County precincts with the highest rates of discarded ballots did not show votes for at least some candidates during a test vote that was conducted minutes before the polls opened. Elections department supervisors said they believed precinct workers conducted the tests improperly and the machines performed properly. The precinct workers whose initials appear on the test ballots insisted that they performed the tests properly but did not realize the machines had failed the tests.

In any case, the machines at Dunbar Elementary in Overtown and Lillie C. Evans Elementary in Liberty City—both areas predominantly black—were not taken out of service as they should have been. On November 7, the precincts each had an eight-person crew consisting of a clerk, an assistant clerk, a sheriff's deputy, and five inspectors. According to elections department records, most workers at both precincts had several years of experience, and both clerks have worked for more than twenty years. Poll worker Sherrill Blue initialed three test ballots at Evans Elementary. Two of those tests were perfect, but the third lacked all ten punches in the presidential race. Blue had no explanation for that. "I don't know why that would have happened," Blue said. "We always make sure the holes go through."

County election officials insist that the machines should have worked. Gisela Salas, the county's assistant election supervisor, said the testers probably didn't press hard enough or didn't hear the numbers when they were called out. John Clouser, another assistant supervisor, said that the test is only a backup, similar to one conducted at a county warehouse in the week before an election. "We punch through every single position just to make sure everything is OK," he said. "If it's OK, we send [the machine] out." Every machine sent to the precincts passed those warehouse tests, he said.

Had precinct workers realized that the tests had produced failing results, and had they then acted on that, they might have been able to avert serious ballot problems. The two precincts in question—Dunbar and Evans Elementaries—had the highest rates of discarded presidential ballots, both undervotes and overvotes, in the county. The Evans precinct had a discard rate of 13 percent of presidential ballots, or 113 of 868 ballots cast; Dunbar's was 12.8 percent, 105 of the 820 ballots cast. The results were more than double the rate of discards in the 1996 presidential election. That year at the Evans precinct, 819 presidential ballots were cast and 54 were not counted, a discard rate of 6.2 percent. At Dunbar, 754 presidential votes were cast and 46 were not counted, a 5.8 percent discard rate.

In a check of the ten presidential candidates on the 2000 ballots, two test ballots—one in Dunbar and one in Evans—lacked punches for any candidate. A ballot at Evans failed to register a mark for the number assigned to Gore. By comparison, test results were flawless in the precinct with the county's lowest percentage of discarded ballots—St. John Neumann Catholic Church in Kendall.

Larry Williams, an Evans worker whose initials appear on five test ballots, said the machines were tested fifteen minutes before opening. He and Blue were surprised when they learned that punches were missed on their test cards. "We take [the ballot] out, check it, and initialize," Williams said. "We make sure it's all right, and we turn it in to the clerk." When told that a ballot he initialed was missing punches, he said he had some difficulty using one of the machines but finally managed to push the stylus through the slot. "I had to work it a little," he said, "but it went through."

Two studies—one by the *Herald* and another by an independent researcher—also found that as many as 1,700 Miami-Dade voters invalidated their presidential ballots because they mistakenly punched the chads immediately below those corresponding to their preferred candidates. Anthony Salvanto, a faculty fellow in the University of California at Irvine's political science department, said those voters penetrated meaningless chads—chads that didn't correspond to any candidates—probably because their punch cards were not properly aligned with ballot books in the voting booth. In some cases, Salvanto believes, voters simply inserted their ballots incorrectly. But, he said, the slots in some voting machines might have been misaligned, defeating the efforts of even the most expert voters.

The finding added to the growing body of evidence suggesting that many voters whose ballots showed no presidential preference actually did intend to vote. The thwarted votes found by Salvanto represent more than 15 percent of Miami-Dade's 10,650 undervotes. Engaged in a national study of voting behavior, he had arranged before the election to obtain data for every ballot cast in Miami-Dade. The machines that read ballots can be programmed to provide digital representations indicating how each card was voted. The data come only from ballots that can be cleanly read by the machines, ballots that include no hanging or dimpled chads. The pattern Salvanto found favored Gore: 1,012 voters punched number 7, one below Gore's number 6 position; 696 voters punched number 5, one spot below Bush's position at number 4. So, if the cards had been aligned properly, Gore might have gained 316 more votes than Bush would have gained.

Often the pattern was repeated throughout a voter's ballot, Salvanto said. On about 400 ballots, voters also punched unassigned holes precisely one spot below those for Democratic candidates for U.S. Senate, commissioner of education, and insurance commissioner—leading Salvanto to conclude that those voters meant to support a straight Democratic ticket. "It's particularly telling when they punch other unassigned chads that are one down from the Democratic candidate," Salvanto said. "This happened all the way down their ballot."

Even if the U.S. Supreme Court had not stopped the recount of undervotes in Florida, it's unlikely that these ballots would have helped Gore, because they were obviously punched improperly. But Salvanto, who studies voter behavior in polling booths, said the phenomenon shows how some voters can become confused by voting systems—to the point of ruining their ballots. "The voting machine is not an everyday appliance," Salvanto said. "That's why some people have advocated moving to more of an ATM-like system, which people see and use every day. You're taking a piece of cardboard and sticking it into a slot. The vast majority of people do this correctly. But what we do see is that the system, by virtue of the fact that you have to take this flimsy piece of cardboard and put it correctly into the slot, is just flawed enough that it can impact a close election."

Salvanto believes that some voters may have been unable to push their ballot cards all the way into the slot on the voting machine, causing the holes on the ballot book to sit over the wrong chads. But Miami-Dade Elections Supervisor David Leahy, while concurring with most of Salvanto's findings, said the voting machines have a safeguard that makes it impossible to punch through any chads at all unless the ballot card is fully inserted: a plastic shield blocks the stylus from punching through the card in invalid spots.

Leahy hypothesizes that those voters who punched meaningless chads simply placed their ballot cards on top of the ballot book. If voters had aligned the bottom of the card with the bottom of the frame holding the book, they would have achieved the same one-spot-down misalignment, with the arrows corresponding to candidates' names pointing to invalid chads. Thus a Bush voter would punch number 5 instead of the correct spot at number 4. But that scenario would require voters to ignore the fact that the numbers beside the candidates' names were different from the numbers on the punch cards themselves.

Salvanto had not examined any machines and could not say whether mechanical problems might account for the mispunches, but he said the possibility requires investigation. If, for instance, slots were slightly misaligned, or a mechanical problem on a particular machine caused mispunches only intermittently, that might explain the relatively small number of examples that appeared in each precinct. "I would like to know how bad the problem is, if there is one. Does it happen every time a machine is used or just once in a while?" he said. "Even if there is a small problem, it's a problem. Every vote is supposed to count."

Mechanical problems were reported around the state but not at a particularly high level. State law requires each of the sixty-seven county supervisors of elections to complete a one-page report titled "Report on Conduct of Election." Among the three questions they had to answer soon after the election: "Did you have any problems which occurred as a result of equipment malfunctions either at the precinct level or at a counting location?" Seventeen of the sixty-seven responded affirmatively. Five of those counties use punch cards, but in general, all of the reported problems were minor: a jammed ballot or a balky card-reading machine. Ballot-reading machines connected to optical scan systems seemed particularly troublesome, sporadically failing to register votes at some precincts or central tabulation points, but no supervisor reported serious problems or votes lost because of faulty equipment. Palm Beach County didn't officially report any mechanical problems.

LePore realized early on Election Day that something was wrong, but she did not learn until much later that many of her machines were malfunctioning. Much more immediate at the time, and much more obvious to all involved, were the profound problems caused by the butterfly ballot: overvotes that disenfranchised thousands of people, and votes intended for Al Gore that were accidentally given to Pat Buchanan. It turned out that voters in LePore's county were handicapped by faulty machines *and* a confusing ballot design, the perfecta of imperfect elections, and nothing short of electoral chaos resulted.

Carol Roberts, a member of Palm Beach County's election canvassing board, didn't see the ballot until she voted at 8 A.M. She didn't have any trouble with it, but she suspected that others would. "I knew what I was going to do, and I did it," she said. "I turned it over and found a dimple, so I put [the ballot] back in, checked it, and pushed it out. When I became aware that there were problems, I went to the Century Village polling places and was basically besieged by poll workers [reporting problems]."

At the same time, phones started jangling at Palm Beach Democratic Party headquarters. "Little old voters were upset that they were confused," said Party official Peyton McArthur. "Some said, 'There's something wrong with the ballot; it doesn't line up.' At nine forty-five, a woman called and really explained it, so I knew exactly what she was talking about, and I thought, 'Oh my God.' "

In nearly every case, people complained that they had accidentally voted for Buchanan instead of Gore or that they had voted for both. In some cases, they said they were denied the replacement ballots that are authorized by law. In other cases, they said they did not realize they had made a mistake until after they left the polling place.

Tony Enos, LePore's close aide, handled some of the complaints. Months later he remained convinced that they were overblown. "It has to do with it being a close election," he said, "so people were mainly venting, then they felt better. I don't usually get defensive, because it has to do with people's feelings. I'd say, 'How do you know you voted for Buchanan?' They heard it on TV so they thought it too. Buchanan would have gotten a hundred thousand votes if all the people who thought they voted for him really did."

Still, a *Herald* computer analysis of election returns from Palm Beach County and neighboring Broward County revealed an enormous disparity between two very similar Democratic strongholds. In the massive King's Point condominium development in the Broward city of Tamarac, Buchanan received 1 vote for every 851 cast for Gore. In the equally massive King's Point development in the Palm Beach County city of Delray Beach, Buchanan received 1 vote for every 72 Gore votes. The populations of both places tend to be elderly and predominantly Jewish. "If Palm Beach County is a Buchanan stronghold, then so is my synagogue," said David Goldman, former chairman of Florida's Reform Party.

Isa Friedman, a retired engineer from New York, said he watched his anguished neighbors in West Palm Beach's Century Village development leave their polling booths after they realized that they might have miscast their ballots for Buchanan. "Everybody I spoke with that made that mistake was just crying—crying tears," said Friedman, eighty-seven. "Some came out of the voting booth saying, 'I think I voted wrong. I think something is wrong here.' I heard people saying that. They certainly never intended to vote for Buchanan."

Kurt Weiss, who voted in precinct 60 at Century Village in West Palm Beach, is president of the United Civic Organization, a community group in the complex. Weiss said his community is between 65 and 70 percent Jewish—with a population entirely over the age of fifty-five. "My parents were killed by the Nazis, and almost every other member of my family," said Weiss, seventy-seven, who fled from Vienna in 1939. "They all perished." Yet Weiss feared that he voted for Buchanan by mistake. "I hope I didn't. I pray I didn't. But I'm not sure," he said. "We wouldn't vote for that man for anything. Even Alzheimer's victims wouldn't vote for Pat Buchanan."

It was much the same story in the black communities of Palm Beach County. At a polling station in a predominantly black neighborhood of Riviera Beach, Buchanan received 13 out of 709 votes—1 for every 50 cast for Gore. Throughout Florida, Buchanan fetched 1 vote for every 167 votes cast for Gore. In addition, Buchanan has opposed virtually every civil rights law of the last generation. "I do not believe thirteen of my neighbors knowingly voted for Buchanan," said Judy Davis, forty-five, a county school board employee who lives in that neighborhood. "I am so angry. I am very, very upset about this."

At the Greater Bethel Primitive Baptist Church polling place in Riviera Beach, Buchanan received 17 out of 1,262 votes—1 vote for every 71 cast for Gore. Margaret Doss, a church secretary who voted in the primarily black district, was astounded by that result. "I don't know what could have happened," she said.

Suddenly thousands of people wanted to know what was happening. They jammed phone lines in LePore's office, and the more technologically savvy resorted to e-mail. Some samples from LePore's e-mail logs:

Allison Nazarian of Boca Raton identified herself as an Ivy League–educated, working mother of two. "I was so confused by the physical format of the ballots and the booklets that (I later found out) I pierced the wrong holes and mis-voted. . . . There was no one to show me how to properly use the ballot, and I went at it alone, assuming I was doing it correctly. I would imagine that given our large senior citizen population, among other groups, I'm not the only one who wasted my time and my vote because of a confusing, antiquated ballot system. . . . The worst part is that some planning and forethought on the part of those administering the elections in our county and state could have prevented such a disaster."

Sandra Schultz e-mailed that she couldn't reach LePore's office by phone. She voted at Fire Station #3 in Boynton Beach, Precinct #148G. "When I had completed my ballot, I went to deposit it in the box. The woman attending the box took it from my hand and I asked why she was doing that—she said she had to check the ballots. I do not believe this is true. I think what she was doing was checking the holes on the back to see who I voted for. I told her that I did not think she had the right to touch or inspect my ballot. Isn't this true?"

Sy and Joan Rifkin of Boynton Beach: "The ballot was awful. I am not sure that my vote for president was recorded properly. The alignment of the presidential ballot was very confusing. Many people that I spoke with later in the day also experienced difficulty."

But by then, what could anyone do?

On the night of November 6, 2000, Theresa LePore left the office at about 10 P.M. The next day was Election Day. The once-every-four-years presidential race would be close, and turnout would be heavy, but she figured everything was under control. She thought the day would be so routine that she and her husband didn't even discuss it. Still, Election Day is when it all comes together, all those months of work, so after only a few hours of sleep, she awakened at 2:00 A.M. and was back at the office by 4:00 A.M.—after the required stop at Dunkin' Donuts. "I get six dozen doughnuts and a big box of Munchkins," she said. "It's an election morning routine."

She turned on the phones. Voters began calling at 5:00 A.M., wanting to know what time the polls were opening. Her staffers arrived about an hour later. The phones rang steadily, but there's nothing unusual about that on Election Day. Voters call. Poll workers call. The media call. Nothing out of the ordinary.

By 9:00 A.M., the phones were getting busier. People were complaining about the butterfly ballot, but the complaints had not yet reached critical mass and were not brought to LePore's attention. About ninety minutes later, a few voters appeared in person to complain, and the media overheard them. Now events started taking off. Something bad was happening out there, and LePore knew it.

By 2:30 P.M., that delegation of Democratic politicians arrived. LePore: "They were not happy, because they were Gore supporters. They wanted me to fax something to all the precincts. I said I can't do that because they don't have faxes. Then they said, 'Call them,' but I said, 'I can't do that because the phones are very busy.' But when poll workers called in, I made up a little script for staff to tell them to remind voters to punch the hole next to the arrow next to the name of the candidate they wanted to vote for. But that wasn't good enough, so I made up an information sheet and staff copied them, and I said, 'If you have a way to get them out there, go ahead,' and they agreed. . . .

"They [the politicians] did not make me feel very comfortable. They were accusatory, and there was a problem, and they wanted it fixed. I know them all very well. I was taken aback. Everyone had gotten copies of this [ballot], and nobody said anything. If they had, maybe I could have done something about it. I was surprised, and the later we got into the evening, the more surprised and disappointed I got."

Soon, other election supervisors also came under fire, among them Jane Carroll, who had overseen two hundred elections during her thirty-two years as Broward County's supervisor of elections. The second most populous county of Florida (after Miami-Dade), Broward is home to Fort Lauderdale, Hollywood, Pompano Beach, and the mushrooming suburban cities of Weston, Coral Springs, Pembroke Pines, and Miramar. It has a large black population and a growing Hispanic presence, as many immigrants and their children join an exodus from neighboring Miami-Dade that began in the aftermath of Hurricane Andrew in 1992. Broward's population more than doubled between 1970 and 2000, from 620,000 to more than 1.5 million. Carroll, seventy, was experienced, respected, and, as it turned out, prophetic. This is what she said on November 6, 2000, the day before the election, her last before retirement:

"The electoral college. We need to revamp that. It says that some people's votes are more important than others. It was created in the colonial days because in remote areas to gather every vote and count it was much harder. They probably missed some. Today that is not true. If one candidate wins the popular vote today and the other wins the Electoral College vote, people will rebel. It's time to say that every American's vote counts the same. And we need to somehow stop announcing the results of elections before the polls have closed on the West Coast and people are still voting. It's discouraging.

"And in Broward, we need a computerized voting system. Other counties have more modern systems. Our system is twenty-six years old, and we have to gather and count paper ballots from 618 precincts. . . . Broward County commissioners so far have refused to purchase a new system, but maybe they will for my successor."

The polls had just closed when Carroll arrived at the Voting Equipment Center in downtown Fort Lauderdale. She wore a red, white, and blue sweater she saved especially for Election Day. In what Carroll described as "an orderly sort of chaos," the ballots started trickling into the warehouse from nearby precincts. Staffers unsealed ballot boxes and carried punch cards into the computer room to be counted. The building was chilly, as is so often the case in computer centers, and some workers wore latex gloves to warm their hands. A machine tallied the ballots at a rate of 1,000 per minute. Just as the count began at 8:00 P.M., television networks projected that Gore had won Florida.

This was Carroll's last election as supervisor, and—just as she had feared—her county's antiquated voting system proved unable to record and measure her voters' choices accurately. In her line of work, nothing could be worse. It is not the way you want to go out.

By midnight, chaos reigned over order, she said. First the networks retracted their projection for Florida. Then one television report claimed that Carroll's office had lost ballots from nine precincts. Carroll knew that the ballots simply hadn't arrived yet. "I went out and told [the media] that this is not true, that we have not lost any precincts, but that wasn't exciting, so they didn't pay any attention to me," Carroll said. The "missing" ballots arrived at midnight from Pembroke Pines, but now other news outlets were running with the erroneous story.

Broward's count wrapped up at 4:19 A.M., giving Al Gore a 209,239-vote advantage over Bush. The winning margin was one of the largest in the country. But the vote was astoundingly close statewide. Florida Attorney General Bob Butterworth ordered a statewide recount by machine. That step is mandated by state law whenever a margin of victory does not exceed 0.5 percent of the vote.

After being awake for twenty-four hours, a weary Carroll went home for two and a half hours of sleep. She returned to the warehouse at 1 P.M. Wednesday, finding a choice parking spot among a growing cluster of cars. A sheriff's deputy told her she couldn't park there. The spot, he said, was reserved for the county sheriff. "I think I outrank him here," Carroll told the officer. Her red Mercury Cougar stayed.

But soon Carroll would leave again, twice heading out of town and sparking charges that she abandoned her post at critical times. In addition, her pre-election planning—particularly the distribution of election machines and polling places in Broward—would be attacked by critics who claimed that extremely long lines on Election Day discouraged many potential voters and essentially disenfranchised them. More specifically, Democrats blamed Carroll for failing to divide the county's most populous precincts. At least sixteen precincts were jammed with more than 3,000 voters each. Two in booming southwest Broward encompassed 7,000 voters. But others served 1,000 or 1,500 registered voters, and one had only 51 voters.

Precinct boundaries must be reviewed at ten-year intervals, after each U.S. Census, but the county can change them at any time. More precincts were drawn in ever-growing Pembroke Pines, for example, before the 1996 presidential election. Said Russ Klenet, a lobbyist and Gore fund-raiser: "You drive up, see a line and decide, 'Why do I need to do that?' This could have been done a lot better."

Carroll held her office from 1968, when she was first elected, until January 1, 2001, making her one of the longest-serving officeholders in Broward and one of the only Republicans to survive in the predominantly Democratic county. Born Jane Roberts Conner in Newport News, Virginia, on October 26, 1930, Carroll graduated from Southern Seminary Junior College and received her bachelor's degree in sociology from the University of North Carolina at Chapel Hill. She and her husband, Herb, moved to Broward in 1957. She taught fifth grade at Colbert Elementary School in Hollywood. She registered to vote as a Republican, having come from a family that didn't have any kind words for Democrats like Franklin Delano Roosevelt. In 1964, while her two children were toddlers, Carroll worked on Barry Goldwater's unsuccessful presidential campaign. The following year she was elected vice president of the Broward Republican Party.

Party activists urged her to run for supervisor of elections in 1968—the year Richard Nixon took the White House. Although she was the underdog in the general election against a former school board member, she won by 8,010 votes. Running elections was a lot simpler back then. Broward had only one district, so everyone used the same ballot. By contrast, the 2000 election required eighty-eight different ballots to reflect various races for state legislators, Congress, the school board, and the county commission.

Carroll's first major project was to replace the old voting system, in which voters pulled levers on 950-pound machines the size of telephone booths. In 1974 she purchased the punch-card ballot system still in use.

Remarkably, Carroll was only the second supervisor of elections in Broward history. Her predecessor, Easter Lily Gates, renowned for wearing colorful wide-brim hats, held the job for forty years. "I've been elected eight times, and I think that's pretty good," Carroll said.

Over thirty-two years, election fraud never tainted Carroll's office, though minor glitches surfaced. During the March 2000 primary, for example, poll workers in three precincts went home without sending their ballots in; a few absentee voters received the wrong ballots; and some residents of the city of Sunrise found themselves voting on a ballot measure for the city of Tamarac. Carroll said she worked diligently to avoid those snafus, but errors are inevitable in a county with 618 precincts staffed by temporary employees.

Before November 2000, the most serious controversy she endured revolved around her travel habits: Carroll developed a taste for travel at taxpayer expense. She took fourteen business trips during her last year in office, including journeys to Phoenix, Key West, San Francisco, and Cleveland. The trips cost $13,750, according to expense reports. Those seminars, Carroll said, helped her do a better job. "If I'd just been sitting here, I wouldn't know any more than I did the day I started," she said. "You don't want to reinvent the wheel all over the country. I pick up all kinds of things about ways to streamline operations."

Asked why she would need to attend workshops during her last year in office, she said, "I bring a lot of information back to the staff, and hopefully the staff will stay after I'm gone."

Mary Cooney, who worked for Carroll for seven years as a candidate qualifying officer, said Carroll's absences never caused any problems. "She's always had good people in place, so when she's not here, things still run smoothly," Cooney said.

But questions about Carroll's wanderlust paled in comparison with the criticism she absorbed in the weeks following the 2000 election. Voter turnout ended up at 66.23 percent in Broward, lower than Carroll anticipated and only slightly higher than the 64.86 percent in 1996. Yet the county had grown rapidly in the past four years, and her operation seemed largely unprepared for the crowds of voters.

Long lines snaked around polling places throughout the county. Many voters and precinct workers who called Carroll's office seeking confirmation of voter registration experienced busy signals. "This system was set up horribly," said Janis Hernandez, a poll watcher at a Pembroke Pines middle school where 2,695 voters cast ballots. "They were terribly understaffed. People were waiting for two hours. They would come in the morning and see the line was too long and try and come back at lunch. Then they would have to come back in the evening."

Several poll workers turned away voters because they were unable to verify their registration or change of address. At a precinct in Lauderhill, poll workers estimated they sent home at least 20 voters because they could not reach election officials. "There was not an answer but once, at seven-thirty in the morning," said poll worker Nat Rothenberg. "I felt so bad for these people who wanted to vote. I don't care who they wanted to vote for; they wanted to vote."

Carroll insisted that for every voter turned away, there was an explanation. Many voters didn't register in time to meet the state-mandated deadline for the election, while others moved from another county and forgot to change their voter registration. Still other residents who avoided jury duty by saying they no longer lived in Broward County were automatically deleted from the voter rolls.

Two days after the 2000 election, with controversy still brewing, Carroll boarded a plane to travel to her second home in Beech Mountain, North Carolina. This proved inconvenient. She was one of three members of the county's canvassing board, which was asked that day to consider a demand by Democrats for a hand recount of previously uncounted votes. Not only was she out of town, but she couldn't be reached. She didn't own a cell phone.

As it turned out, Carroll and her husband had missed their connection in Atlanta. They were waiting for another flight when they overheard a television broadcaster announce that Democrats were asking for hand recounts in four Florida counties, including Broward. Carroll immediately called her office—from a pay phone. She could hardly hear over the din of the airport. "What is going on?" she asked her assistant, David Beirne. "I can't believe this." She and her husband tried to return home, but had trouble finding seats. The next day she ended up participating by speaker phone in a meeting of the canvassing board.

The board conducted a partial recount and later a countywide recount of undervotes. But halfway through that countywide recount, Carroll abruptly quit. She told colleagues at lunch that she would not return to the Emergency Operations Center the next morning. She was going to Orange County, California, to spend Thanksgiving with her son.

About two years earlier, she had contracted Valley Fever, a fungus infection, while on a business trip to Sacramento. Although she fully recovered, the disease left her with easily irritated eyes and high blood pressure. She said the strain of fourteen-hour days spent squinting at hanging chads, dangling chads, and dimpled chads aggravated both problems.

"My husband finally called my doctor, and he said, 'Get her out of there,' " Carroll said. "This is the right thing to do. . . . I'm flattered that people think I'm indispensable, but I'm not." The canvassing board wrapped up earlier than usual that day, at around 7:00 P.M., with a farewell cake for Carroll.

One colleague joked: "It's made out of chocolate chads." By now, though, laughter was in short supply, and soon new disclosures would further rattle the foundations of Florida's electoral system.

6

DIRTY REGISTRATION ROLLS, TAINTED PRESIDENTIAL VOTES

Before most people outside of government had ever heard of a hanging chad, Florida's inadequate polling standards should have set off alarm bells for officials responsible for assuring the integrity of elections. For thirty-six days after November 7, America and the rest of the world would come to learn of the difficulties facing those attempting to count votes that—everyone assumed—had been cast legally. But the problem, in fact, ran much deeper than that. Magnetized by the rare, it-could-go-to-either-of-them struggle for the top prize of American politics, millions of Floridians joined the electoral chorus. But many contributed sour notes: they were unregistered voters, and they improperly influenced the outcome of this election.

The *Herald* discovered that thousands of Floridians cast illegal votes on November 7; they swore they were eligible to vote, but they were not. The ballots, all of which were counted, came from unregistered voters, ineligible felons, and a handful of senior citizens who voted absentee first, then voted again at their local precincts after swearing they hadn't voted before.

One of them was Cora Thigpen of Madison County, which

borders the Georgia state line. She is ninety years old and apparently quite a fan of Al Gore. She said she voted for him twice, once on an absentee ballot and again in person. "I do remember something about the absentee ballot, and I do remember going to the polls," she said. "If I voted a half-dozen times, I would have voted every time for Al Gore." Most votes, of course, are secret, and it will never be known precisely which candidate most benefited from illegal voting, but fraudulent votes were found primarily in large, predominantly Democratic counties.

That tainted votes were cast at all exposed the failure of a comprehensive new state campaign to prevent election fraud by purging registration rolls of dead and illegal voters. How did it happen? Overwhelmed by waves of voters, plagued by inadequate resources, reluctant to trigger conflict, inclined to err on the side of inclusion rather than exclusion, many poll workers proved indiscriminately hospitable. In many cases, voters merely had to sign statements swearing they were eligible to vote. No challenge, no check, no problem. "A lot of our poll workers are elderly, they are human, and they make mistakes," said Joseph Cotter, assistant elections supervisor in Broward County. "They were dealing with a huge turnout, people in line screaming in their faces, and they made mistakes."

Fort Lauderdale and the rest of Broward County represented a case in point. More than 850 illegal ballots were cast in Broward, hundreds by felons who lost their right to vote and hundreds by nonfelons who, intentionally or not, violated election laws. Records also show that one man voted twice—once by absentee and once at the polls—while another may have voted at two different precincts. Time after time across Broward, poll workers violated safeguards intended to defeat voter fraud. They were supposed to call election headquarters in Fort Lauderdale to verify registrations, but in dozens of instances the calls were not made. Other times, poll workers tried to call but to no avail. All they got were busy signals or long hold times. One frustrated poll worker, Jerry

Utter, said that many people showed up at his polling station in Dania Beach, near Fort Lauderdale, with driver's licenses or other picture IDs, but their names were not on the register. A veteran election worker with six years of experience, Utter followed his instructions and called headquarters. He pulled out a jogger's stopwatch and began timing the waits. Fifteen minutes. Twenty minutes. Thirty-five minutes. Forty minutes. Meanwhile, would-be voters hovered and grew incensed. "But you see, voting is important to people, so they'd wait a lot of the time," Utter said. "But sometimes they'd say, 'I can't wait anymore.' They had to get back to work or home to their kids. I felt really bad. So in those cases, I'd take their phone numbers, and if we got it sorted out, I'd call them. I don't know if they were all able to get back to the polls, though."

The last hour of Election Day, between 6:00 and 7:00 P.M. when the after-work rush descended, was the worst, he said. "The day ended with me on the phone, on hold, listening to classical music. I've never seen anything like it." Other workers finally surrendered, deciding to give some unregistered voters the benefit of the doubt—and also ballot cards. "I quit trying," said veteran clerk William La Fontaine, who supervised two precincts in Hallandale, twelve miles south of Fort Lauderdale. "It was impossible to get through on the phone." The illegal ballots were among 587,928 cast in Broward, which experienced a 66 percent turnout.

Poll workers overseeing the ballot boxes received four or fewer hours of training and were paid $95 to $125 for a fourteen-hour day. Election supervisors throughout the state complained that they had trouble recruiting such workers—low pay and long hours are not alluring enticements in a time of nearly full employment. Florida's election supervisors rely on an auxiliary army, almost a citizen militia, of poll workers willing to turn out for one grueling day of work at minimum wage. It is primarily an army of the elderly, subject to all the frailties that come with age, and supervisors are forced to recruit new battalions of workers each year as many of the last season's soldiers fade away.

Pam Iorio puts three thousand of these people to work on Election Day. She is supervisor of elections in Hillsboro County, which includes Tampa, and also president of the Florida State Association of Supervisors of Elections. A former county commissioner, Iorio has served two terms as supervisor. She is smart and civic-minded and very aware of the problem. The average age of the poll workers in Hillsborough County is sixty-seven. From year to year, she loses five hundred to a thousand people who worked the last election. "It's a chronic problem for supervisors," Iorio said. "We rely on a person who has a great degree of patriotism and dedication to volunteer work, even though we pay them. The person who is a retiree is the likely recruit. My poll workers are conscientious, they have a wonderful work ethic, but it is a challenge. It's a constant recruitment struggle."

Cotter, Broward's assistant elections supervisor, said that 400 illegal ballots turned up during a department review of voters who signed in at precincts where they weren't registered. The *Herald* found another 452 votes cast by felons. "Yes, there was a problem with the phone system—it got overloaded," he said. "But regardless, our poll workers are instructed not to let anyone vote without verifying registration with our office."

Most did not heed the order. They were overly benevolent or overworked or sloppy or all three, but *they did not heed that order,* and the integrity of the electoral system began crumbling at this very first checkpoint. Broward's illegal voters included 219 people who were registered in Miami-Dade, Palm Beach, other Florida counties, or out of state. Most appeared to have recently moved to Broward but had failed to register in their new home county as required by state law. Forty-four unregistered voters were allowed to cast ballots without providing photo identification; instead, they signed sworn statements attesting to their identity. Another 164 people voted even though their names were purged from

Broward's voter rolls because they had moved away and registered elsewhere or failed to respond to letters attempting to verify their registration.

An example of the things that went wrong: One Fort Lauderdale resident voted twice—once with an absentee ballot, then in person at Precinct 32Z. Corey Cornelius Green, twenty-eight, filed an affidavit with a poll worker swearing that he had not yet voted. But election records show that the registered Democrat cast an absentee ballot on November 2 using a different address. Had the poll worker checked Green's registration, she would have known he had already voted. She did not, blaming a busy signal. "Unable to get through," she wrote on Green's affirmation.

And another: Records show that two ballots were issued to George A. Harris, eighty-three, who stopped at two different precincts. But Harris, a Republican, insisted he only voted once, for Bush. "The elections department can't keep its records straight," he said. Harris said he ordered a voter card before the election because he had moved to a new home, but the card never arrived. He said that on Election Day he filled out an affidavit to vote at precinct 75R, which corresponded with his new address. The clerk turned him away, he said, because he was not registered there. So Harris said he drove to his old precinct, 59R, filled out another affidavit, and voted. "I'm glad you're exposing this," said Harris, a retiree from Pittsburgh. "The elections department is all wrong. There is no way I voted twice."

And yet another example: James and Irish Kendall voted for Gore, although they were not registered to vote in Broward. James Kendall said the couple had moved recently to Hallandale and failed to make the registration deadline for the November election. They were still registered in Miami-Dade. "We really wanted to vote," said James Kendall, thirty-three. "We showed the clerk our IDs from Dade, and [the poll worker] said, 'I don't know if I should do this,' but the supervisor said it was OK. We didn't know you couldn't do that."

La Fontaine, the poll worker, acknowledged that he signed the couple's affidavits. He said he felt obligated to let everyone vote. "I did not want to turn anyone's vote away," said the retired insurance broker and a World War II veteran. "I remember some folks came in from Dade. But I didn't have a right to turn their vote away. At least they got an opportunity to vote." To discourage fraud, La Fontaine said he made everyone without proper voter registration sign an affirmation swearing to their new address. "I did the best I could do," he said. "If someone lied, they'll have to take it up with God."

Similar irregularities were found nearly everywhere the *Herald* looked. Few counties were spared problems, and thousands of voters were implicated. They presented themselves in the wrong county or were otherwise unregistered, yet vote they did. "Numbers like that are very troubling," said Kurt Browning, the election supervisor in Pasco County, where 64 illegal votes were found. "What this does is chip away at the credibility of our whole elections system."

In Orange County, which included Orlando, Nathaniel Wiseman, thirty, said he voted although he is not a registered voter. Wiseman, a window tinter, said he moved into the county a year and a half ago from neighboring Seminole County but never bothered registering. "I told them I was not registered," said Wiseman, a Democrat who said he voted for Gore. "They looked around at each other and asked the precinct deputy for advice, and they let me vote." Nearby, in the tiny town of Ocoee, Keith Evans voted for president—although he told poll workers he lives ninety miles away in Tampa. "I feel more comfortable voting back home," said Evans, nineteen, a computer technician and college student who said he voted for Gore. "I was born and raised there. I know the issues. I just didn't know I couldn't vote there. The poll workers didn't say anything."

In Madison County, Elections Supervisor Linda Howell said the signature on the absentee ballot submitted by Thigpen, that ninety-year-old Gore supporter, matched her signature on the voter register in Precinct 3. Howell said the poll worker ignored the notation on the register showing that Thigpen had already voted absentee. "I was so shocked when I saw it," Howell said. "Why the clerk allowed it, I cannot tell you. I guess we are always going to have mistakes, because we are human."

In Lake County, in the heart of central Florida, James K. Rogers voted for president, although he admitted he lives in neighboring Sumter County. "I moved to Sumter, but I've been too busy with work to register there," said Rogers, twenty-eight. "So I drove back to Lake so I could vote." Rogers declined to tell the *Herald* for whom he voted except to say: "I was happy with the outcome."

In Daytona Beach and the rest of Volusia County, election officials discovered 277 bad votes, almost all from nonregistered voters. Seventy-three bad votes came from a precinct at Bethune-Cookman College. "Students were allowed to vote although they were not registered," said Denise Hansen, assistant supervisor of elections. Weldon Blake, a college employee and longtime vote-drive organizer, said that the Rev. Jesse Jackson appeared at the predominantly black campus on October 10—the state registration deadline for the presidential election—urging students to register. Blake said that many registration forms were filled out quickly and were missing required information: signatures, dates of birth, and proof of citizenship. That day, the Volusia elections office was flooded with boxes filled with applications. Many were rejected. Hansen said the elections office could not reach many students who applied at the last minute. As a result, many students went to the polls believing they were registered. "The poll workers could not get through on the phone, so they erred on the side of protecting someone's right to vote," Hansen said.

In Jacksonville and elsewhere in Duval County, poll workers allowed 327 unregistered voters to cast ballots, precinct registers show. The tally includes 162 people who filled out voter registration applications at the precincts—nearly a month after the October 10 registration deadline. Assistant Elections Supervisor Dick Carlberg said poll workers took matters into their own hands. Robert Kurtzke, a retired construction worker, oversaw voting at The Tides at Marsh Landing, where 15 nonregistered voters cast ballots. "There are really no safeguards," Kurtzke said. "The system is set up to allow people to vote. Think about it: You don't even need a voter's card to vote anymore, just a picture ID. But what could you do when someone showed up without a picture? To make things worse, it was impossible to get through on the phones to check if someone was registered, so we let them vote. What could you do?"

In Miami-Dade, reporters discovered that 473 illegal ballots were cast at 498 of the county's 617 precincts by voters who were allowed to sign in at polls where they were not registered. In one case, a ballot was cast in the name of an El Portal man who had died three years earlier. Local prosecutors and the Florida Department of Law Enforcement opened investigations.

It gets worse. Large numbers of felons voted for president, even though they lost their right to participate in any election when they were convicted. A computerized review by the *Herald* of 2.3 million ballots from twenty-two counties found 1,241 votes cast by felons. If the pattern repeated itself statewide, more than 2,500 felons most likely cast illegal ballots. "This just goes to show that the most expensive voting equipment in the world is worthless when the voting rolls are that filthy," said Deborah Phillips, president of the nonprofit Voting Integrity Project in Arlington, Virginia. "It's just an invitation to lower the integrity of the election." About 75 percent of the felons were registered as Democrats. Several civil groups have charged, in legal actions and through the media, that black voters were harassed, intimidated, and prevented from voting. There is considerable evidence of this, and the claims are being investigated. Some also claim that many legitimate voters—of all ethnic and racial groups, but particularly blacks—were illegally swept from the rolls through the state's efforts to ban felons from voting. There is no widespread evidence of that. Instead, the evidence points to just the opposite—that election officials were mostly permissive, not obstructionist, when unregistered voters presented themselves.

To find felony voters in Broward and elsewhere, the *Herald* compared lists of voters with the names on a database from the Department of Corrections. The newspaper then checked those names against a list of felons who had been granted clemency and are now allowed to vote. Only those who were sentenced to at least a year in state prison and have not received clemency are included in the *Herald's* tally of felony voters. Many election supervisors around the state said they weren't surprised that some felons and other illegal voters found ways to cast ballots, but they were unnerved by the magnitude of the problem. "No felon should be voting," said Broward's Cotter. "We try to keep the rolls clean, but I know the problems and limits of the information we're working with."

Many supervisors faulted the state's new antifraud effort, which they branded as nearly worthless because it is so polluted by error. Too many illegal voters slipped through, they said, and a few legal voters were mistakenly entangled like dolphins in tuna nets. The program grew out of a corrupted Miami mayoral race in 1997, exposed in a series of *Herald* stories that overturned the election and won a Pulitzer Prize. In response, the Florida Legislature in 1998 adopted sweeping reforms intended to scrub the rolls.

The reforms did not work. Among the felons who cast presidential ballots, the *Herald* found 62 robbers, 56 drug dealers, 45 killers, 16 rapists, and 7 kidnappers. At least two who voted were pictured on the state's on-line registry of sexual offenders. "There are a ton of us out there," said William Herman, thirty-seven, of

Lake Worth, sentenced to five years in prison in 1989 for negligent homicide with a motor vehicle. "It shouldn't be that way, but when they give you a voter registration card, hey, what are you supposed to do?"

Deerfield Beach resident Douglas Griffin said he has voted regularly since he was released from prison in 1990 after serving time for an aggravated child-abuse conviction. In the 2000 presidential election, the registered Democrat said he voted for Gore. "I just went [and] my name was on the [rolls] so I just voted," Griffin said. "I wasn't supposed to? Well, I didn't know that."

Clarence Williams, seventy-seven, of Pahokee in rural Palm Beach County also voted, even though he was convicted of sexual battery on a child in 1992. He never petitioned to have his voting rights restored. Charles Bodziak of Fort Lauderdale said he was released from prison in 1993 after serving time for several convictions, including burglary and theft, but he registered to vote when he applied for a driver's license six years ago. "I told them I was a felon, and I said, 'You sure I can vote?' She said, 'Yes, I don't see any problem with it,'" Bodziak said. "I was surprised, but then I thought, after I served my time, why shouldn't I be able to vote? I didn't mean nothing wrong by it."

In any event, this is clear: the $4 million statewide program to clean up the voter rolls collapsed in failure on Election Day, largely because county election supervisors had little faith in the purge list and treated it skeptically, removing only one of every five targeted voters. The list had been created by Database Technologies Inc. of Boca Raton under a contract with the state Division of Elections to compare voter registration rolls with criminal databases and lists of dead people. "We wanted these lists to be fairly broad and encompassing," said Emmett "Bucky" Mitchell, a former Florida Division of Elections lawyer who headed the purge effort. "It was never intended to be a cure-all." The company agreed, saying it was just a starting point.

Several months before the election, the state, through Database Technologies, sent local supervisors the list of nearly 58,000 registered voters who might be felons. Records show that the sixty-seven county supervisors of elections were told of the list's limitations, that the matches were graded as "possible" and "probable," and that they were responsible for verifying the accuracy of the matches. Social Security numbers weren't required on voter registration forms until recently, so the matches were sometimes limited to names and birth dates. The supervisors were wary from the start, and their confidence dropped another notch when the company told them it had mistakenly identified 8,000 Florida voters as having felony convictions in Texas.

Duval County Elections Supervisor John Stafford said he never trusted the purge list. One reason: a worker in his own office found her husband listed as a felon by mistake. "We weren't going to take that chance and delete everybody," Stafford said. "We'd have been in a world of trouble. It is almost a joke because there are so many errors in it." Duval had one of the highest turnouts among felons, with at least 258 voting illegally.

Many other counties—including Broward, Palm Beach, Leon, and Volusia—largely ignored the lists and did little with them. In other counties, such as Sarasota, the only felons purged from the rolls were those who acknowledged letters and admitted they were ineligible to vote. Some counties—including Miami-Dade, Hillsborough, Leon, Pinellas, Pasco, Manatee, Orange, Brevard, and Polk—worked the list hard, trying to verify matches and contact people through letters and newspaper ads.

But the confidence level plummeted again when the letters generated 7,837 appeals to the Florida Department of Law Enforcement, the state's official repository of criminal records. Of those, nearly half—3,729—turned out to be mistakes resolved in favor of the voter. Those voters were never purged, and—despite the county supervisors' concerns—the FDLE received only 8 valid complaints from people misidentified as felons on Election Day. One of those came from Michael Aron Murphy, a Tampa resident who never committed a crime but was invited to leave his polling place after mistakenly being labeled a felon. "I found out a long time ago when your last name is Murphy, Murphy's Law certainly applies," said the twenty-nine-year-old firefighter, a registered Democrat and Ralph Nader supporter. He landed on the list of felons because someone used his stolen driver's license in a crime spree. "I got some papers back from the state," he said. "But it was too late."

On the other hand, in Pinellas County, which includes St. Petersburg, a cautious stance allowed at least 212 ineligible felons to cast votes, the *Herald* found. Broward officials sent four thousand certified letters to targeted voters, but amid an outcry over unreliable data, the county adopted an honor system. "The state itself said we could not depend on the accuracy of the data," Cotter said. "We got hundreds of calls from people saying they were not felons. So we told people it was their responsibility to have us remove them from the list if they actually were felons who had not had their rights restored." Which leaves Floridians with exactly what the $4 million effort should have made unnecessary: felons on the honor system.

Not that all—or even most—felons intentionally breached elections laws. Joseph Bonner, twenty-one, with a felony drug conviction, voted in Pinellas County even though state law prohibited him from doing so. Later, he wrote this note to his elections board: "I wish to apologize for voting. Please understand that my error was made in good faith." Miriam Oliphant, Broward's newly elected supervisor of elections, said she believes that people like Bonner truly didn't know they were ineligible to vote. "They think it is all OK after they serve their time," Oliphant said. "My job now is to educate people, improve communication with the state, intervene, and prevent it from happening in the future." She believes technology is the answer. She wants poll workers to have laptops to check the sworn statements against Broward voter databases instead of having to phone elections office workers for confirmation. And she wants the state to provide counties with the ability to tap into the state's primary criminal databases so they can spot-check and verify information on the purge list.

Cotter agrees. He said his office is investigating what went wrong and will take corrective action. And while he and Oliphant have heard arguments about such a system being too costly, both wonder if Florida—and very possibly other states around the nation—can afford not to fix the problem. "We all need to look at the cost this has to the whole integrity of the election process here in Florida," Cotter said.

Meanwhile, Florida's policy of excluding felons from the voting booth has provoked complaints of civil rights violations. The ban was imposed in Florida after the Civil War, and twelve other states have similar policies. But by the end of the 1990s, Florida led the nation in disenfranchised adults, according to a report by Human Rights Watch and the Sentencing Project. By some estimates, at least 400,000 former prisoners—20 percent of them black—are still barred from voting.

Felons can restore their civil rights only by navigating a bureaucratic obstacle course. They must apply to the state Office of Executive Clemency in Tallahassee, a process that can take eight months to a year. And to qualify for restoration of their voting rights, they must have no more than two felony convictions, no pending criminal charges, and no outstanding penalties in excess of $1,000. The vast majority of felons have not yet sought that action.

The Justice Department began investigating whether Florida's purges of voting rolls unfairly targeted minorities. One group of civil rights advocates filed a federal class-action lawsuit against

Florida, and another prepared a state suit. It is perhaps no surprise, then, that the phrase employed by Cotter—"integrity of the election process"—also began sounding in other quarters, many other quarters, and often with the simmering anger generated by generations of second-class treatment.

7

"WE'RE GOING TO BE YOUR NEW VOICE"

It is lunchtime in Palatka, near Jacksonville in Florida's northeast corner, and the election is still five months away. Gray clouds darken the sky and trouble approaches from the horizon. Twenty people gather in the Bethlehem Baptist Church on Madison Street. Finally, Kendrick Meek and Tony Hill arrive. They are here to share the gospel of get out the vote.

Six months earlier, the two state legislators (Meek, a state senator from Miami, and Hill, a state representative from Jacksonville) had staged a twenty-hour sit-in at the office of Florida's lieutenant governor, protesting Gov. Jeb Bush's order to gut many affirmative action initiatives. The pair's peaceful act of defiance, so reminiscent of past battles won by earlier generations, galvanized Florida's 2.5 million black residents. Now Jeb Bush's brother is running for president, and it's payback time. Meek and Hill are leading an evangelistic statewide crusade to boost voter turnout by racial minorities and women—and to defeat George W. Bush. They call it Save Florida: Arrive with Five. Five other voters, that is.

"We don't want to be caught disconnected again," Hill tells

the congregation. "We want to stay connected, not just for this election but from here on." The audience leaps to its feet and seals a pledge with high-fives and a chant: "I'm going to stay connected! I'm going to stay connected!" Outside, thunder booms and rain pounds the stained glass windows. Inside, the fire-and-brimstone sermon rolls on for ninety minutes.

Blacks and women, Hill and Meek tell the audience, must elect candidates who will support issues vital to them—equal pay, affirmative action, education, and health-care reform. The two exhort the audience to organize shuttle services to polling places. They encourage absentee voting. Whatever it takes, they say, do it. Vote. A low turnout, they say, is a step backward. "I didn't have to sit in the back of the bus," Hill says, "and I'll be damned if I go back."

He also says this: "We're going to get people to ask questions in this election. It's going to be something else." He had no idea how right he would be.

Within little more than two months after the election, allegations that Florida blacks were disenfranchised in grossly disproportionate numbers triggered an inquiry by the U.S. Justice Department, a full-scale investigation by the U.S. Commission on Civil Rights, and a hearing conducted by the NAACP and other black groups. A federal class-action lawsuit, filed on behalf of all NAACP members and twenty-one individuals, alleged that in predominantly black precincts, votes were wrongfully disqualified, individuals were erroneously deleted from voter rolls, and voter registrations were improperly processed.

Adora Obi Nweze, president of the NAACP's Florida chapter, claimed that many minority precincts were understaffed, run by poorly trained workers, and unprepared for a deluge of black voters. She and others said these voters did not receive assistance to which they were entitled and that might have prevented voting errors. Four days after the election, during a hearing in Miami sponsored by the NAACP, Nweze shared her own Election Day experience. She testified under oath that she presented her voter registration card and a confirming piece of identification to a poll worker. "She went to speak to someone and she came back and said, 'You can't vote,'" Nweze recalled. "I said, 'Excuse me? What do you mean I can't vote?' She said, 'You have been sent an absentee ballot, and therefore you can't vote. Step aside, get out of line, and you may go see someone.'"

That someone, Nweze testified, said he was too busy to deal with her at that point, but he would get to her later. She told him she never received the absentee ballot and thus could legally vote in person. She told him: "Listen, I'm willing to wait all day if I have to, but I'm going to be voting or else you're going to have to send me to jail because I'm not leaving until I vote today." Still no action. After some delay, Nweze approached him again and requested a challenge ballot—one that can be used on the spot but is subject to subsequent confirmation by the county elections office. "If not," she told the man, "give me a regular ballot and let the elections department decide if I've committed fraud." Nweze said the man called the absentee section of the elections department, which proved unhelpful. Finally, after ninety minutes, she was given an affidavit to sign—and then a ballot, which she promptly cast. "I tell you, it took me every bit of the rest of the day to get over this because I wanted everybody in this community and throughout the state to know that whatever it takes, when you know you have your registration card, know you have everything in order, you must stand until you are allowed to exercise your right. I never understood what it meant to have the feeling that you were being disenfranchised."

In addition, allegations surfaced that, in at least one county, a roadblock by the Florida Highway Patrol intimidated black voters. "It's consistent with the overall plan and the overall actions in this state and in this country to treat blacks as though we don't count," Nweze said. "All of it falls under one banner, the disen-franchisement of the black and minority voter."

Atop all of this, the U.S. Supreme Court's decision to halt the statewide recount of undervotes—a ruling that ultimately sealed Bush's victory—aroused protests from many blacks. For one thing, a disproportionate share of the antiquated machines that produced undervotes had been located in minority precincts. For another, civil rights activists and black politicians noted that the Court, to support its ruling, leaned heavily on the U.S. Constitution's equal protection clause, which was originally intended to protect the rights of former slaves.

So, in the end, the hopes of most black leaders and individual voters were dashed. Despite unprecedented efforts to stimulate civic interest and get out the vote, thousands of their ballots were not counted, and blacks did not provide the winning margin for a candidate they considered hospitable to their concerns. Many emerged from this experience angry, discouraged, and disillusioned. Some, like Paulette Sims Wimberly of Miami, resolved not to support the new president. Bush was "selected, not elected," she said. "He's not a legitimate president. . . . I won't recognize him." And some learned a hard lesson: get-out-the-vote drives can prove unrewarding unless they are accompanied by voter education drives. "All this voter registration without education has caught up with us," said Irby McKnight, a Miami civil rights activist. "Every black person wants to do registration without telling them what it means. We have ourselves to blame for a part of this."

But not all of it. An analysis by the *Herald* of uncounted ballots substantiated many complaints raised by black leaders and voters. According to the study, presidential ballots were invalidated at higher rates in nearly all of Florida's majority-black precincts than in majority-white neighborhoods. The examination of precinct-by-precinct trends showed that the lopsided loss of black votes occurred throughout Florida and at shocking rates: nearly one of every ten ballots in majority-black precincts went unrecorded. In majority-white precincts, the discard rate was less than one ballot in thirty-eight.

Of Florida's 463 majority-black precincts, 82 percent had discard rates above the statewide average of about 3 percent. By contrast, 41 percent of majority-white precincts had higher-than-average discard rates. Moreover, the analysis also found that poor and less-educated voters of all races were more likely than better-off voters to spoil their ballots. Ballots in poverty-stricken precincts were discarded at a rate nearly twice that of better-off precincts, suggesting that socioeconomic factors formed the root of some of the problems.

David Bositis, senior political analyst at the Washington, D.C.–based Joint Center for Political and Economic Studies, which focuses on issues of concern to minorities, said balloting disparities were magnified on Election Day by a surge in black turnout that carried tens of thousands of new or infrequent voters to the polls. The problem was compounded by the lengthy, ten-candidate presidential ballot, he said, because voter error is enhanced by long lists of names and the odd ballots that must be designed as a consequence.

In addition, many blacks start off with an apparent disadvantage based solely on where they live. A higher proportion of black voters than white voters reside in the twenty-four counties that use error-prone punch-card machines. More than half of Florida's black voters are concentrated in five large urban counties—Miami-Dade, Broward, Duval, Hillsborough, and Palm Beach—that use punch-card systems.

Nowhere was the trouble with punch cards more obvious than in Duval County, where voters seemed confused by those inaccurate sample ballots—with all presidential candidates on one page—that were published in the newspaper. On the actual ballot, presidential candidates appeared on two different pages. "A lot of people thought that if you didn't vote on every page, your ballot won't be counted," said Rodney Gregory, an attorney working with the Democratic Party in Duval. About 9,000 of Duval's 21,942 overvotes came from majority-black precincts. In fact, nineteen of the twenty precincts with the highest spoilage rates in the state sat in heavily black neighborhoods of Duval. All had at least a fifth of their ballots tossed out.

Conversely, black voters are slightly less likely than white voters to live in the twenty-six counties equipped with optical-scan readers that alert voters to errors—places with the lowest discard rates in the state. Such machines, which read fill-in-the-oval ballots at the precincts, are typically programmed to return the card if a voter marks more than one candidate in a race. In some places, the machines also return the ballot if they fail to register a vote in a race. Statewide, when these electronic readers were used in predominantly black areas, the discard rate dropped to 3 percent. In contrast, the discard rate rose to 16 percent in predominantly black precincts that used scanning systems without the correction feature, and 11 percent in those that used punch-card machines.

Tiny Bradford County, a rural area and home to the Florida State Prison in Starke, has a modern fill-in-the-oval system. But voters don't get a chance to correct errors, because the ballots from the county's twenty precincts are read at a central location rather than at individual precincts. In Bradford's Precinct 7, where two-thirds of the voters are black, 88 ballots out of 464 were not counted. That is nearly 19 percent of the total, a figure that worried Bradford Elections Supervisor Terry Vaughan. "I don't want anyone to think there was any systematic way that any group was targeted," he said. "There is nothing sinister going on, but we need to figure out why this happened and come up with a solution."

Some counties have already hit on one. In Brevard County's

Precinct 98, where 95 percent of the voters are black and two-thirds of school-age children are so poor they qualify for free school lunches, only about 2 of every 100 votes were discarded. Scanners at all Brevard precincts return double-punched ballots to voters. Brevard replaced its old punch-card system with the optical-scan machines about eighteen months before the election. "Absolutely it's better," said Gayle Graham, Brevard's assistant supervisor of elections. "The voter isn't being disenfranchised if he makes a mistake."

Yet only 1,720 of Florida's 5,885 precincts were equipped with optical scanners that alert voters to mistakes. Many experts believe that counties have an ethical obligation to make voting as simple as possible for voters, which means using the best available equipment, regardless of cost, and adopting a clear, evenly applied policy of offering extra assistance to those who need it. "The fundamental problem is we have a history of discouraging people from voting, and that history is very clear," said Henry Thomas, chairman of the political science department at the University of North Florida in Jacksonville. "Casting a vote ought not be rocket science. Ordinary folks should be able to do it."

Many ordinary folks certainly tried, more than ever before. A dramatic development almost exactly one year earlier triggered the surge in black turnout. On November 9, 1999, Gov. Jeb Bush announced his One Florida Initiative, which called for an end to a state university policy that employed race as one of several criteria for admissions. For two decades, that affirmative action policy had helped balance the racial composition of the student body while aiding students who might have come from disadvantaged circumstances. Bush also issued an executive order that prohibited executive branch agencies under his control from using racial or gender set-asides in the awarding of contracts. In return, he promised to lead Florida to unprecedented diversity and opportunity—but without laws mandating it. In an attempt to lessen the blow to underprivileged communities, he offered state university admission to all high school seniors who finished in the top one-fifth of the class. That plan, later endorsed by the Board of Regents, reduced the importance of SAT scores, which critics say are culturally biased.

At first the announcement yielded little more than confusion. In an age of often strategically planned news leaks, no word of the One Florida Initiative trickled out before the public announcement, and immediate reaction was muted. But by the next day, skeptics began denouncing the policy as naive and forgetful of history. "The governor's plan doesn't eliminate the good-old-boy system, which is still alive and well," said U.S. Rep. Carrie Meek, D-Miami. She reminded Bush of Florida's "long history of blatant, legal, and official racism. The affirmative action law was all we had for a chance at equality of opportunity. Poor as it was, it was something."

Other black legislators joined in, including state Rep. Tony Hill, a Democrat from Jacksonville. He noted that less than 1 percent of Florida's $12 billion in state services contracts went to minority-owned businesses. "We had a law in place and it wasn't working, and now we are going on the assumption that people are just going to do the right thing?" he said. "It's not going to happen."

Even before Bush's initiative, tensions had been mounting. California businessman Ward Connerly, who is black but is an avowed opponent of affirmative action, threatened to sponsor a ballot initiative to end the practice in Florida. Jeb Bush's new policy was partially intended to blunt a potentially divisive fight over Connerly's plan.

And so, at 3:30 P.M. on January 18, 2000, Kendrick Meek (the son of Carrie Meek) and Tony Hill found themselves at the office of Lt. Gov. Frank Brogan to discuss Bush's new policy. The lawmakers wanted Brogan to ask Bush to rescind the One Florida

y unlikely" Bush would agree. The
ere prepared to remain in Brogan's
few minutes later, Bush appeared
"If you think I'm going to rescind
blankets." An hour later, one of
s for two.

press aide, in comments overheard
o be a living hell. Kick their asses
he was referring to news reporters,
, Meek and Hill insisted that they
opped his new plan, but they ended
agreed to meet with them. "We've
Meek said as he emerged from the
de sacrifices for us to reach where
that will infringe on our rights, we
have to protest.

The incident attracted widespread attention and enlisted
many new opponents to Bush's initiative. "A week ago, you would
have asked people about One Florida and they would have said,
'What is that?' " said Nweze, the state NAACP president. "A lot
of people didn't know what it was. Now they get to see what it's
about." Bishop Victor T. Curry, president of the Miami-Dade
branch of the NAACP, took to the airwaves on a local radio station and spent five hours urging the audience to reignite its tradi-
tion of peaceful protest, though with a modern touch. He called
on them to e-mail, fax, and call Tallahassee. "It's not as though
people haven't been dealing with it," he said. "We just needed a
wake-up call."

Message received. The public outcries compelled Bush and his
aides to arrange public hearings hastily in Tampa, Tallahassee, and
Miami. At the first meeting, in Tampa, hundreds of people
showed up, requiring officials to extend the hearing from four to
seven hours, and the session turned angry. Some speakers characterized Bush, who was not present, as a hypocrite who only pre-

tended to care about black Floridians. "You tell Governor Bush that I say if he does not resolve this, he'll be a one-term governor," Marvin Davies of Saint Petersburg's African-American Action Alliance said to thunderous applause. Then he linked One Florida to the overarching struggle for civil rights. "I've given you a list of people who have died over this issue, and I'm willing to die over this issue."

In Miami, a dispute flared over the meeting site. Bush's aides selected the county commission's chambers, a rather small auditorium. Miami-Dade Mayor Alex Penelas, concerned that limited access could inflame already heated passions, offered as an alternative the much larger Miami Arena. Finally, in the nick of time, everyone compromised on Gusman Hall, a downtown Miami theater more often the site of concerts than political action meetings.

A raucous crowd packed Gusman, once again transforming a forum on One Florida into an emotional civil rights rally spiced with verbal attacks on Bush. By the end of the seven-hour meeting, more than four thousand people had filed through the auditorium. This time, Bush listened from the front row as speaker after speaker blasted One Florida. He endured three hours of testimony, then left. "There's a lot of misunderstanding," he said, but he would not change his plan.

They called it A March of Conscience, and on March 7, 2000, the opening day of Florida's legislative session, tens of thousands of affirmative action supporters paraded up Apalachee Parkway to the Old Capitol Building in Tallahassee. Equal parts political rally and church revival, the demonstration bridged age, race and gender. Many had traveled overnight, among them Kenneth Pace, twenty-six, a minister at a Hollywood, Florida, church, who required six hours to complete the 450-mile journey. "This is a state-of-emergency situation," he said.

Civil rights and labor leaders gave the crowd its marching orders: maintain the pressure on Jeb Bush, smother his One Florida initiative, then defeat his brother, George W. Bush, at the polls in November. "When the playing field is equal, we can always make it," the Rev. Jesse Jackson told the crowd. "Level the playing field." Then he uttered a phrase that months later would still serve as a rallying cry for Florida blacks: "Stay out of the Bushes." Along the route, families walked in unison. Men held children on their shoulders. Mothers pushed infants in strollers. Some older marchers, their endurance no longer able to keep pace with their enthusiasm, hailed taxis and rode to the rally site instead of walking up the parkway.

For many in the sea of faces, the march represented far more than a battle with Bush over affirmative action. It was a pilgrimage, a personal renewal of the civil rights movement, the acceptance of an inheritance—the legacy of peaceful protest. This was reflected in words spoken by a Miami teenager to his grandfather, just before the young man left for this March of Conscience. "Papa," Douglas Sanders said to his grandfather, Kenneth Williams, "I wish you were going, but we're going to be your new voice."

Energy generated by the One Florida hearings and the protest march spread through black communities across the state. From radio talk shows to churches in Miami, Fort Lauderdale, Tampa, Tallahassee, and Pensacola, a unified call to action sounded: Make your voice heard. Register to vote. "If there's a large turnout, and if George W. Bush wins, then there's a large constituency that he has to deal with," Nweze, the state NAACP president, said at one point. "But if we don't vote, then he will write us off. If we don't vote, then he ought to write us off."

Representatives of the NAACP and People for the American Way had already stationed voter registration tables outside Bush's community meetings. During the Tallahassee session, volunteers signed up more than a hundred people, most of them students from predominantly black Florida A&M University. In addition, national organizations began supporting state efforts. The NAACP and the AFL-CIO pledged personnel and financial support to nourish the registration drives. Nweze had joined the national governing board, and the group pumped $400,000 into Florida's registration efforts. The group carefully noted that the effort was nonpartisan, though virtually everyone agreed that black voters were far more likely to vote Democratic than Republican.

Similarly, churches—among the most potent of forces in the black community—received aid and comfort from their parent organizations. The National Primitive Baptist Convention and several statewide religious organizations condemned Jeb Bush's initiative and supported registration campaigns and other efforts that might salvage affirmative action.

These efforts had startling results: between February 2000 and Election Day, 59,126 new black voters registered in Florida, adding to a flood of people who would vote in their first presidential election. Between 1996 and 2000, the number of black voters in Florida soared from 747,000 to 934,000—an increase of 25 percent.

"The black vote," said Kendrick Meek, "is smack in the middle of the election."

So hopes were high in June when union workers trudged down the dirt roads of tiny Gadsden County, along the Florida-Georgia line. Their goal: sign up 2,000 new voters and motivate them to visit the polls on Election Day. It was part of the statewide effort, but the recruiters here had an advantage. Gadsden is one of Florida's most Democratic counties. It has 22,016 registered Democrats and 2,593 registered Republicans. It was the only county to vote Democratic when Ronald Reagan won Florida in 1984. It gave the highest percentage of votes of any county to Hugh Rodham, President Clinton's brother-in-law, when he ran unsuccessfully against U.S. Sen. Connie Mack in 1994. And Clinton won 66.3 percent of Gadsden's vote when he recaptured Florida in 1996.

Alas, the recruiters also had a problem. Gadsden is the state's third poorest county, a place with rusting tin roofs and dusty farms and more history than future. Nearly 26 percent of its 47,000 people live in poverty. In one of its four high schools, 94 percent of the students read below the minimum standard, and the other three high schools aren't much better. It is also Florida's only majority-black county. Still, the goal was achieved: 2,000 new voters registered in Gadsden County—most of them as Democrats—and many of them would cast votes in November.

Elsewhere, dividends of the organizers' work were realized around the state. One day before Election Day, hundreds of blacks and other voters stood in line for hours to fill out absentee ballots. It was an early indication of how strongly people felt about the election and how determined they were to vote. Many of those people said they voted early because they planned to work on Election Day, at precincts or elsewhere, inspiring others to participate in the election. At Miami-Dade County Hall, election supervisor David Leahy observed a line of people that snaked through the lobby and out the door. "We have never had this kind of turnout," he said. "This election is bringing people out in droves. You can tell the intensity of this election."

Annie Clayton waited for two hours so she could vote absentee in Miami-Dade. Why? "We work tomorrow getting people to the polls," she said. As she finished voting, someone motioned her to a van filled with other voters. It was time to return to the community center and pick up another load.

But back in Gadsden, no one bothered to show new voters *how* to cast ballots, a problem that repeated itself around the state and undermined the entire black registration drive. Exactly 2,085—12.4 percent—of the 16,812 votes in Gadsden were ruined and thrown out. This was by far the highest percentage of discarded votes for any county in the state. Gadsden County uses an optical-scan system but does not marry it to a precinct-based tabulation system that alerts voters to their mistakes.

At least 1,900 people in Gadsden marked more than one choice for president. Many of them selected all ten presidential candidates and then scrawled Gore's name in the box used for write-ins, creating overvotes that were discarded. This undoubtedly cost Gore many votes and possibly the election. Among the votes that counted, Gadsden awarded 66 percent of its support to Gore.

"Ninety-five percent of those [lost] votes were for Gore," said Gadsden-born Jeanette D. Wynn, president of the Florida council of the American Federation of State, County and Municipal Employees. She watched Gadsden's canvassing board inspect rejected ballots one day after the election. "They were enough to give Gore Florida, from little Gadsden County," she said.

The *Herald*'s review of undervotes in Gadsden showed that 29 in that category—ballots rejected by counting machines because no clear vote for president could be found—would have gone to Gore and 15 to Bush, if voters had properly filled in their forms. A reporter inspected a total of 64 presidential votes in Gadsden that did not count because residents improperly filled out their ballots. Some voters used a ballpoint pen instead of the required No. 2 pencil. Others drew an *X* in the oval instead of filling it in. The placement of the oval in the race for president may also have confused voters. Because two candidates were listed—president and vice president—the bubble in that race appears between the two candidates. In the other races, the bubble appears directly to the left of the candidate's name. A number of voters put marks—similar to filling in an oval—next to Gore or Bush's name but did not properly fill in a bubble. "Our problem here is functional illiteracy," said Nikki Beare, seventy-two, a former Miamian who runs a used bookstore in Gadsden's tobacco-growing community of Havana. "It's that, and the fact that we're just about the state's poorest county."

Many blacks in Gadsden also alleged that white officials conspired to diminish the strength of their vote. Vivian Kelly, eighty-one, a leader of civil rights marches in Quincy in the 1960s, said that Denny Hutchinson, the elections supervisor, dealt with many of the 2,000 new voters in what she characterized as an intimidating manner. She said that Hutchinson, who is white and was defeated when he ran for reelection in 2000, also made it difficult for elderly people living in rural areas to get absentee ballots. When she brought them to his office to request ballots, "He asked them, 'What do all these old people want?' " she said. "I said, 'I'm watching you. I see how you are intimidating people.' "

Hutchinson, sixty-three, said that nothing improper happened. "It's all a matter of people going to the polls and not being informed," he said. "People get confused." Why would people vote for all ten presidential candidates? "Some people used a shotgun effect to make sure they got at least one candidate," Hutchinson said. "There are a lot of older people in this county that maybe don't have the level of education. But I adamantly deny there's anything wrong anywhere."

Still, many results from many counties—small and large—raised concerns, and some blacks reported experiences that raised eyebrows. In rural Gulf County, on the southern flank of the Panhandle, one precinct reported a spoilage rate of one in every five ballots. Precinct 8 is 88 percent black and a pro-Gore stronghold in a county that went solidly for Bush. Sally Jenkins, a member of Gulf County's Democratic Committee, drove voters to the polls and, when asked, accompanied them into the booth. She said she told voters to ask poll workers if they needed assistance, but some had too much pride. "They don't want you to know that they don't really understand," she said.

In urban Miami-Dade County, machines voided as many as one in nine ballots cast in some black precincts in the inner-city neighborhoods of Liberty City and Overtown because voters apparently punched holes for two or more presidential candidates. Countywide, only 2.7 percent of Miami-Dade's ballots were discounted because of overvoting. But in about two dozen disadvantaged neighborhoods, between 8 percent and 11 percent of ballots were fouled. At least fifty Miami-Dade precincts in such areas had rates of 7 percent or higher. "There has to be something wrong there," said Gus Garcia, a Democratic Party activist.

Other complaints percolated from Miami-Dade. Haitian-American activist Marleine Bastien said she fielded calls from Haitian voters who were turned away from precincts. She said she visited one precinct to investigate a report that a supervisor was mistreating Haitian-American voters. Bastien said she was intercepted by the poll worker in question. "She and her mother came to assault me," Bastien said. "She was cursing, talking about Haitians want special treatment, and who do we think we are? I was just responding to telephone calls from voters who were crying that they did not know what to do. We will not be satisfied until justice is done, and it will be done."

In Okaloosa County's mostly black Precinct 12, Election Day brought out many new faces from the black community, according to poll clerk Aljonia Porter, who lives in the neighborhood. The precinct reported 35 uncounted ballots out of 364 cast. That's a discard rate of nearly 10 percent. Porter noted that elderly white voters might have made errors on their ballots, but "most of our problem was first-time voters or those who had not voted in a long time." And most of those voters, because of the registration drive, were black.

Some optical-scan ballots registered as completely blank because voters made their marks outside the borders of the ovals,

Porter said. Those errors were caught, but the counting machines were not programmed to prevent other mistakes. "I had one woman tell me on the way out that she colored in one oval and then wrote in the name of the candidate," Porter said. "That's an overvote. She was just making sure. But it didn't count."

Okaloosa Elections Supervisor Patricia Hollarn contends that giving voters a chance to redo an erroneous ballot can slow down voting. While acknowledging that the precinct has "probably the lowest educational levels" of the county, Hollarn said that voters, not elections officials, are responsible if they fail to follow directions. "As simple as our system is," she said, "if people are functionally illiterate . . . Look, if the directions say fill in the oval, then you fill in the oval. What's so hard about that? If you screw it up, you screw it up. When you pander, low expectations make for low results."

The NAACP hearing held in Miami four days after the election attracted prominent members of that organization and other groups in the tight-knit civil rights community. The NAACP had already joined with People for the American Way, the Lawyers Committee for Civil Rights Under Law, and the Advancement Project to investigate complaints lodged by blacks and other minorities. The national cable network C-SPAN carried the five-hour proceeding live.

In an opening statement, NAACP President Kweisi Mfume said the hearings were intended to establish a public record of the allegations. "We expect to have a fair and unfettered election and a fair and unfettered process," he said. Even before Election Day, he said, black and Hispanic voters reported misleading phone calls from supporters of George W. Bush—calls that erroneously claimed the NAACP had endorsed the Republican. Bush aides later denied those allegations. Once the polls opened, Mfume said, "We received scores of calls from Florida complaining about irregularities, intimidation, and the inability to vote." By 2:00 P.M. Election Day, Mfume said, his group had dispatched more than two hundred additional volunteers to precincts in Florida. They were assigned to observe conditions, interview aggrieved voters, and report their findings to the NAACP's national office.

Barbara Arnwine, executive director of the Lawyers Committee for Civil Rights Under Law, said that Florida has a "rich history of voting rights abuses." Still, "what we actually saw on November 7 was an unprecedented turnout of voters who sought to exercise their rights, and too many of those voters were turned away at the polls as they sought to vote. This is a tragedy. It is an American tragedy. Those who have raised these concerns about their opportunity to exercise their franchise must be heard."

Thomasina Williams, a lawyer for the NAACP, said that state statutes clearly protect voters from threats and intimidation. In addition, they allow voters to receive up to two replacement ballots if they make a mistake, and they endorse assistance for voters who do not speak English. Yet dozens of people from around the state testified about encountering just those problems on Election Day.

One witness, Ernest Duval of West Palm Beach, said he sought a new punch card after realizing he had mistakenly voted for presidential candidate Pat Buchanan. The request was denied, he said. Determined to vote for Al Gore, he went back to the booth with the same card and punched his "real choice." That invalidated his ballot, and Duval, a Haitian-American, said he felt cheated of his rights. "I lost my vote," he said.

Fort Lauderdale resident Fumiko Robinson said she helped register more than 3,000 people in three counties as part of the NAACP's drive and spent November 7 shuttling Broward County voters to precincts. She said that precinct workers told elderly black voters their names were not on the list and asked them—in front of others—if they had committed a felony since they last voted. She said this profoundly embarrassed would-be voters, and

many left without casting ballots. "They don't need my vote,' "
she recalled some of them saying.

All of this attracted the attention of federal officials. The U.S.
Justice Department launched an inquiry that remained active
months after the election, and the U.S. Commission on Civil
Rights stepped in, seeding Tallahassee with subpoenas. The independent bipartisan commission, with seven members appointed
by the president and Congress, has no enforcement power but can
subpoena witnesses and documents during fact-finding missions.
The commission often makes recommendations to the Justice Department.

In January 2001, commission chairwoman Mary Frances
Berry conducted hearings to "analyze the conduct of the election
in Florida, with a view toward assessing the validity of the allegations and making recommendations for improving the election
process if warranted." The panel subpoenaed Gov. Jeb Bush, Secretary of State Katherine Harris, Attorney General Bob Butterworth, and Agriculture Commissioner Bob Crawford, a member
of Florida's Elections Canvassing Commission, the final authority
on election matters in the state. Also under subpoena were several
North Florida elections supervisors, Florida Highway Patrol officials, and several citizens who had filed complaints.

Even as the hearings began in Tallahassee, the commission itself came under fire. The panel was created under the Civil Rights
Act of 1957 to investigate complaints of voting rights denied because of race, color, religion, sex, national origin, or disabilities,
and it was instrumental in the development of further civil rights
legislation during the 1960s. Officials said that three staff attorneys explored complaints in Florida before the commission voted
in December to investigate. By then, four Democrats, three Independents, and one Republican sat on the panel, and three-quarters
of the commission had been appointed to six-year terms by Bill

Clinton or Democratic congressional leaders. Some Republicans grumbled that the group was likely to harbor political grudges and pursue an agenda that could prove damaging to Bush's presidency. In fact, by the end of the first round of hearings, some panel members had grilled Florida officials intensely and uttered unusually candid criticism.

Florida's governor was the first state official to take the hot seat. But Jeb Bush refused to accept any blame for the problem-plagued election, testifying instead that "the duties of carrying out an election are not the responsibility of the governor." The mechanics of voting, Bush said, were controlled by Katherine Harris, her state elections director, and the sixty-seven county election supervisors. Under questioning by panel members, he also testified that neither he nor his staff consulted with election officials in advance about the projections of high voter turnout. Although 70 percent of registered Floridians voted in 2000, up only slightly from the 67 percent in 1996, more than 700,000 people had been added to the voter rolls during those four years, enough to swamp a system that had hardly been modernized or otherwise improved.

During the hearing, Berry asked Bush why he hadn't appointed a task force to investigate the complaints of disgruntled voters. Said Bush: "I was confident that with the attorney general investigation and the Department of Justice investigation ongoing, those were the proper officials to deal with these issues." He did concede that he learned of problems the day after the election. One of the most widely reported complaints came from one of his own employees. Roberta Tucker, a forty-nine-year-old state worker from Tallahassee, said she was intimidated after being stopped by five white Florida Highway Patrol troopers about two miles from her polling place near Tallahassee. She said the officers asked for her driver's license, but nothing else. "It was an election day and a big election, and there were only white officers there," she said. "It was suspicious to me." Highway Patrol Director Charles C. Hall later testified that the officers were conducting a road safety checkpoint that had not been authorized by their superiors. He denied that the police action was intended to scare voters away from the polls.

Another Tallahassee resident, minister Willie D. Whiting, told the commission that he was one of the people mistakenly identified as felons. He said he had never spent a night in jail. He had been in court only once in his life—as a federal juror. Nevertheless, he testified, election workers told him he had been purged from the rolls in October 1999 and had lost all his civil rights. Suddenly voting was only one of this concerns. What other trouble did he now face, wrongfully? "I was slingshotted into slavery," Whiting testified. "I thought of all the things that had happened to African-Americans that I knew about, and I thought of all the possibilities of what could have happened had I been stopped by the wrong policeman. It didn't feel good." Whiting's wife, son, and daughter accompanied him to the precinct. Upon hearing of his difficulties, they were reluctant to vote, he said. Finally, he called the Leon County election supervisor's office and was told that another man with the same first and last name but a different middle initial and birth date was on the felons list. Whiting threatened to sue. Election officials allowed him to vote.

Linda Howell of Madison County also testified in a rather personal way about the problems with the felons database. She also was on the list mistakenly. Howell is the Madison County election supervisor. "You get that on your record and how do you get it off?" she said. "You're hurting people for the rest of their lives."

By the end of the first set of hearings, Katherine Harris, the by-now prominent secretary of state, had also distanced herself from the process of voting and the subsequent recounts. During ninety minutes of testimony, she answered few questions, deferring repeatedly to Clay Roberts, director of the state's Division of Elections, who works for her and appeared with her at the hearing. "I don't have expertise in the management of these activities," said Harris, who described her role as ministerial. "The way I've chosen to administer our office . . . I've chosen [to delegate]."

Now, near the end of two days of hearings, some commissioners became exasperated and flayed Harris. "I'm on this merry-go-round called denial," commissioner Victoria Wilson told Harris. "Supervisors were desperate for your help, and you abandoned them. They wanted money. They wanted guidance. Voters ended up having to pay the price." During a break, Berry, the chairwoman, said, "Testimony leads me to believe that voting in Florida is like [getting to] a goodie in a box. If you aren't persistent, you can't vote. If you don't file a complaint, no action is taken. A lot of public officials do not think of how they can ease the way for voters." Berry also called Harris's description of her role in the election "laughable." During the public hearing, she questioned how someone in charge of a multimillion-dollar state agency could have so little knowledge of its workings.

It was not the first—or the last—criticism endured by Harris, a woman who held a job so inconsequential that it had begun to be phased out long before the election, a woman who nonetheless emerged as one of the most prominent and memorable figures of the affair.

8

THOU ART COME TO THE KINGDOM FOR SUCH A TIME AS THIS

Katherine Harris's special state bodyguards stood on alert twenty-four hours a day. A security guard joined her when she stepped outside her two-story brick colonial home to carry out the garbage. Normally only the governor merits protection by the Florida Department of Law Enforcement, but these times were not normal.

Harris, the Florida secretary of state, shouldered the ultimate responsibility for regulating and certifying the state's presidential election. She was a registered Republican and a dedicated and ambitious one. She served as a cochair of George W. Bush's campaign. In her official state capacity, she hewed to rigid interpretations of state law that, coincidentally or not, aided Bush's position during the post-election political and legal maneuvering. As the controversy played out, she came under pressure from all sides, stirring strong emotions across the political spectrum, and particularly among her detractors.

"It became real tiring," Harris says. "People sent e-mails as they would send . . . an anonymous phone call, just vent and hang up." She says she considered some of them threatening, though only one such message was found during a survey of her e-mail by the *Herald*. One threat arrived by telephone, she says, and was traced to a crack house in Austin, Texas. No suspects were ever identified.

It is late February, and she is curled up on a burgundy leather sofa in the sitting room of her home in one of Tallahassee's oldest and most stately neighborhoods. The home is paneled, furnished, and floored with dark wood. The furnishings include oriental rugs, wooden paddle fans, and her odd lamp from Africa. Made from metal, heavy as a barbell, it is carved in the shape of a palm tree, and its small shade is crafted from black and tan vertical slats of dyed camel bone. She calls it her "Chad lamp," a reference both to the country and to the ballot disputes that brought her fame, or maybe notoriety.

Harris tucks her feet under her. She appears relaxed, and no, she is not wearing a lot of makeup. In fact, she says lightly, she normally puts on her makeup while driving to work, and not with a trowel either. A mild southern accent tinges her voice, which like her demeanor is all honey and sugar. But it is not always like this.

When she becomes cross—or senses a double-cross or a trap or even just probing questions—she can lash out. At one point during two substantive interviews with *Herald* reporters, questions about her e-mail annoyed her. "If you're going to write about me, there's a heck of a lot more at stake about what went on than e-mail," she said. "I'm not going to give you an interview on e-mails. This is stupid. You're being stupid. You're missing the forest for the trees."

Tom Lyons, a columnist for the *Sarasota Herald-Tribune*, has observed Harris for the past decade. When she was preparing to run for the State Senate in 1994, they met for lunch and he told her he would be writing about her from time to time. Lyons, who is known for his scathing columns, said Harris asked him to go easy on her. "I told her if she was corrupt or bamboozled the voters I'd write it," he said. "She seemed very worried, and I asked her why. I learned that it wasn't because she planned to do anything bad. It was because she couldn't bear anything even slightly negative or questioning."

If Harris was ultrasensitive then, he said, she has become even more so during her tenure in the national limelight. "She wants to be seen as an icon, and she sees anyone who doesn't see her this way as a foe," he said. "With her, there is no in-between. If you ask the questions that need to be asked, you're the foe. If you let her stick to her script—she has been well coached—then she likes you."

Not everyone agrees with that assessment, and the mood is lighter tonight, even as she discusses another perceived threat, one that was broadcast nationally in the guise of a joke. She calls it her darkest moment. On November 30, comedian Bill Maher, host of ABC's *Politically Incorrect*, said, "Now earlier today, a rental truck carried a half a million ballots from Palm Beach to the Florida Supreme Court there in Tallahassee. CNN had live helicopter coverage of the truck making its way up the Florida highway, and for a few brief moments, America held the hope that O. J. Simpson had murdered Katherine Harris." This was said on a major television network during a time of extreme political tension.

Harris's public appearances during the election controversy were carefully choreographed and scripted, but one-on-one, when she is comfortable, she speaks the way a powerful river runs—quickly and in great torrents. Emotions cascade rapidly across her face. A swift smile, a frown, another smile, another smile, regret, smile, frown, frown, smile, frown.

Harris: "When that guy, I didn't know he was supposedly a comedian, when the trucks were driving down the road, and he says, 'Oh America lies in hope that O. J. has murdered Katherine Harris' . . . I read it in the clips the next day. That was so . . . heinous . . . because I was having death threats, and to have someone say that . . . I am never afraid, but that is not something you make fun of either."

She tells that story a lot. Katherine Harris, forty-three years old and a multimillionaire at the time of the election, sees herself as a victim of circumstance and as a martyr. She believes she sacrificed her privacy and to some extent her political future by rejecting every plea for vote-count flexibility from the Democratic support-ers of Al Gore. She says this was not a matter of political games-manship but simply the proper course of action, one that was required by law. At the same time, though, e-mail traffic exam-ined by the *Herald* suggests that Republican partisanship seeped into her office.

Under Florida's sweeping Sunshine Law, all written commu-nications to, from, or between state employees are considered public documents and must be made available for public inspec-tion. That includes e-mail.

On Election Day, when Harris sat at her desk to look at the morning's e-mail, she was greeted by a note from Jillian Inmon, a friend at Republican headquarters and chief Florida coordinator of the George W. Bush campaign. ''. . . Leave no stone unturned . . . [then] Florida will be in the WIN column and Governor George W. Bush will be President-Elect. . . .'' Inmon's note, apparently sent to a group of Bush supporters, concluded, ''We have one very big battle left today—getting everyone to the polls to vote. We've won the others, but this one is it—WINNER TAKES ALL. SO PUT ON YOUR ARMOR ONE LAST TIME AND LETS WIN THIS WAR! ! ! ''

That Inmon would employ war imagery and suggest the don-ning of armor would become strangely prophetic. For as time went on and the election's outcome remained unknown, Harris would endorse the views of supporters who came to see her as a modern-day crusader, a biblical figure following the will of God, a woman with no choice but to place herself in actual or at least metaphoric danger as she served her nation and performed what she viewed as her duty.

Within the first twenty-four hours after Election Day, Harris received dozens of e-mail notes. Most commented on the closeness of the election and demanded a manual recount of votes, or even a revote in Palm Beach County. Very few, other than those from friends and staff, earned a response from her. The most notable came from Bob Leatherman, a forty-seven-year-old father of seven who lives near Chicago. He told Harris he saw the election in biblical terms, with her playing the role of Esther, the beautiful queen who saved the Jewish people from genocide. Leatherman said that he prayed Harris would oversee the recount process and help place Bush in office, otherwise "thousands and thousands of unborn children would not get to see the light of day."

Harris, who describes herself as a dedicated Christian, wrote Leatherman back the next day. "This was the exact conversation and prayer that I shared with my sister last night," she wrote. "I reread a book about Esther last night. She has always been the specific character in the Bible that I have admired. Thank you so much for your encouragement and your prayers."

During the next week, she received more e-mail that cast her in Biblical terms. She frequently responded to those e-mail notes—and very few others, telling her correspondents that it was Esther who inspired her.

A few months later, Leatherman and Harris were asked about that initial exchange.

Leatherman: "When I knew Bush could become the next president and Katherine could make it happen as secretary of state, I thought about how she could be directly responsible for saving the unborn children in the U.S., and I wanted to tell her this."

Harris: "Before I ever ran for office, in my church, someone had been praying for me, and they said, you know, 'You will be in the position to change the heart of the angry king, like Esther.' They said, 'We just hope you will keep your sense of virtue and principle no matter what the cost.' So Esther made a big impression on me." She adds that the message exchange "wasn't about the unborn children. It was about Esther."

In the biblical Book of Esther, Mordechai, a Jewish leader driven into exile with many of his people, begs his cousin, Queen Esther, to intervene on their behalf. Her husband, King Ahasuerus, intends to kill them all, but he does not know that Esther is Jewish. Now she must tell him. Esther is in the right place at the right time, and though she senses danger, her time has come. Sacrifice might be required, but the cause is vital.

Mordechai says: "Who knoweth whether thou art come to the kingdom for such a time as this?"

Esther says: ". . . So I will go unto the king, which is not according to the law; and if I perish, I perish."

Katherine Harris was born into the closest thing Florida has to aristocracy. She grew up around power, enthralled by her grandfather, Ben Hill Griffin Jr., a wily man, as sturdy as the citrus groves that made him a millionaire many times over. It was a legacy for which she cultivated an abiding respect, a birthright she never took for granted. Her friends, her mentors, even her detractors agree on this: Harris was always willing to study more and work harder than any colleague or competitor.

"Katherine always was ambitious, and I think she enjoyed her grandfather, and that had a strong influence on her," said Evelyn Laurent, who taught Harris honors English during her senior year at Bartow High. "Ben Hill Griffin Jr. was quite a politician, and I think that had a bearing on her. But she never expected the tides to part just because of who she was. Nobody worked harder than Katherine."

In a state legendary for its rough-and-tumble politics, Griffin was among the toughest, a conservative Democrat who served in both houses of the state legislature, successfully pushing an agenda that leaned toward the reactionary. That same will to win was evident in his granddaughter's 1998 campaign for Florida secretary of state—a crusade against one of her own, Republican incumbent Sandra Mortham. Harris vanquished Mortham in the GOP primary.

Her opponent in the 1998 general election, Miami Democrat Karen Gievers, considered Harris's conduct during the election controversy "more consistent with campaign politics than following and applying the law in a neutral way for all Floridians rather than just Republican Floridians."

"That's disappointing. And that's wrong," said Gievers, who served as an attorney for the state Democratic Party.

Harris and her family dispute that portrayal, insisting that she is not a political operative. They take umbrage at the slashing portraits drawn by late-night talk hosts and pundits, and they take solace from the dozens of flower arrangements and supportive messages that flooded Harris's office.

Nearly 750,000 e-mail notes arrived in the secretary of state's office on Election Day and in subsequent months, she says. Most came from Republican supporters, and some came from members of her own largely Republican staff. A survey of her e-mail notes suggests that many of these people, working in an office that was supposed to be a neutral arbiter of election results, could not contain their partisan zeal.

For public consumption, Harris portrays herself as determined to remain above political temptation. "The downside of all of this for me, and really the only thing that was bad in the aftermath, was from my perspective being so pegged as a political hack," she says. "Because I have never been the partisan one on the floor. . . . That is the only downside, that the world thinks I'm so partisan and that I am a party hack, or that in any way I would have confounded my oath that I swore that I would uphold, or that somehow—and this is what just defies the imagination—that I would distort the law so that my preference in the election won.

"That is just unimaginable. Integrity is doing the right thing when nobody else is looking. But when the world is looking, the concept that I would actually not follow the letter of the law is so preposterous that maybe it becomes believable. I guess Hitler said if you say a lie enough, people start to believe it."

Still, as the results of exit polls and other indications of voter attitudes came in on Election Day, Harris received e-mail from her staff expressing concern over the apparent closeness of the election. Chief of Staff Ben McKay relayed an e-mail to her in the afternoon: ''We're down by 6 in FL [Florida]. We're losing in MI [Michigan]. Look fine in WI [Wisconsin]. No word on PA [Pennsylvania] yet. Keep praying . . . this will be very, very close.''

"We're down by 6" means that, at that early juncture, Bush trailed Gore by six percentage points in exit polls. Was this type of communication, including the phrase "keep praying" and the word "we're," appropriate within a state agency that regulates elections? Harris: "Ben e-mailed me what the Drudge Report said. We were watching it [the election] very closely."

That morning, when Harris arrived at work, waiting for her was an e-mail from Maureen Garrard, her speechwriter. It included speaking points for a three-minute speech Harris was scheduled to deliver at that night's anticipated victory party for George W. Bush: ''Thank faithful . . . bedrock of freedom and democracy . . . closest race in

history, their efforts have/will make the difference. . . ."

As cochair of the Bush campaign in Florida, Harris certainly devoted herself to victory for her party and its candidate. Though she described her title as "honorary" and minimized her duties, she served as a Bush delegate to the Republican National Convention and campaigned vigorously, trudging through snow in New Hampshire and traveling through North Florida in a motor home.

It must be remembered that she was not alone in this sort of campaigning. On the other side, for instance, Florida Attorney General Bob Butterworth served as Florida chairman of Al Gore's campaign and as a Gore delegate to the Democratic National Convention. But as events unfolded, it was Harris's office and her actions that proved central to the election dispute, and thus the trail of communications to and from her office becomes instructive.

At 4:11 A.M. on that long Election Night, Garrard messaged Harris: "Good grief! I have never in my life seen anything like this—the networks are now putting Fla.
in the undecided column—so the race ain't over yet.
The Gore campaign just said they consider the campaign still ongoing. . . ."

At 5:00 A.M., the Bush campaign's Latin America adviser, Will Perry, messaged Harris directly: ". . . I have to think we
will ultimately emerge victorious in the electoral
college. . . . On that basis, my heartiest congratu-
lations for having won this triumph on Jeb's home
ground. . . . Please be in touch so we can chat personally and begin to think how to treat the transi-
tion with respect to Latin America."

Later, Perry said he was referring to the impact a Republican administration in the White House would have on her role as Florida secretary of state, specifically in the context of cultural and economic agreements with Latin America. He was not, he said, referring to any new role she would play in a George W. Bush administration. "There was no quid pro quo set up for Katherine Harris that I knew anything about," Perry said.

At 9:15 A.M., November 8, when the winner was still unknown, a staff secretary sent Garrard this note: ''The world is gathering at the Secretary's office. CNN is there. . . . All eyes are upon Florida. As chief elections officer KH is certainly in the limelight. . . . This will turn out for us.''

Thirty minutes later, Garrard sent this note to Harris's staff: ''. . . Congressman Wexler on CNN . . . said the ballot listed the candidates alphabetically . . . and alleged that the 3400 votes Buchanan received in Palm Beach were INTENDED for Gore. This is NOT the same as a mechanical problem on the key punch. . . .''

This would be a crucial distinction. As lawsuits mounted and the days passed, Harris insisted that state law mandated time extensions for manual recounts only in response to fraud, natural disasters, or proven mechanical problems with voting machines. Without evidence of these hindrances, she would say, she had no discretion to allow more disputed votes to be examined and counted.

Friends and relatives say loyalty and persistence were branded on Harris, the firstborn of three siblings, just as surely as the marks she emblazoned on cattle at her grandfather's rambling estate, Peace River Ranch. Born in Key West, she spent her formative years in Polk County, the Griffin clan's home turf. She was joined there by her brother, George, who now owns a restaurant in Aspen, Colorado, and her sister, Fran, who helps manage the singing career of her husband, a country-and-western artist named Wes King.

Their father, George W. Harris Jr., ran Citrus and Chemical Bank—named for the orange and phosphate industries that dominated their part of Central Florida. Their mother, Harriett, presided over a vibrant Girl Scout troop and for fifteen years taught white-water rafting in North Carolina. "It's like this," said George W. Harris Jr., still chief executive at the family bank. "When people work hard around you, you learn to work hard. I still put in fifteen hours a day or so, and enjoy every bit of it."

After spending three years at a private school in Lakeland, Katherine Harris decided she wanted to graduate from her hometown school and transferred as a senior to Bartow High. She filled the yearbook with a constellation of accomplishments—National Honor Society, the Anchor Club (a service organization), the tennis team, and a stint on the student council. "She was active, oh my goodness, in athletics, in all of the beauty queen contests," said Beverly Conner, who taught Harris pre-calculus. "She was that capsule of one of the perfect little high school seniors, the sort of person you hope to teach."

Like her mother before her, Harris spent her undergraduate years at Agnes Scott College, a small women-only liberal arts school near Atlanta. During college she held two internships in Washington—one with Republican U.S. Rep. Andy Ireland, the other in the office of Lawton Chiles, a Democrat who was then a U.S. senator and would later become Florida's governor. In 1979 Harris graduated with a bachelor of arts degree in history and came home to Florida to work in real estate and as a sales representative for IBM. She settled in Tampa, eventually migrating to Sarasota, her first husband's hometown.

It was Sarasota, and specifically the Ringling Museum of Art, that provided the seedbed for her political activity. A student of art and, by her father's account, an accomplished artist in oils and acrylics herself, Harris joined Ringling's board of directors and danced the tango often required of those who would court the wealthy and the powerful. In her position at Ringling, Harris forged connections that energized her first bid for elected office—a State Senate seat in 1994.

She defeated her Republican opponent in the primary and, in the general election, wrested the seat from a Democratic incumbent. She did it with help from her friends—and family. On Election Day 1994, her dad drove over from Bartow, wearing an Uncle Sam costume. George Harris Jr.: "When I first showed up at the campaign office that morning, she said, 'Oh golly, Daddy, you're not going to wear that, are you?' They put me on the busiest corner, and they got so many calls about me at the campaign office that when I came in for lunch, she said, 'Dad, can I go out with you on that corner?' "

During her term as a state senator, she continued as a champion of the arts—and as a patron of arts groups. It was during a night at the Sarasota Opera in 1996 that she met her second husband, Anders Ebbeson, a millionaire whose business equips yachts. Ebbeson has a teenage daughter, Louise. After the election, when things calmed down a bit, Harris pointed to her husband as the source of her strength. "My husband is Swedish. He just became a citizen last summer, and this was the first time he voted, in Florida. . . . Anders is an extraordinary man. He is just a wonderful man. I said, 'Anders, what am I going to do?' All of a sudden, the first forty-eight hours, everybody was screaming, 'We're not going to have a president.' We were just totally in the weeds. I mean it was a fog. He came up here to be with me. He said, 'It's real simple. You absolutely have to conduct yourself with the utmost integrity.' "

In between sessions of the legislature, Harris pursued a master's degree at Harvard's John F. Kennedy School of Government. That is where she cultivated her interest in international trade. Many students at the Kennedy School are policy wonks in the making. The faculty wishes more of them wanted to run for public office, which is why they encourage elected officials to seek degrees there. Joseph J. McCarthy, associate dean at the Kennedy School, recalls hobnobbing with Harris several times at the receptions and lectures that are ubiquitous at the school. "I remember that she was Republican and that she was very interested in Republican politics and going forward in Republican politics," McCarthy said.

He was right too. Within months of getting her master's from Harvard in 1998, Harris decided to run for statewide office. She chose the post of secretary of state, the least visible of the cabinet posts. And it looked like an easy run to her party's nomination, with the incumbent, Mortham, plucked by Jeb Bush to be his running mate. But when Mortham stepped aside from her bid to be lieutenant governor and instead sought another term as secretary of state, Harris was faced with this dilemma: run for another term in the State Senate or stay in the race for secretary of state, knowing she would confront a popular incumbent in the primary. She decided to fight—and a fight it was.

Harris's campaign ads tarred Mortham for taking illegal contributions from Riscorp, an insurance company that federal prosecutors concluded made nearly $400,000 in illegal campaign contributions to candidates. Company executives pleaded guilty to felony and misdemeanor charges. Mortham received $5,825 from Riscorp in 1993 and 1994. Harris had received $20,292 in illegal contributions from the company during her 1994 State Senate campaign—more than any other legislative candidate. Her campaign managers at the time said the contributions never influenced Harris's votes. Both candidates said they did not know the contributions were illegal. Ultimately, Harris and Mortham each made $1,500 contributions to a state fund to fight election fraud.

Harris won 61 percent of the vote, sending Mortham into political retirement. She defeated Gievers by a narrower margin in the general election to become Florida's secretary of state.

One of the first signs of Election Day trouble arrived in Harris's office at 12:29 P.M. Paul Craft, Florida's assistant supervisor of elections, sent an e-mail to Clay Roberts, the state's supervisor of elections. Both reported to Harris, and a copy ended up in her e-mail inbox. Craft wrote: ''We're getting pounded with national press inquiries regarding an accusation that . . . Gore votes are going to Buchanan.'' Shortly afterward, a secretary sent Craft an e-mail: ''Call Mr. and Mrs. Rosenzweig. This has to do with Palm Beach.''

At noon, Gloria Rosenzweig voted in the clubhouse of her Platina condominium in Boynton Beach, a city in Palm Beach County. She complained to precinct workers that the ballot did not fit correctly on the prongs that held it in place, causing her to vote for the wrong person. "I punched it, and it slipped so that I realized my choice hadn't lined up with the numbers, and I voted for Buchanan when I meant to vote for Gore," she told the *Herald* later. "It was not a case of being too stupid or confused to punch it correctly. The problem was with the voting equipment."

A week later, Harris's staff would pass around an e-mail joke suggesting that Palm Beach County voters were simply too dim to cast proper votes. A fake ballot featured photos of Bush, Gore, and Buchanan. It was entitled "Voting for Dummies . . . Specifically Designed for Residents of West Palm Beach County, Florida." Each photo came with instructions. Under Buchanan, it said: "You have chosen Pat Buchanan. This candidate is NOT Al Gore. Are you sure you want to vote for Pat Buchanan?" The ballot repeatedly asked if the voter really wanted to select Gore instead of Buchanan or Bush, and then asked: "Do you think the residents of West Palm Beach County, Florida have enough common sense to elect a President of the United States?" The choices were: "No" or "Huh?"

But on the day that she voted, Rosenzweig thought her intent, as well as the intent of hundreds of other people at her condominium, should have been honored. She said she called Tallahassee to find out what they needed to do to have their votes count. Craft told her that investigators would look into the problem, she said.

A few days later, Rosenzweig and hundreds of her neighbors signed Democratic Party affidavits saying that they had not voted for the presidential candidate of their choice, that they had "miscast" their votes. "It didn't occur to us that the language of the affidavit would mean anything," Rosenzweig said. "I should have said that I miscast my vote because of problems with the voting apparatus. As it was, it sounded like voter stupidity, which ultimately gave the secretary of state a reason not to recount, because she said it wasn't machine error." In reality, although concerns over the county's butterfly ballot arose quickly, no one in Palm Beach County officially reported any mechanical problems to state officials. County Election Supervisor Theresa LePore did not become aware that many of her punch-card machines were faulty until many weeks after the election was settled, and then only when the *Herald* called her attention to them.

After the election, as the controversy deepened, it became clear that conservative forces felt compelled to demonstrate their support for Harris. Before November 13, much of her e-mail featured demands from Democrats that she extend the recount. On that day, though, she announced that she would certify the election on November 14, and a vast shift of sentiment is evident in her e-mail beginning just after 2:00 P.M. What explains this? Harris: "That is a silly question. There is no software that filters my e-mail. Maybe it was a paradigm shift. Maybe the country realized we were following the law. Maybe all of the misrepresentations in the media were starting to materialize to show we were following the law."

Actually, another explanation seems more likely: several popular conservative media personalities mobilized their followers to show support for the secretary of state at this critical juncture. Just before 2:00 P.M., radio talk show host Rush Limbaugh publicized Harris's e-mail address. Some of the thousands of e-mail notes of support referred to Limbaugh. Also, at about 1:45 P.M. that day, Mike West of Pensacola sent a batch e-mail to 17,000 people who monitor his popular conservative Web site. He suggested that they write notes to Harris, which he offered to relay to her. Over the next three days, more than a thousand of those e-mail notes hit Harris's mailbox. Many echoed the message he suggested: ''Thank you for upholding the rule of law. Continue to stand strong.''

"I was happy to forward the e-mail to the secretary," West said. "I'll forward just about anything to anyone except for the kind of vulgar, perverse pornography that underground liberal Democrats send me." Of the thousands of e-mail notes Harris received, about a hundred used the expression "stick to your guns" as suggested by members of the National Rifle Association. About a hundred others asked Harris to do God's work and stop the recount. Some quoted Bible verse; many said they were praying for her. "The mention of prayer makes sense," said West. "The hard-shell conservatives, who support Harris, tend to be hard-shell Christians too."

Harris says she had no idea that many of the e-mail notes in her favor were related to religion or to any conservative or Christian groups. "I don't know what you're talking about," she says. "I got seven hundred and fifty thousand e-mails. I don't know which ones I read. Maybe you read them. Maybe you had time, but I didn't."

She did continue to respond to those who cast her in a Biblical role. One, which she received on November 13, referred to verses from Ephesians: ''Put on the whole armour of God, that ye may be able to stand against the wiles of the devil. For we wrestle . . . against principalities, against powers, against the rulers of the darkness of this world. . . . Take unto you the whole armour of God, that ye may be able to withstand in the evil day, and having done all, to stand.''

Harris replied in all capital letters: ''THANKS FOR YOUR EN- COURAGING E-MAIL—ESPECIALLY TODAY. ACTUALLY, MY SISTER AND I PRAYED FOR THE FULL ARMOUR THIS MORN- ING . . . AND QUEEN ESTHER HAS BEEN A WONDERFUL ROLL [sic] MODEL. PLEASE PRAY FOR OUR NATION AND FOR ME— FOR WISDOM AND UNDERSTANDING. MANY THANKS. KATH- ERINE.''

She also responded to an e-mail that said, ''WELL DONE, THOU GOOD AND FAITHFUL SERVANT. JESUS IS THE DELIV- ERER.'' She wrote, ''Please keep me and especially our country in your prayers. Queen Esther is a powerful role model.''

On the evening of November 13, after Harris announced that all sixty-seven counties must have their returns in by 5:00 P.M. the next day, recount or not, she returned to her office. There, her e-mail inbox contained an "automatic reply"—the electronic equivalent of a form letter, typically programmed to respond in- stantaneously if impersonally to incoming e-mail—from Jeb Bush. It was time-stamped at 8:22 P.M., indicating that she had e-mailed him right before that. Yet in her "sent mail" file, there is nothing to him. Harris has no explanation. "I didn't e-mail him, and he didn't e-mail me. We put up a fire wall, so we wouldn't be influenced." A search of Jeb Bush's e-mail revealed nothing in his inbox from her on that day.

Seven years younger than George W. Bush, Jeb Bush is an e-mail addict, traveling with a laptop, writing and answering e-mail notes at dawn and near midnight at home and at work. After the election, his e-mail account would also come under pub- lic scrutiny.

In late September, he exuded confidence about the election in

an e-mail reply to a *Herald* inquiry about the election. ''REMEM-
BER, I LIKE THE FLYING BURRITO BROTHERS,'' Bush re-
plied to one question about rock and roll aimed at breaking the
ice. ''THE REST OF THE QUESTIONS CAN BE ANSWERED BY
THE FACT THAT GEORGE WILL CARRY THE STATE. I HAVE
BELIEVED THAT FROM THE BEGINNING,'' Bush wrote in all
upper-case type. ''I HAVE ALSO BELIEVED THAT IT WAS
GOING TO BE CLOSE. I HAVE NEVER TAKEN THIS RACE FOR
GRANTED. WE HAVE A GREAT PLAN TO TURN OUT THE VOTE
AND OUR BASE IS VERY MOBILIZED. WE ARE GOING TO
WIN.—JEB.''

In the basement of Florida's capitol, hard-copy piles of the
governor's post-election e-mail are consigned to blue cartons
stacked near filing cabinets. ''Jeb, Keep the faith,''
e-mailed a supporter named Kimberly Ann Blevins, director of
distance learning at the University of South Florida's College of
Public Health. The note arrived at 10:25 P.M. on Election Night.
''God's grace will be manifest this night.''

The Associated Press asked Jeb Bush on Friday, November 10,
what "if anything" he was doing behind the scenes. The AP had
heard he might have called a couple of supervisors of elections.
True? ''I am at the office and I have not spoken to
any supervisors of elections,'' Bush replied to the AP
at 11:56 A.M., November 10.

The next day, newly elected Education Commissioner Charlie
Crist wrote to his fellow Republican. ''I'm amazed by how
many times (2 so far) your brother is being required to win Florida!'' Crist wrote. ''This will all
work out and he will be President! Your Loyal
Friend, Charlie Crist.'' Bush replied, ''Way to go
Charlie. I would love to see you or talk to you when
you have a chance.''

Bush's dawn-to-dark personal e-mail regimen can seem stag-
gering, and it was unaltered by the events unfolding around the

capitol. To John Donovan, who wrote the governor on November 12 and attached a *Wall Street Journal* article that opposed a manual recount in Palm Beach County: ''I saw it and it makes a good point. We should not have a manual ballot in one county.''

Often the communications were less . . . cosmic. A Fort Myers man wrote the governor about a state park enforcing a leash law for dogs at a park where for years pooches have run free on a sandbar that is exposed only at low tide. Bush fired off an e-mail to an aide Sunday afternoon, November 12: ''What is the deal about pets in state parks?''

The next day Bush received an e-mail from Dona Hannagan of Sebring, complaining about a phone call she was repeatedly receiving at home warning her that "Your vote along with 19,000 others was thrown out. Call Gov. Bush to find out why." The calls apparently originated with Democratic supporters.

''Are 'we' doing anything to counteract this?'' Hannagan wrote the governor. ''Is there any way this can be stopped? I had several on my answering machine. I live in Highlands County. There was not a problem here at all. I think the recount wasn't that much different. What can I do about these calls? It is very irritating.''

Bush, at nearly eleven that night, in a note to Katie Baur, his communications director: ''This is a concerted effort to divide and destroy our state.'' Baur's reply: ''Ve have our vays also. . . . I'm working on this.'' She later said she had responded overzealously, and no harm was intended in her jocular mimicry of Colonel Klink–style prison camp vernacular.

Still, it was Katherine Harris—not Jeb Bush—who played a starring role in this electoral drama. A few months later, she was just beginning to put it into perspective.

Katherine Harris, unfiltered:

- On her image—"If you were to ask me what the worst outcome of this is, it was so surreal and so intense and so unnatural. I am not a spotlight person. I am never the one grandstanding on the floor. I am never the one giving press conferences. I am not a spotlight person. It sounds disingenuous for a politician to say that, because we are supposed to be such spotlight seekers. But in reality, it was surreal. I still get popped in the press occasionally. The personal attacks were really, really hard. But following the law was simple."

- On her makeup—"When they said my makeup needed a daytime and a nighttime, I wanted to tell them, 'Hey, it is nighttime.' It was so silly, all the makeup stuff, and it hasn't stopped. 'Katherine Harris wears too much makeup and wears that mask to hide her insecurities.' I thought, 'Oh, man.' "

- On what was at stake—"I always had the sense that America, the United States, the world was waiting."

- On her future (the elected position of secretary of state will be eliminated in 2002 through a state cabinet reorganization approved by voters in 1998)—"I can tell you, first of all, another big press misconception; what I wouldn't do is be an ambassador. I would like to do that someday. But one day isn't two thousand and one. One day is if I've had a dignified political career, and it makes sense. That's what you do after active public service. I'm the one who said they'll probably make me ambassador to Chad, and they never give me credit for the quote. I really do have this idea of giving back. It's not an act of power. It's just that we're really passionate. Somebody said I'm really ambitious. I never thought of myself as ambitious."

- On what she could have done differently—"That's all I thought about over all of December and over vacation. Our test was, if the situation was reversed, would we be doing the same thing? What I've tried to do is go through my mind and think over and over again, what would we do differently? And people have said, if I had come out more, people would have thought differently.

"But it wasn't about me. Everybody wanted to be a talking head. Everybody wanted their fifteen minutes of fame. We only went out when we had to bring everything in for a landing.

"I realize that it made me the brunt of the issue, but I felt like my job was to carry out the law as secretary of state, not to defend myself or my makeup. It wasn't about me. It was about a presidential race. I felt like one of the players in it. I didn't feel like I was the central figure. The media made me the central figure, or the administration didn't like what I was saying, and they were very good at packaging information for the media to print. I had to take it with the territory.

"I backed into it. I have been through situations, particularly with the press, where I didn't feel I was well represented and, particularly, maligned, but you can't be bitter. It can really break you, or you can be better. We did a Nexis search of [printed stories about] me—fourteen thousand hits. What are you going to do, have a coronary? I'm really calm. It's a better way to live. If you're broken, then learn to be better from it, not bitter."

January 21, 2001. Washington, D.C. The Florida Inaugural Ball. Purple and turquoise lights and no snide comments about Katherine Harris stealing an election and no cruel jokes about her makeup, and no tough questions about her motives. Country singer Larry Gatlin steps to the microphone.

"In France, it was Joan of Arc," Gatlin says. "In the Crimea, it was Florence Nightingale." Now applause is beginning. "In the Deep South, there was Rosa Parks. In India, there was Mother Teresa." The applause is reaching a crescendo. "And in Florida, there was Katherine Harris!" The place explodes with acclaim.

Harris takes the microphone. She smiles. She says, all honey and sugar, "We just thank you so very much, for your prayers, your letters of support, your flowers, your encouragement during the count and the recount. . . . It is going to be a great next four years. Eight years.

"God Bless America."

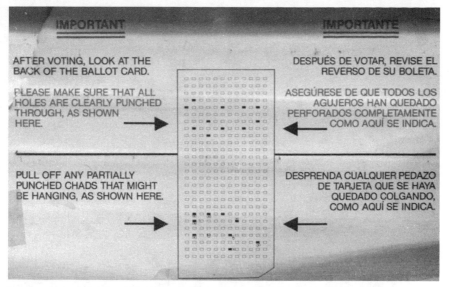

Instructions for using Miami-Dade's punch-card ballots, placed inside election booths throughout the county. During the 2000 elections, one of every nine votes for President had to be thrown out in some inner city communities due to ballot irregularities. *The Miami Herald*

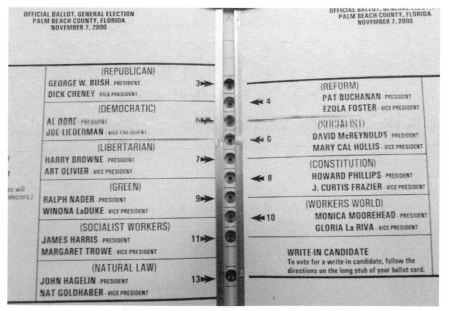

Palm Beach County's infamous "butterfly ballot." Confusion over the placement of the holes may have resulted in more than five thousand ballots cast with holes punched for two presidential candidates: Al Gore and Pat Buchanan. *JAMES W. PRICHARD, The Palm Beach Post*

Seventy percent of registered Floridians voted in 2000, up slightly from the 67 percent in 1996. But more than 700,000 people had been added to the voter rolls during those four years, enough to swamp a system that had hardly been modernized or otherwise improved. Here, inspector Ann Portnoy helps a voter at Miami Beach's Fire Station #3. *Tia Chapman, The Miami Herald*

Elections supervisors throughout the state complained that they had trouble recruiting workers—low pay and long hours are not alluring enticements during times of nearly full employment. Here, Miami-Dade election workers approaching the 24-hour point in their workday—November 8, 2000, 3:00 A.M.—await instructions from election headquarters. *Marice Cohn Band, The Miami Herald*

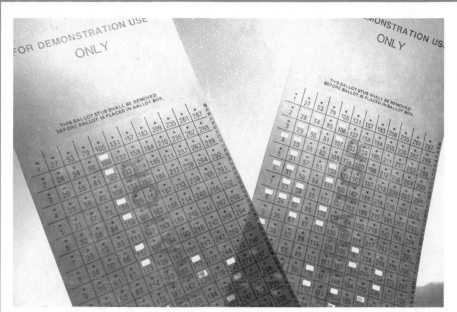

Two test ballots from Overtown, in inner-city Miami, displayed at the Miami-Dade elections office. These two should have exactly the same chads punched out, but obviously the one on the left has many omissions. Machines that produced errors in Overtown—and elsewhere—were not pulled out of service before polls opened.
DAVID BERGMAN, The Miami Herald

A properly punched chad (145) and a dimpled chad (144). Election officials were aware of the Votomatic's shortcomings since it was first marketed in the 1960s.
PATRICK FARRELL, The Miami Herald

Florida Republicans on Election Night, celebrating the television networks' reversal of the earlier prediction that Gore would win Florida. *CHUCK FADELY, The Miami Herald*

Two days later, Democrats were up in arms. In Palm Beach County, many demanded a revote after the debacle with the butterfly ballot cost Vice President Al Gore critical thousands of votes. *WALTER MICHOT, The Miami Herald*

Many Republicans felt their candidate had been wrongly deprived of legitimacy because of election irregularities and five weeks of ballot recounts. These Bush supporters demonstrated outside the Broward County Courthouse while a recount was being held inside. CANDACE BARBOT, *The Miami Herald*

One week after the polls closed: Judge Lawrence D. King, Chairperson of the Miami-Dade Canvassing Board, *center*, reviews a questionable ballot along with Democrat Jarrett Barrios, *left*, and Republican Miguel A. De Grandy, *right*, during the Miami Dade recount. *JEFFREY BOAN, The Miami Herald*

November 16, 2000: The Broward County recount. *WALTER MICHOT, The Miami Herald*

November 22, 2000: Recount workers in Miami-Dade take a stretch break. *CARL JUSTE, The Miami Herald*

November 24, 2000: Judge Robert Rosenberg examines a punch card ballot at the Broward recount. *WALTER MICHOT, The Miami Herald*

December 1, 2000: Ballots en route from Miami to Tallahassee. Two more weeks would elapse before the U.S. Supreme Court's decision ended all recounts in Florida, thus handing the election to George W. Bush. *CANDACE BARBOT, The Miami Herald*

After they arrived in Tallahassee, the ballots were placed under the guard of the Leon County Sheriff's Department. *WALTER MICHOT, The Miami Herald*

9

"How Can I Ever Top This?"

Michael Leach sat at a folding table in a back office of the Seminole County Elections Department, huddled over a laptop computer that ran a program called Victory Suite. He worked every day for two straight weeks, making notations on pieces of paper, one after another after another after another. He was participating to the max in participatory democracy, but he saw no point in dressing up. No one was watching. He wore a T-shirt, flip-flops, shorts, and a baseball cap emblazoned with a sheriff's office badge. He was stocky and sported a blond buzz cut. He listened to Rush Limbaugh on the radio, which broke the monotony and enhanced his sense of purpose as he performed his duty.

Duty was important to Leach. He was twenty-nine years old and already a U.S. Air Force veteran and a former police officer. He worshipped Richard Nixon and believed that Nixon paid too dear a price for the Watergate scandal. Leach was also an ex-janitor. Now his sense of duty required an entirely different type of cleaning up.

On the orders of the Republican Party and with the knowledge of the county's Republican-registered election supervisor, Leach, a Republican field worker, purified more than 2,200 defective applications for absentee ballots from Republicans, transforming the requests into proper applications. Voters ended up casting 1,926 of those ballots. Statisticians later estimated that at least 85 percent of those voters chose Republican Goerge W. Bush, and he won Florida's election—and thus the presidency—by 537 votes.

Behind the scenes, in that back room, Michael Leach played an instrumental role in the outcome of the election, and though few know his name, he qualifies as a major character in this saga. Before long, and after extraordinary tag-team trials in a Tallahassee courthouse, his actions and those of two county election supervisors would be criticized but not overturned by a judicial team with the historically resonant names of Lewis and Clark, and George W. Bush would reside in the White House. "Every time I see Bush now, I have a sense of awe and pride," Leach said several months after the election. "And I think about what I did to get him elected. I think he's going to accomplish great things for the country."

Many unusual circumstances coalesced to produce Florida's tight election and Bush's ultimate victory, none more unusual than those surrounding Michael Leach and some colleagues farther south in Martin County. Together, they corrected nearly 3,000 requests for absentee ballots from Republican voters, and those ballots helped turn the election.

As November 7 approached, both political parties mailed out many tens of thousands of absentee ballot applications to voters in Florida. Under state law, this was perfectly permissible. Anyone could send out these applications and customize them for individual voters, who only needed to sign and return them. Once they were signed and returned, however, they were legal documents and public records. According to most interpretations of state law, they would now be out of bounds to anyone other than the voter or a government official. Soon this would become a key issue.

The objective of these mass mailings was to increase voter participation and, of course, support for each party. Who could argue with that? For decades voter turnout rates had been dropping, a perennial concern of political scientists and commentators. People led busy lives, and they complained that candidates were uninspiring, and they had computers to play with and cell phones to program. Something had to be done. Maybe if the system made it easier to vote—yes, even from citizens' own living rooms—more people would avail themselves of the opportunity. This opened up a new front in the battle for political support, and both parties launched major initiatives. At one point even Gov. Jeb Bush endorsed the outreach program, saying in a mass mailing that Republicans should cast "mail-in" ballots "from the comfort of your own home."

Voters who completed and sent in applications were supposed to receive absentee ballots in the mail. But for the Republicans, something went wrong. Thousands of requests arrived at elections offices in Seminole and Martin Counties lacking crucial voter registration numbers. Some applications showed birth dates where registration numbers should have been. Others showed random characters in that space or nothing at all. Such numbers have been required on Florida absentee ballot requests since 1998, shortly after the Miami voter fraud scandal in which absentee ballots were sold on the street. Without those numbers, the applications were invalid, and ballots could not be mailed out.

Republicans discovered the mistake in Seminole when voters began calling party offices in the weeks just prior to the election, asking why their ballots hadn't arrived. Party officials looked into it and paled. The Republicans' printing company had omitted the registration numbers, and in some cases a computer glitch had inserted other, random numbers. Everyone knew that Florida's race would be close and possibly decisive, and now a printing error threatened to ruin everything for the Republicans. This was a disaster in the making. Many of these Republican voters, a good number of them homebound and elderly, would only vote if they could do so by absentee ballot.

October 17, 2000. The final Bush-Gore debate was scheduled that night, and Michael Leach drove to On The Border, a Mexican restaurant in Tallahassee. He was one of ten Republican field workers in Florida, and he planned to drink margaritas with two Republican friends as they watched Bush take on Gore yet again. The election was only three weeks away, so of course Leach's cell phone was on standby, and then it chirped, and Michael Leach's life changed forever.

Leach was born and raised in Pensacola, the son of a telephone repairman. During high school, he devoted more attention to the licks of hard-rock guitarists than to his studies. After graduation in 1989, with few other options, he enlisted in the U.S. Air Force. During the Gulf War, he served as a military policeman in Iceland. After his two-year enlistment, Leach worked as a janitor for minimum wage. He moved through a series of odd jobs, eventually becoming a $19,000-a-year policeman in the Florida Panhandle town of Gulf Breeze.

He began finding his way in 1994, while watching the televised funeral of Richard Nixon. Leach vaguely knew that Nixon was a tainted president and that something called Watergate had been responsible for much of his notoriety. But during the funeral, Leach heard speaker after speaker praise the deceased president, especially complimenting his work in foreign affairs. Intrigued, Leach began studying Nixon's life. The more he read, the more he became convinced that Nixon was one of our greatest presidents, a misunderstood, unappreciated statesman of the first order.

Here was the role model he craved, and Leach decided to become active in the Republican Party. He also decided that he needed a university degree if he expected to achieve greatness. He enrolled at Florida State University in 1996, graduating four years later with a degree in criminology. He began working for the Florida Republican Party in the summer of 2000, while serving in the U.S. Air Force Reserve and in the Jefferson County Sheriff's Office Reserve Drug Task Force. With little prompting, he would describe, illustrate, and celebrate Nixon's virtues, along with those of Ronald Reagan. "When I see him, I think of the shining city upon a hill and the eternal optimism of America," Leach would say of Reagan. He also admired Harry Truman. "His character, his honesty, his damn guts," Leach explained. "He was one tough son of a bitch. I love the guy to this day."

So now, Leach lifted the cell phone to his ear. The person on the other end was his boss, Todd Schnick, political director for the Florida Republican Party. "We have a problem in Seminole County," Schnick told Leach. "I need you to go there tomorrow and meet with the supervisor of elections and take care of the problem." Schnick told Leach about the absentee ballot foul-up, and Leach made the four-hour drive to Sanford, a quiet, generally refined little city that serves as Seminole's county seat.

Seminole had acquired a strong Republican identity as it filled with affluent suburbanites from Orlando, the metropolis to the south. Its election supervisor was Sandra Goard, a tall, slender, seemingly frail woman. A native of West Virginia, she moved to Seminole County in 1966 and began working for the elections office as office manager in 1977. Then-Gov. Bob Graham, a Democrat, appointed Goard election supervisor in 1983. Goard, a Democrat, switched to the Republican Party two years later and was repeatedly reelected to the post.

It turned out that it was Goard who first spoke publicly about the problem with the Republican applications. In mid-October, she told listeners of a local radio program that if voters wanted to

receive ballots by mail, they would have to make sure their voter
ID numbers were filled in. To some Democrats, it seemed that
Republican elections chief was engaging in a bit of covert campaigning. Gerald Richman, a Democratic attorney who would
later lead a legal battle against Goard, said, "She was basically
trying to get the message out" to Republican voters.

According to court testimony and depositions, a short time
later Republican officials called Goard to ask if they could remove
faulty ballot requests from her office and correct them. Goard said
they could not. Then they asked if they could "resolve the situation by having an individual come into the office to place the
information on the cards," Goard said in a deposition. She said
they could do that, so long as they used the party's voter database
rather than the county's. She would say later that she had never
before allowed a party worker to perform that kind of work during her twenty-three years with the office. Democratic ballot requests had been printed properly, so no special action was
required, but Goard did not tell the Democrats that Republican
visitors were on the way and would be working in her office, unat-
tended.

Schnick had told Leach he would need about two days to complete the work. Then Leach was to head to Broward County and
perform other duties for the party. But when Leach first glimpsed
the huge stack of applications he had to process, his jaw dropped.
"This is too much for one man," he thought to himself. "I got a
college degree so I wouldn't have to do things like this." For a
moment Leach considered abandoning the job, but that would
not be the action of a patriot, a man with a sense of duty. "I'm
serving a cause greater than my damn self-interest," he reminded
himself. "We're trying to win the state of Florida for George W.
Bush." He plugged in the computer and reached for the first application form.

Day after day, Leach filled in voter registration numbers he found on a Republican Party computer disk that also contained the names and addresses of every voter in Seminole County. He completed nearly a hundred applications every day, but each mail delivery brought more and more. At times he felt like Lucille Ball in that classic comedy routine about the assembly line: the faster he worked, the more behind he became. Sometimes it seemed as though he wasn't making any headway at all, but he plodded on. "I'm in the military," Leach reminded himself. "I've been sent here to accomplish a mission." With Goard's office open on weekends, he worked diligently and finally completed his work. On November 2, the Thursday before the election, Goard told him time had run out. No new ballots could be mailed out anyway.

When he packed up his laptop computer and left Goard's office for the final time, "I felt like I had accomplished my mission," Leach recalled later. He remained in the Orlando area for the final days of the election. On Election Night, he was crushed when the networks initially awarded Florida to Gore. But later, he and his Republican friends at the Orlando Marriott celebrated when the networks withdrew that call. Florida was now too close to call.

Harry Jacobs was that rare breed: a wealthy political donor who also wanted to roll up his sleeves and work for the campaign. On the day after the election, when the Democrats needed people to monitor the first recount of votes cast in Seminole County, Jacobs volunteered. At the elections office, Jacobs overheard a conversation between an elections employee and a canvassing board member—something about Republicans who visited the office daily to "correct" absentee ballot applications. Shocked and angry, Jacobs reported the story to party leaders, unearthed more details, and announced that he was filing a lawsuit.

The Democrats assembled a fifteen-attorney team of volunteer lawyers in the Tallahassee offices of the Florida teachers union.

Gerald Richman, named the lead attorney, was a Palm Beach County Democrat who had run an unsuccessful campaign for Congress from Miami-Dade in 1989. The Democratic Party and the Gore campaign were noticeably absent, keeping a safe distance from the suit. Elsewhere they were arguing for recounts on the basis that every vote must count. How could they publicly support this suit, even if privately they welcomed it? Jacobs wanted to throw out every absentee ballot cast in Seminole County—10,006 for George W. Bush, 5,209 for Al Gore. A victory might have delivered Gore an effective gain of 4,797 votes.

Martin County sits beside the Atlantic Ocean, just north of Palm Beach County. The Internet site for the Republican Party there boasts: "Martin County—Where all the elected officials are Republican!" It is a place of beachfront mansions, low-density developments, cattle ranches, and citrus groves, though the hustle and bustle of South Florida is beginning to intrude. It is one of the state's wealthiest counties, and Democrats are a definite minority. George W. Bush carried Martin County with 55 percent of the vote. Democratic attorney John Kennedy, a Martin resident, grumbled, "If you're a Democrat in this county, you don't usually even get to vote. The seats are all decided in the primary." One of those Republican office holders was Peggy Robbins, the Martin County election supervisor. She is a former kindergarten teacher and a kindly grandmother: when something surprises her, she exclaims, "Jiminy Cricket." But before long, she also stood in the glare of the media spotlight.

Just as in Seminole, thousands of incomplete absentee ballot applications had been mailed to Republicans in Martin County. When they came back, the forms had voters' birth dates where ID numbers were supposed to be. They were no good. Once again, Republicans called to ask if they could take the invalid forms to their party office and correct them. This time they struck pay dirt. Robbins said yes.

The enterprising staff of the *Stuart News,* a local newspaper, landed the story shortly after the election. Government reporter Melissa Holsman asked Robbins about it. The election supervisor said she had allowed Thomas Hauck, a Republican official for Martin County, to visit her office regularly over several weeks to pick up incomplete forms and bring them back later with ID numbers filled in. "Tom came in every day to see if there were any incomplete," Robbins told Holsman. "I don't know of any law that speaks to this. I don't think it was wrong, because they were assisting Republican voters, and the reason the form was incomplete was that the state party didn't fill out all the information. It was Republican, Republican, Republican."

Later, Hauck said in court documents that he worked with Charlie Kane, a retired CIA man who is now Republican county chairman for Martin. Hauck and Kane ultimately corrected 670 ballot applications. Robbins and her staff said they didn't believe the forms were public records because they hadn't yet been processed by her office. If they weren't public records, what did it matter if the Republican Party borrowed them for a day?

The account outraged Ronald Taylor, a resident of Stuart, an electrical contractor, and a longtime union man with a passion for the Democratic Party sharpened by memories of a run-in with a Republican president decades ago. Taylor was among the striking air traffic controllers fired by Ronald Reagan in the 1980s. Taylor also filed suit. He demanded the rejection of all 9,773 absentee ballots in Martin County—6,294 votes for Bush and 3,479 for Gore.

The Seminole and Martin cases were moved to Tallahassee, though they were not exactly consolidated there. A generally quiet, even genteel capital city that thought it had already seen it all now saw this: tag-team trials involving some of the same lawyers, most of the same issues, and two different judges, under way on the same day in adjoining courtrooms at the Leon County Courthouse.

Proceedings in the Martin County case began at 7:00 A.M. December 6 in Courtroom 3-C before Circuit Judge Terry Lewis, a soft-spoken jurist who writes mystery novels in his spare time. At 8:15 A.M., Lewis declared a recess so that lawyers could move next door to Courtroom 3-D for opening arguments in the Seminole County case before Circuit Judge Nikki Clark, the first black judge ever appointed in Tallahassee. That case dragged along until 7:00 P.M., when Clark declared a recess until the next day. After a short break, Lewis resumed the Martin case in 3-C, which continued until 12:35 A.M.

The Democratic lawyers built their lawsuits around a 1998 law that focused closely on absentee ballots. That law said that "the person making the request" and no one else must fill out vital information on the form, including the eight-digit voter registration number. The courts, however, interpreted this to mean that vital information could be pre-printed on the form, by political parties or others, so long as it appeared before the voter signed it. Nevertheless, some Seminole and Martin County officials testified that they had mistakenly thought the Republicans had every right to correct the forms—even after voters signed them—because the party had originally printed them.

Public records laws were also at issue. Both major political parties printed absentee ballot applications, but they handled the process differently. Democrats typically had the forms mailed back to the party and then delivered those forms to elections offices; Republicans had voters mail the forms directly to county governments.

Either way, some observers have found the practice distasteful, saying that it blurs the line between nonpartisan election procedure and partisan campaigning. "I think it is inappropriate," said Barbara Petersen, executive director of the First Amendment Foundation in Tallahassee. "Why are these parties sending out these applications?" She emphasized the crucial timing issues: Had the Republicans altered their ballot requests before they were signed by voters, they would have committed no legal foul. But by the time they regained access to them, within county offices, the documents were public records and should not even have been touched by anyone but government officials. A ballot request form becomes a public record when it arrives at the elections office. "To alter a public record is, in effect, to destroy it, because you're changing it," Petersen said. "To me, this was an egregious public records violation."

She said that election supervisors in the two counties erred in allowing the Republicans to change the absentee requests: "As the custodian, it was their job to make sure they weren't altered or destroyed."

Each team of Democratic attorneys argued that its case was the worst of the two. In Martin, Republicans removed the public records from the elections office and did who-knows-what to them before bringing them back. In Seminole, the election supervisor turned her office into a virtual satellite of the Republican Party. But to Petersen, "They were both awful. Equally awful."

Republicans argued that the supervisors' actions represented nothing more than indiscretions based on a desire to preserve the voting rights of as many people as possible. Bush campaign attorney Daryl Bristow said that the wrong, if there was a wrong, merited no punishment harsher than a mild reprimand. "These are fine people," he told Judge Lewis. "They are innocent people. They were trying to do the right thing." Robbins, the Martin County elections supervisor, testified that "it only seemed logical" to let the Republicans take the ballot applications away and correct them, because "the mistake was made by the Republican Party. . . . We did not want to deny the voter the right to get their absentee ballot."

Finally, both judges ruled for the Republicans, though with reservations. They concluded that a missing voter ID number on an absentee ballot *request* wasn't sufficient to invalidate the ballot itself. A tainted ballot request, they reasoned, is not the same as a tainted ballot.

Judge Clark concluded that Goard did, in fact, violate election law by allowing a third party to alter the ballot forms in Seminole County. But she found no evidence of "fraud, gross negligence, or intentional wrongdoing," circumstances that could lead a judge to throw out the results of an election. "While the Supervisor of Elections of Seminole County exercised faulty judgment in first rejecting completely the requests in question, and compounded the problem by allowing third parties to correct the omissions on the forms, no remedy against her is available in this election contest," Clark wrote. "Faulty judgment is not illegal unless the Legislature declares it so."

In the Martin County case, Lewis went a bit further. He said the evidence showed a clear violation both of election law and of public records laws and "that it offered an opportunity for fraud and created the appearance of partisan favoritism on the part of the Supervisor of Elections."

But, he said, "in the present case, the persons who signed the request forms in question were duly qualified and registered voters in Martin County. There is no evidence of fraud or other irregularities in the actual casting of the ballots, or the counting of the ballots." Case closed. The Florida Supreme Court affirmed the Lewis and Clark rulings in a swiftly written ruling released the same day the U.S. Supreme Court ruled against Al Gore and ended the ballot recount. Prosecutors say that criminal charges are not expected to be filed against anyone involved in either case.

On January 20, Leach watched the inauguration on television and his eyes filled with tears. He could not help but reflect on his role in the election. "I felt proud that I made a huge difference in the country, that I saved the country from a bad man, Al Gore," he said. "I also thought, How can I ever top this, helping elect an American president?"

10

UNDERVOTES

Even after Al Gore conceded, even after George W. Bush was inaugurated, provocative questions swirled around Florida's election. Were all recoverable votes counted? Did the intervention of the U.S. Supreme Court tilt the scales? Did Bush really, *really* win?

The *Miami Herald* sought to find out. Acting swiftly after the nation's highest court halted a sweeping recount in Florida, the *Herald* demanded access to all undervotes—ballots on which presidential votes were not detected by counting machines—in the state. At times it had to file suit to examine those ballots. In the end it dispatched reporters and independent accountants to all sixty-seven counties.

They inspected 64,248 ballots. They marked their findings on complex tally sheets that were converted into computerized reports. Then editors, writers, and data analysts dug through mountains of information. Finally, conclusions emerged.

Paramount among those conclusions: *Bush almost certainly would have won the presidential election even if the U.S. Supreme Court had not halted the statewide recount of undervotes ordered by the Florida Supreme Court.* But in one of the great ironies of the

long and bitter 2000 election, Bush's lead would have withered—
and perhaps vanished altogether—if those ballots had been
counted under the severely restrictive standard advocated by some
Republicans.

The review by the *Herald* and its parent company, Knight Ridder, in partnership with *USA Today* found that under the most
inclusive standard, in which every dimple, pinprick, or hanging
chad on a punch-card ballot was considered a valid vote, Bush
would have added 1,128 votes to his official 537-vote lead—for a
final margin of 1,665.

Bush's advantage diminished, however, as the standard tight-
ened: His final lead would have fallen to 884 if dimples were
counted as presidential votes only when dimples appeared elsewhere on the ballots. His lead would have dwindled to 363 if votes
were counted only when a punch-card chad was detached by at
least two corners, perhaps the most common standard applied
nationally. And his margin of victory would have disappeared,
replaced by a Gore lead of only 3 votes, if only clean punches
were accepted. That Gore advantage—0.00005 percent of the 5.9
million votes cast by Floridians—was so tiny that it left the outcome in question. In addition, it was produced by a highly unlikely scenario. The severely restrictive clean-punch standard is
rarely employed. Among two dozen states that impose standards
on manual recounts of undervotes, only Indiana insists on cleanly
punched chads.

Nevertheless, many Republicans advocated that standard as
the *Herald*'s ballot reviewers moved through the state. "The context in which we viewed this entire recount is that the election is
over [and] there is only one legal standard for a vote, the standard
that was in place when people went in to vote, and that was a
clear punch," Portia Palmer, a spokeswoman for the Republican
Party of Florida, told the *Herald* during its ballot review.

In a finding certain to interest Gore supporters, the review also
discovered that many hundreds of ballots were discarded in pre-

dominantly Democratic Broward and Palm Beach Counties even though those ballots contained marks identical to marks on ballots that were officially tallied. That was the apparent result of several factors: Scores of people were deputized to conduct official recounts that were not guided by a common standard. Partisan observers frequently lodged objections to individual ballots. Fatigue eventually gripped nearly everyone involved.

At any rate, the bottom line of that analysis is this: *If not for the inconsistencies in Broward and Palm Beach Counties, Gore might have netted enough new votes to have swung the election— and long before the Florida Supreme Court and U.S. Supreme Court acted.*

Although besieged by Republican claims that they used lax standards to award votes to Gore, the canvassing boards of Broward and Palm Beach Counties could have credited 2,022 more votes to the Democrat if they had counted every dimple, pinprick, and hanging chad as a vote. Those Gore votes would have been enough to make him president—if the fully inclusive standard had been employed on a consistent basis, an unlikely scenario. But even if the canvassing boards counted dimpled ballots only when the ballots contained at least one other dimple, Gore would have netted about 1,000 additional votes in the two counties— again enough to win the election.

As intriguing as that might be, those findings in Broward and Palm Beach Counties are somewhat irrelevant to the main issue examined by the *Herald*, which sought to answer a question asked by many Americans and certain to be examined by historians: What would have happened if the U.S. Supreme Court had not acted on December 13, reversing the Florida court and terminating the official undervote recount?

The nation's highest court said that the lack of a consistent statewide standard for judging ballots raised constitutional issues. It declined to give Florida time to develop such a standard, effectively handing the state's 25 electoral votes and the White House to Bush. And few who endured the election aftermath could argue with this: for anyone attempting to determine the will of Florida's voters on November 7, 2000, the absence of a consistent standard for weighing undervotes proved as serious a problem as inadequate machinery, uneducated voters, and ineffective administration.

The *Herald*'s requests cited the Florida Public Records Law, which makes ballots subject to public examination. The newspaper later retained the public accounting firm of BDO Seidman, LLP, to inspect the ballots.

The comprehensive review of undervotes began on December 18 in Broward County, and teams of accountants and reporters soon visited all sixty-seven counties. The last undervote was inspected March 13 in Hamilton County. Under its agreement with the *Herald*, BDO's accountants noted what kind of mark was present on each ballot and the mark's location, then totaled the marks of various kinds and reported them to the *Herald*. But BDO made no effort to determine voter intent or whether a mark on a ballot was a legally valid vote.

Reporters from the *Herald*, other Knight Ridder newspapers, and *USA Today* also reviewed every undervote ballot and made separate and independent assessments of their characteristics. That effort was designed as a statistical check of variations between observers but was not considered in the tabulations BDO reported.

The project was exceedingly difficult and time consuming, and many complexities had to be resolved. Foremost among them: in order to answer the basic question—what would the Florida Supreme Court's recount have shown—the *Herald* had to recreate electoral and legal conditions that existed on December 8, when the order was issued. That required factoring in certain county results and factoring out others. This is how it worked:

Of the 64,248 ballots inspected by BDO, only 42,897 came

from precincts affected by the Florida Supreme Court order or from counties that did not complete the recount before the U.S. Supreme Court issued its stay. The state court specifically excluded from the statewide recount Broward, Palm Beach, Volusia, and 139 precincts in Miami-Dade where manual recounts had already been conducted. In addition, three counties—Escambia, Manatee, and Madison—completed the count before the U.S. Supreme Court froze the process. Another, Hamilton County, reported that it had no undervotes, although that was proven untrue when the *Herald* inspected its ballots.

Of the 42,897 ballots, no marks for president were found on 20,861. These were true undervotes—with no evidence of any attempt to vote for president. Another 861 ballots showed marks for write-in candidates or for presidential candidates other than Bush or Gore, and 2,912 had marks in ballot locations that were not assigned to candidates. Not included in the tabulation were 1,514 ballots that BDO determined had marks for more than one presidential candidate but that for unknown reasons were presented by canvassing boards as undervotes. State law specifically prohibits the tabulation of ballots with marks for more candidates than are to be elected to the office.

That left 9,114 ballots with marks or write-in notations that might, under the most permissive standard, be interpreted as votes for Bush. And it left 7,637 ballots with marks that, under that same standard, might be interpreted as votes for Gore. The *Herald* also accepted the official results of the recount in Escambia, Madison, and Manatee Counties—an additional 20 votes for Bush and 27 for Gore—and Hamilton's claim of no undervotes. That brought the Bush total to 9,134 and the Gore total to 7,664.

The *Herald* then followed the court's order, adding 174 votes to Gore's total as the net gain from Palm Beach County's official recount. It also added 168 votes to Gore's total as the net gain from the 139 Miami-Dade precincts that had been recounted manually. That left Gore with a potential total after the recount of 8,006, under the most permissive standard.

The *Herald* then added 537—Bush's statewide lead at the time the Florida court acted—to Bush's result, leaving him with a total of 9,671—1,665 more than Gore.

Similar calculations were made to arrive at results for the three other standards most often suggested for gauging the legitimacy of disputed ballots: Dimples when dimples appear elsewhere. Two or more corners of a chad detached. Only clean punches.

Among the *Herald*'s other findings:

• Contrary to popular belief, mismarks for Gore were less likely than mismarks for Bush in punch-card counties. Marks of some type were found in the Bush position on 1 ballot for every 172 valid Bush punch-card votes; marks in the Gore position were found on 1 ballot for every 181 valid Gore punch-card votes.

But the opposite was true in optical scan counties. Marks were found in the Gore position on 1 ballot for every 1,489 valid Gore optical scan votes; marks in the Bush position were found on 1 ballot for every 2,600 valid Bush optical scan votes.

• More specifically, dimples were only slightly more likely to appear in the Gore position than in the Bush position. Statewide, 10,745 dimples were found in chads assigned to Gore and 10,004 dimples were found on chads assigned to Bush, a nearly equal result. This suggests that dimpled punch-card ballots were related more to machine failure than to human error.

• Optical scan balloting does not solve the problem of discarded ballots. While the sheer number of problem ballots was far higher in punch-card counties, 2,119 discernible presidential votes were left untabulated in counties that use optical scan systems. Gore would have received 1,179 of those votes; Bush would have received 860. The large number of seemingly valid votes that went uncounted suggests that election reform may need to go beyond the replacement of punch-card systems with optical scan systems. For example, Florida law says that no ballot may be discarded if the intent of the voter is clear. But the law is less definitive concerning the obligations of canvassing boards to examine discarded ballots to determine if the intent of voters can be ascertained.

The Florida Supreme Court ruled in 1998 that canvassing boards must examine "damaged or defective" ballots for voter intent and further defined the term *defective ballot* as "a ballot which is marked in a manner such that it cannot be read by a scanner." Though some canvassing boards in optical scan counties conducted such reviews on Election Night, most boards around the state did not. Had all canvassing boards in all counties examined all undervotes, thousands of votes would have been salvaged throughout the state long before the election dispute landed in court—and the outcome might have been different—the *Herald* found.

In that scenario, under the most inclusive standard, Gore might have won Florida's election—and the White House—by 393 votes. If dimples were counted as votes only when other races were dimpled, Gore would have won by 299 votes. But if ballots were counted as votes only when a chad was detached by at least two corners (the standard most commonly used nationally), Bush would have won by 352 votes.

The ballot review also accentuated the latitude that local election officials enjoy under state law to establish standards and practices that can differ from those employed in other counties. For example, nearly all optical scan systems can alert voters to errors on their ballots—if scanners are deployed in each precinct. But *Herald* reviewers found that some election officials intentionally don't use the scanning equipment's full capabilities. The result: voters in some counties are able to correct fewer errors than voters in other counties.

One consequence of this latitude was clear in Escambia County, where vote tabulating equipment was programmed to flag as undervotes only those ballots on which no votes were apparent anywhere. Few other counties adhere to that policy. When Escambia was ordered by the Florida Supreme Court to recount its undervotes, it only examined ballots that fit that limited definition—a total of 16: 9 votes went to Gore, and 6 went to Bush, a net gain of 3 for Gore. But when the *Herald* insisted that Escambia identify ballots where no votes were tabulated specifically in the presidential race, the county presented 677 ballots for inspection. Of those, 20 were deemed to be votes for Bush and 45 were deemed to be votes for Gore—a net gain of 25 for the former vice president.

Though the *Herald*'s findings in Broward and Palm Beach Counties could not be considered when the newspaper calculated the likely outcome of the state court's order, those results did allow the newspaper to assess the actions of the canvassing boards in these two counties that played such a central role in the election.

The newspaper's representatives looked at 16,669 ballots in Broward and Palm Beach Counties, and it turned out that both political parties adopted strategies that favored their candidates there. Republicans correctly anticipated that a lenient standard would benefit Gore in those two counties and fought strenuously against it. Democrats unsuccessfully fought to include more ballots as valid votes.

At the same time, consistency was hard to come by. Piles of dimpled ballots never made it to the canvassing boards for scrutiny because election workers and observers agreed that these ballots contained no valid votes. The canvassing boards only scrutinized ballots when teams of two election workers and two representatives of the parties did not agree. "If we missed that many, I'll have to go kill some people," said Dennis Newman, a Boston attorney who represented the Democratic Party in Palm Beach. "That depresses me. Our instructions were very clear. When in doubt, question it or challenge it if you see anything."

Broward and Palm Beach kicked off their countywide manual recounts with basically the same benchmark for judging a ballot: the chad had to be detached by at least two corners to count as a vote. But as the recount battle went to court again and again, and the canvassing board members saw dimpled ballot after dimpled ballot, the basis for judging a vote evolved.

In both counties, board members started looking at the whole ballot rather than just the presidential chad in an effort to determine voter intent. In Palm Beach, the canvassing board counted dimples as votes if the rest of the ballot bore similar marks instead of clean punches. But even that was subject to interpretation. "Generally there had to be some pattern that this was how the person voted," said Judge Charles Burton, chairman of the Palm Beach board. "Out of twenty-two votes if you just had two little dings, we wouldn't necessarily count that."

Broward canvassing board members Robert W. Lee and Suzanne Gunzburger tended to view a dimple as a vote if there were other marks on the ballot for candidates of the same party. Lee even made a list showing which punch-card numbers corresponded to Democrats and which corresponded to Republicans. A quick glance at the list and the ballot could show whether the voter appeared to have chosen a straight ticket. "There had to be a pattern of two or three dimples in the Democratic field for me to feel comfortable to count a dimple for Gore," Lee said. "That's the way I interpreted the law." Lee's rationale: many people vote along party lines.

Republicans and some election law experts strongly objected

to that standard. Daniel Lowenstein, a UCLA law professor and an expert on election law, called the voting pattern standard "profoundly wrong." He said: "If you're going to count marks like that, you're surely going to count some significant number of votes that were not intended." Maintaining even an arguably flawed standard, however, proved impossible. The *Herald* compared similarly dimpled ballots to see if the pattern held up. While many dimpled ballots that were counted as votes did show a pattern of other dimples, others assigned to candidates did not.

During the week and a half of recounting, the boards often worked fourteen-hour days, tediously inspecting one ballot after another. In Broward, the board did not even break for Thanksgiving. The Palm Beach canvassing board worked nonstop before the recount deadline from 8 A.M. Saturday to 7 P.M. Sunday. All of this came under intense media scrutiny. Reporters and television cameras from around the world hovered just outside the glass-paned rooms where the canvassing boards toiled. The late hours, the life-in-a-fishbowl atmosphere, and the overall enormity of the task ahead took a toll on board members, despite their valiant efforts.

Palm Beach had a written policy on recounts, which called for the two-corner standard and left little opportunity for partisan objections. But Democratic and Republican activists whittled away at the canvassing board's resolve. "We blew every policy and procedure with all of that because of the demands placed upon us," said Palm Beach Supervisor of Elections Theresa LePore. "Looking back, we were trying to please everybody. We probably should have said, 'This is the way it is.' "

Compounding the pressure on the boards was the inherent difficulty of assessing punch-card ballots. A chad is no bigger than a freckle. A dimple to one person can be a shadow to another. "It's like reading tea leaves. Everybody sees something different," said

William Scherer, a Fort Lauderdale attorney who represented the Republican Party during the Broward recount.

Even canvassing board members acknowledge they could not be 100 percent consistent over the course of long days. "I'm sure there's a few [ballots] in there now that if I went back and looked, I'd say these are votes, and if I went through the votes, I'd say some are not votes," Burton said.

The order in which ballots came before the canvassing board was another variable. If the board saw a dimpled ballot and called it for Gore, they might be likely to call the next dimpled ballot for Bush. But if a similar dimpled ballot came three hours later, it might be discarded. "At ten A.M. a person might be a little more conservative, and by ten P.M. they may be a little more liberal," said Broward Republican Party Chairman George LeMieux. Multiply the boards' inconsistency times sixty—the number of election workers and partisan observers in each county who reviewed the ballots first. If they reached agreement, the canvassing board never saw the ballot. A ballot ruled as containing no valid vote and not reviewed by the canvassing board had no chance of counting for a candidate.

Ideally, the people looking at ballots would receive the same training and follow it to the letter, minimizing discrepancies. But different teams behaved differently, according to Jeff Darter, information technology manager for the Palm Beach elections office. "There was a huge variation in their intensity, in observing or dissenting," he said.

While the quarrel over standards for manual recounts continues, there's one point on which there is little debate. Said Brigham McCown, a lawyer who represented the Republican Party in Palm Beach: "I think everyone's in agreement it did not work as advertised."

Of course, regardless of the undervote reviews, only one thing is truly clear: Precise numbers released on Election Night mask a world of imprecision and chaos. Responding to *Herald* requests for undervotes, only eight of Florida's sixty-seven counties were able to produce for inspection the exact number they reported on Election Night. Elsewhere, there is no way to know whether the Election Night figure, the number of ballots actually inspected, or some other number is correct. At one point, Pasco County Supervisor of Elections Kurt Browning testified during a hearing that multiple machine recounts in his county produced a different number of undervotes each time: November 8—1,776; December 9—1,712; February 5—1,744.

But it was not machine sorting alone that proved inaccurate. In Duval County, election officials—acting under court order—hand-sorted the county's 291,000 ballots in search of the 4,967 undervotes they had reported on Election Night. They ended up delivering 5,106 ballots for inspection by the *Herald.* That's close, but it also raises the possibility that some of those ballots were actually tabulated in the Election Night machine count.

The data collected by the *Herald* can be analyzed from many perspectives, and a close look at Miami-Dade's undervotes is particularly instructive—and provocative. It shows that if Katherine Harris, Florida's secretary of state, had allowed the four counties targeted by Gore to complete their manual recounts before certifying the election results, Bush most likely would have won the presidency outright—avoiding much of the political and legal warfare. Gore would have netted no more than 49 votes if the Miami-Dade recount had been completed, according to the review. That would have been 140 too few to overcome Bush's lead, even when joined with Gore gains in Volusia, Palm Beach, and Broward Counties—the three other counties where Gore requested manual recounts.

Of 10,644 ballots that the Miami-Dade elections office identified as undervotes, 1,555 bore some kind of marking that might be interpreted as a vote for Gore. An additional 1,506 bore some kind of marking that might be interpreted as a vote for Bush. There were 106 markings for other candidates. Reviewers found no markings for president on 4,892 ballots, and 2,058 ballots bore markings in spaces that had been assigned to no candidate. An additional 527 ballots were deemed to have markings for more than one presidential candidate—overvotes.

A large number of ballots—1,912—contained clean punches. But 1,840 of those were in ballot positions that corresponded to no candidate, including 1,667 ballots where the voter cleanly punched the positions just below the numbers corresponding to Bush or Gore.

Republicans called the Miami-Dade results further proof that Bush was the legitimate winner all along. "President Bush was lawfully elected on Election Day. He won after the first statewide machine recount," said Mark Wallace, a Miami lawyer for the Republican Party. "He won after the manual recount, and he won at the conclusion of the litigation. Now, after a ballot review using liberal standards unprecedented under the law, we find President Bush would still win. At some point, the Democratic National Committee needs to accept that, and that time is now."

Democrats remained bitter and maintained that results showed that neither side could have known how the recounts would turn out. "This underscores how unpredictable the whole recount strategy was, on both sides," said Doug Hattaway, a former Gore campaign spokesman. "This shows Bush's tactics of delaying and blocking vote counts didn't really benefit him." But Hattaway acknowledged that the Democrats too may have been flawed in their approach. "Our strategy of focusing on four counties might not have benefited Gore either," he said with a rueful laugh.

As was the case elsewhere, the Miami-Dade inspection showed a range of problems with the ballots. Some voters in Miami-Dade didn't punch the chads. Instead they marked their ballots with pen or pencil, either coloring in the chads or crossing them out. Some were torn. One voter wrote across the top of the ballot, in bright green block letters: Elián González.

Other voters punched chads that didn't correspond to a candidate. On the Miami-Dade ballot, 736 voters made marks at hole number 5, one below Bush's number 4, and 1,017 voters made marks at hole number 7, one below Gore's number 6. And still others, 2,457 altogether, marked their ballots with only an indentation, or dimple, in the presidential column.

It will never be known if those marks would have been counted as votes by the Miami-Dade canvassing board, since it reviewed only about a quarter of the undervotes before halting its hand count of all ballots on November 22. The board said it could not finish the job by the state's deadline of November 26, a decision that pleased a boisterous crowd of Republican demonstrators who opposed the recount.

Throughout the course of the statewide ballot review, from December until mid-March, representatives of the Republican Party trailed *Herald* ballot reviewers throughout the state. And they all saw many strange things. Criticize Floridians, if you must, for their voting skills during the presidential election of 2000, but at least give them points for style and creativity. In spoiling their ballots, many demonstrated considerable ingenuity.

Some voters inserted punch-card ballots upside down into the machines. Some didn't punch the cards at all, instead circling or underlining the tiny numbers. Some scribbled candidates' names or indecipherable notes on punch cards. One voter in Tampa used clear nail polish to paste a chad back into an absentee ballot. Others used tape. Some ballots contained reversed chads, in which the paper tabs had been punched out, then placed back in the ballot—backward.

Some ballots had no markings whatsoever—for any candidate

in any race. These "voters" traveled to precincts (or, in at least one case, filled out and mailed back an absentee ballot) but chose not to vote. Many ballots were punched in spots that did not correspond to any candidate; in some cases, this was mechanically impossible with the card placed in the machine. These voters must have punched those chads before inserting the cards. And all of this was in addition to the familiar epidemics of pregnant chads, hanging chads, dimpled chads, and pinpricks found in nearly all twenty-four punch-card counties.

Even the highly regarded optical scanning system proved little match for resourceful misvoters. Forty-one counties employed such systems, but only twenty-six of them provided immediate on-site scanning that alerted voters to their mistakes and gave them a second or even third chance. The other fifteen optical scan counties tabulated ballots at a central location, and voters there generally had no way of knowing they had fouled their votes.

Some residents of these optical scan counties filled in the bubbles of their lottery-like ballots with pencils instead of the special black marking pens that were supplied and required. Some used their own pens filled with red or blue ink that, to the color-blind scanners, might as well have been invisible ink. Elsewhere voters used pens instead of the pencils that were supplied and required.

Some inked out the name of the party to the right of the candidate's name rather than the bubble to the left. Some scrawled Xs through bubbles instead of coloring them in. Some drew their own bubbles in the wrong places. Bradford County Supervisor of Elections Terry Vaughan called these "created ovals." He said: "Some people just like doing their own thing." On ballots that required voters to connect the heads and tails of arrows, some people proved unequal to that task.

Ballots in Pinellas, Columbia, and several other counties suggested that some voters needed a "practice round" to polish their skills. They botched their first selection of the day—the presidential race—but seemed to get the knack of it as they worked through the lengthy ballots. This was particularly apparent in optical scan counties, where some voters made their marks to the left of presidential bubbles but then cast clean votes through the rest of the ballot.

All of this left election officials appalled. Regardless of their political persuasions, most election supervisors are passionate about this: Everyone should vote, and every wasted vote is a shame. "We put up the instructions on the booths," said Don Hersey, Putnam County's supervisor of elections. "We tell them, 'Fill in the ovals. A check or an X may not work.' But that's the problem we're having—some people just don't follow instructions."

Said Mark Andersen, Bay County's supervisor of elections and a former U.S. Navy SEAL: "I've run into people who have just been naturalized and they are burning to vote. An Iranian guy I know said he was very proud of being able to cast his first ballot as a U.S. citizen.

"When I was overseas, I was in Beirut pulling bodies out of a building, and it didn't matter if you were Republican, Democrat, Green Party, whatever. But it does matter that you vote."

During the *Herald*'s ballot review, reporters and accountants from BDO found that some election supervisors were accommodating but others were inhospitable.

Lake County Supervisor of Elections Emogene Stegall, for instance, refused to sort her ballots, compelling the *Herald*'s reporter and accountant to comb through 92,000 votes in search of 245 undervotes. In Marion County, election supervisor Dee Brown glowered at the assembled observers. "We're going to the vault where the ballots are sealed," Brown announced in a taut voice as the review began. "There will be no conversation with my staff whatsoever. There will be no conversation with the [spectators] back there. We will work from nine to noon and from one to four daily until we get done." She placed the three official observers at a wood-veneer table in one corner of a large room crammed with black metal ballot boxes. She cordoned off spectators in three rows of folding chairs behind another wood-veneer table, several feet away from the punch-card ballots. "We should have brought our binoculars," one woman joked.

Though their level of enthusiasm and cooperation varied, all election supervisors were required by state law to make their ballots available for inspection. Under Florida's Sunshine Law, ballots are public documents, and the media and other organizations have the right to examine them. But, also under the law, the ballots could not be touched by anyone other than election officials, who tediously offered them one by one for visual inspection.

Nearly every county required the *Herald* to reimburse it for expenses incurred by the review. The amounts ranged from $57.50 in Gulf County to $5,784 in Orange County. Overall, including travel expenses and data-processing fees, the review has cost the *Herald,* Knight Ridder, and *USA Today* more than $430,000, not including salaries of the people involved.

In some counties, the ballot examinations required weeks. In Miami-Dade, for instance, the review consumed eighty hours over nearly three weeks. Day after day, the *Herald* team sat at a government-issue utility table under fluorescent lights, listening to soft background music as election worker Jesus Arrechea displayed the ballots.

In Broward County, the review consumed more than fifty hours that spanned seven and a half days in December and January. It was conducted at the Voting Equipment Center in Fort Lauderdale, a chilly warehouse filled with boxes of ballots, hundreds of voting machines, and the county's vote tabulating computers.

In other counties, the review took a day or less. In sparsely populated Calhoun County in Florida's Panhandle, the *Herald* team needed under an hour to inspect 78 undervotes. There, election supervisor Martin Sewell simply stood behind the counter in his office and presented each ballot.

Among the other things *Herald* reporters learned: the typical dimple in a dimpled chad, at least in Pinellas County, was exactly one-hundredth of an inch thick, according to a precision measuring device carried by one observer.

In every county, Republican observers monitored the *Herald*'s reviews or conducted parallel reviews. Some election supervisors allowed the GOP workers to join the *Herald* at the tables; some required the observers to remain some distance away though still within view of the process. In Collier County, for instance, six elderly Republicans took turns peering at ballot dimples and chads. In Lee County, the Republican observer asked: "Oh, are you finding any of these imaginary votes?"

In Columbia County, local Republican activist Remzey Samarrai monitored the review, as he had in other counties. "We consider them all illegal," he said. "But we're keeping count, like everyone else."

Palmer, the spokeswoman for the Republican Party of Florida, said her party was concerned about the integrity of the process and the standards being employed by both the *Herald* and, separately, by a consortium of newspapers including the *Washington Post* and the *New York Times*. "Obviously, everything that goes on in the counting rooms can't be reported," she said. "Things are edited out. Some things are more interesting to editors or reporters. We thought it was important to know everything that went on in the room—who was handling the ballots, how the ballots were being handled, and what happened with the chads."

Democratic Party workers occasionally monitored the ballot reviews, but far less frequently and comprehensively. Tony Welch, a spokesman for the Democratic Party of Florida, said his party harbored some interest in the outcome but did not want to interfere. In addition, he said, Democrats had little to lose and thus did not need to scrutinize the review. "The Republicans have been trying to condemn all the counts since it started," he said. "One way was to cry that this is a bunch of chaos. Putting us there with Republicans, with additional problems, didn't seem to make much sense. The counts were supposed to be independent, so why would we want to sit there to try to color it at that time? We think that is why the Republicans are there, so that they can cast aspersions on the *Miami Herald* count or the *Washington Post* count. We wanted to be able to say, 'Look at what the counts say,' without interfering in it."

From time to time, interested voters—including some from out of state—wandered into the reviewing rooms to observe the process. William Walters and Bob Schenck, both from York, Pennsylvania, both Republicans, and both in their seventies, decided to drive down to Fort Myers to watch the review there. They had little sympathy for those who spoiled their ballots. "When you use the machine and you make an error, it is your responsibility," Walters said. "The instructions are laid out. Once you make an error, you are on your own, and it doesn't matter whether you are educated or not, Democrat or Republican."

In Marion County, a Republican spectator and a Democrat spectator engaged in good-natured ribbing.

Desmond Austin, Republican: "The election is over."

Ed Rancourt, Democrat: "The election is over. Stolen."

Austin, pulling out a pocket-sized copy of the Constitution: "The election is over. I've got my authority right here."

Rancourt: "You can wrap yourself in the Constitution all you want. Stolen is stolen."

At one point, an observer of the review in Palm Beach County shouted, "A waste of money. This is all the Democrats' fault."

In many places, the media review aroused media interest. In

Panama City, two local television stations and the local newspaper
sent reporters and photographers to record the Bay County review. In Clearwater, Florida's News Channel, a cable-TV news operation, filmed the Pinellas County review. In Ocala, the Marion
County review led a local TV news broadcast, and a front-page
headline in the *Ocala Star-Banner* said, "Miami Herald takes look
at Marion's undervotes."

In general, election supervisors conducted the reviews with care
and professionalism, often with humor, and sometimes with
pomp and circumstance.

Bay County's Andersen swore in four local citizens—a retired
FBI agent, his wife, an elections office worker, and a local house-
wife—as "inspectors of the review of ballots." They raised their
right hands and promised "to endeavor to prevent all fraud, de-
ceit, or abuse in coordinating the count." Later, he said: "I'm
patriotic at heart. The flag will make my eyes glass over."

In his county, the *Herald* examined 529 undervotes and 134
overvotes, all concealed within 59,520 ballots. "Be very thorough
in looking through them," Gene Crist, a Bay County deputy election supervisor, told the four assistants. "Look for undervotes,
those blank ballots in the presidential race only, and also the overvotes in the presidential race. Whether they are circled or whatever, you will have to make the determination. Be very careful.
Don't miss anything."

In Collier County, election supervisor Jennifer Edwards conducted a formal welcoming ceremony that included references to
"the aborted inspection" ordered by the Florida Supreme Court
and ended by the U.S. Supreme Court. Reading from a statement,
she said her lawyers were satisfied that the media review was legal.
Then she turned the process over to employee Dave Carpenter,
who occasionally offered withering observations. Noting that
many undervotes from a wealthy Marco Island precinct populated

by former residents of Manhattan showed no votes for president, Carpenter said: "None was good enough for them."

In Okaloosa County, reviewers attempted to decode an optical scan ballot that contained filled-in ovals for most races but only a tiny dot of ink in the oval assigned to Bush. "This was a mild supporter, as I look at it," election supervisor Pat Hollarn said. "He wasn't a hundred percent for him."

On the other hand, *Herald* reporters found that many thousands of Florida voters were rather overly involved in the presidential election. They cast overvotes, ballots that—for whatever reason—contained votes for two, three, four, or even more candidates, and the volume of these overvotes swamped the number of undervotes.

11

OVERVOTES

Al Gore's lawyers, and eventually the courts, focused much of their post-election attention on the mounds of undervotes because Democratic partisans and some experts believed that legitimate votes could be mined from there like nuggets of gold. But nearly twice as many people ruined their ballots by overvoting—accidentally or sometimes intentionally selecting more than one candidate for president.

At least 110,000 people—nearly one of every fifty voters in Florida—cast overvotes, according to the official machine count. Nearly all of those ballots were lost, rejected by mechanized tabulating machines and never included in certified election results. But weeks after the election, actual ballot inspections by *Herald* reporters and some election supervisors found that hundreds or even thousands of valid votes were hidden among the overvotes, and many of these votes would have been redeemable, if only someone had examined them in time.

For instance, in some counties that use optical scanning equipment, people managed to vote for Gore and then again for his running mate, Joseph Lieberman, or for Bush and then again for his running mate, Richard Cheney. Throughout the state, many people voted for Bush or Gore—and then did so again in the write-in category. All such votes were rejected by machines as overvotes. However, many election supervisors agree that many of those votes could have been rehabilitated. Manual recounts by canvassing boards employing nothing more than common sense might have done the job.

When undervotes and overvotes are considered jointly, an unavoidable conclusion emerges: *If Florida law had clearly mandated a manual examination of all machine-rejected ballots between Election Day and official certification of the election, thousands of additional votes would have been salvaged and the outcome of the election might have been different.*

It is important to note, however, that neither Gore nor Bush requested a recount of overvotes. In addition, the Florida Supreme Court did not include overvotes in its recount order, a fact cited by the U.S. Supreme Court as one of several errors committed by the state court. So overvotes were never legally subject to recounts—and thus did not play a vital role during the post-election controversy.

Moreover, the *Herald* found that most overvotes are lost forever, including 5,264 cast in Palm Beach County for Gore and the Reform Party's Pat Buchanan, 2,862 cast there for Gore and Socialist David McReynolds, and 1,319 cast there for Gore and Libertarian Harry Browne.

Logic and statistical studies suggest that most of those voters intended to select Gore but were confused by the county's now-infamous butterfly ballot. Gore's name and assigned punch hole were surrounded by those belonging to Buchanan, McReynolds, and Browne. If even 10 percent of those people had voted solely for Gore, he would be president today. Many of these ballots came from districts that were heavily Democratic and largely populated by blacks or elderly Jewish voters, none of whom were likely to support Buchanan or the other two minority party candidates.

Nevertheless, no one can definitively determine the intent of those voters or most others elsewhere in the state who—through error, confounding ballots, or faulty machines—chose more than one presidential candidate.

That also applies to most of the astounding 22,000 overvotes cast for various candidates in Daytona Beach and the rest of Volusia County, apparently as the result of confusion over the ballot design there.

Who suffered most? A *Herald* analysis of ballots from nine of Florida's largest counties suggest that Gore lost more votes than Bush when voters there selected more than one presidential candidate. The punch-card counties of Miami-Dade, Broward, Palm Beach, Highlands, Hillsborough, Lee, Marion, Pasco, and Pinellas accounted for nearly 2.9 million votes, or 49 percent of the state's total. The *Herald*'s analysis was based on computerized files that show the location of each punch on the ballot. The files do not show other problems such as hanging chads, dimples, and pinpricks. They also do not show any handwritten notations that might have indicated voters' intentions.

But according to the analysis, 58 percent of the 59,481 presidential overvotes in those counties were cast by people who voted for three or more Democratic candidates elsewhere on their ballots. Another measure: those who cast overvotes in the presidential election in these counties were 2.7 times more likely to vote for the Democratic candidate for U.S. Senate, Bill Nelson, than for the Republican candidate, Bill McCollum, also suggesting support for the Democratic ticket.

The analysis also suggests that overvotes proved particularly costly to Gore in South Florida. In the Democratic strongholds of Miami-Dade, Broward, and Palm Beach Counties, those who voted for two or more presidential candidates were nearly three times more likely to have voted for Nelson, the Democratic candidate for Senate, than for McCollum, the Republican.

Of those 59,481 overvotes in the nine large counties, 6,863 people voted for Gore and Harry Browne of the Libertarian Party, who was listed right below Gore on the ballot. Some election supervisors believe that these voters, not recognizing the names of Browne or any of the seven minor party candidates who followed him on the ballot, thought that all eight of them were running in a nonpresidential race.

*H*erald reporters found that bewildering ballot designs in many other counties also helped create overvotes that siphoned support from both major candidates.

In DeSoto County in south-central Florida, for instance, 608 people punched more than one hole in the presidential section of their punch-card ballots, which were larger and designed quite differently from the cards that were used in Miami-Dade, Broward, and Palm Beach Counties and which became familiar to Americans. Nevertheless, these ballot cards and the Datavote machines that accompanied them caused their own problems.

Many residents appeared to be torpedoed by the ballot's design, which listed eight presidential candidates on the front of the first page and two on the back—Howard Phillips of the Constitution Party and Monica Moorehead of the Workers World Party. The result: a large number of votes for Bush or Gore *and* for Phillips or Moorehead. These voters apparently believed that Phillips and Moorehead were competing in a different race entirely. No one can know for certain, and those presidential votes were forfeited.

But 186 of those 608 ballots—31 percent—were salvageable, if they had been promptly examined. The Datavote ballots featured relatively large entry fields for each candidate, and the machines allowed voters to punch multiple holes in those fields. The result: 94 people punched the Bush box two or more times; 92 people punched the Gore box two or more times. But more than one punch—even in the same field—counts as an overvote and voids the ballot. Though machine tallies rejected these ballots, manual recounts almost certainly would have rehabilitated them. "I don't think there's any question about voter intent," DeSoto Supervisor of Elections Mark Negley said as he inspected those ballots.

In Levy County in north-central Florida, 708 people overvoted in the presidential election. Many of them also appeared baffled by the layout of the ballot, which placed the ten presidential teams in two columns. Phillips and Moorehead appeared at the top of the second column—with no explanation. About 100 people voted for Gore or Bush and Phillips or Moorehead. In addition, a blank spot for a write-in candidate also appeared in the second column, leading to a common, critical, and costly error. Some people filled in the oval for Bush or Gore in the first column, then filled in the oval for a write-in vote and added the name of Bush or Gore. The machine read those ballots as overvotes and didn't count them, but a human blessed with common sense would have overruled the machine—if the ballots had been examined with that in mind, and they were not. "It's sad," said Levy Elections Supervisor Connie Asbell. "These are people who really wanted to vote for president."

DeSoto and Levy Counties are largely Republican, so it is likely that Bush would have gained ground there. Duval County, in northeast Florida, also tilted toward Bush, but Gore might have lost thousands of votes there—and potentially the election— because of overvotes. Nearly 22,000 people in Duval voted for more than one presidential candidate. Some later said they were confused by the presidential ballot, which was split into two pages. Many more may have been misled by an erroneous sample ballot that told them to "Vote all pages." A disproportionate number of the overvotes in Duval—four out of every ten—came from predominantly black areas where Gore overwhelmingly defeated Bush.

In predominantly Democratic Okeechobee County, 774 of the county's 10,722 ballots—more than 7 percent—were rejected as overvotes. Here too the ballot design appeared confusing. Presidential candidates were spread across two columns. Only well-versed voters would have recognized the names listed in the second column as belonging to presidential candidates. Again, many of those casting overvotes may have believed they were voting in two separate races.

Another anomaly turned up by the *Herald*'s analysis was a surprising number of voters, particularly in Miami-Dade and Palm Beach Counties, who voted for four, five, six, or more presidential candidates. "That to me is someone who doesn't understand the process at all and is just voting for everyone who they would approve of being president," said Anthony Salvanto, a University of California professor who studied computerized summaries of ballots from both counties. "There's always going to be someone who doesn't get it. The question is whether you have a system that catches them and prevents them from messing up."

The large number of presidential candidates—ten plus a write-in slot—certainly appears relevant to the high rate of over-voting in that race. The *Herald* found that people spoiled their votes in the presidential race three times more often than in races with fewer candidates. "This probably is the most confusing ballot we ever had," said Babs Montpetit, the supervisor of elections in Union County. "We've never had that many names on the presidential ballot."

Regardless of who was hurt and who was helped by all of this, the magnitude of Florida's overvote—by some estimates thirty times larger than typical rates during a presidential election—overwhelmed experts. Kimball Brace, president of Election Data Services, a Washington, D.C., election consulting firm, called the state results "phenomenal," and he did not mean it as a compliment. In forty years of tracking presidential election results, he said, he'd never seen such an astounding overvote rate. "What the heck is happening down there?" he asked.

How vulnerable to failure were some voting systems in Florida and elsewhere? Here's one benchmark: some voters managed to create undervotes and overvotes simultaneously on the same ballot.

In Gadsden County, which uses the optical scan system, one voter placed marks next to the names of Bush and Buchanan. An overvote, right? Wrong. The voter managed to miss the ovals for both candidates, so the ballot was read as no vote for president—an undervote. In Citrus County, also an optical scan county, an absentee ballot arrived with marks for Gore and Ralph Nader. But it was so stained with coffee that the machine considered it unreadable—another undervote.

Across the state, many voters apparently felt strongly—or weakly—both ways. Of all the overvotes analyzed by the *Herald*, 10 percent showed votes for both Bush and Gore. "I can't figure out some of my voters sometimes," said David Leahy, Miami-Dade's supervisor of elections.

He and his colleagues have been discussing one possible explanation. "When somebody doesn't want to vote in a race, he or she may not want to leave it blank, thinking that someone else will come along and vote for them on the ballot," Leahy said. "So to prevent that, they overvote. Hey, anything's possible."

Indeed, it is.

• Bradford County, which also uses the optical scan system, had 694 overvotes. Some people voted for every candidate except Bush or Gore. One circled Cheney—and filled in ovals for Gore and Nader. Said Bradford Supervisor of Elections Terry Vaughan: "The Cheney-Gore-Nader administration would be fun to watch.

Do you think they could all get along? Some people appear to be under the impression you can mix and match your presidential candidates."

Some voters appeared to realize their mistake. One voted for Bush and Phillips, then apparently tried to erase the mark for Phillips, but the resulting blur was read by the machine as a second vote for president, spoiling the ballot as an overvote.

In many cases, voters marked ovals for Bush or Gore, then marked write-in ovals and wrote the same names in those spaces. Emphatic votes, but rejected votes. "I hate it," Vaughan said, shaking his head over one such ballot. "It's just sad."

• In Levy County, some voters also tried to mix and match Five people wrote in "Al Gore and Dick Cheney." (None went for Bush-Lieberman.) One wrote in "All Gore," another "Larry Dennison, Issac Gillespie," whoever they may be.

In Levy County, as in Bradford and other optical scan counties, some voters unsuccessfully attempted to correct mistakes. They erased errant marks, not realizing that the powerful optical scanner is far less forgiving than the human eye. If Levy or Bradford Counties had used precinct-based scanners, these voters would instantly have known they had ruined their ballots and would have been offered another try. Neither county deployed scanners at the precinct level. Bradford Supervisor of Elections Connie Asbell shrugged when she saw these attempts. "They could have just asked for another ballot," she said. But it was unclear whether voters realized that. Signs posted in precincts on Election Day cautioned voters to fill in the ovals completely. They did not specifically offer replacement ballots.

• In Citrus County, which recorded 54 overvotes, some people defiantly marked giant *X*s through the names of all presidential candidates. One voter simply wrote: "None of the above." A *Herald* reporter also found all sorts of combinations: Gore and Buchanan, Bush and Buchanan, Gore and Browne, ballots marked for everyone but Bush, and ballots marked for everyone but Gore.

The reporter found several with five, six, or more candidates selected, and one on which the voter laboriously selected every other candidate, starting with Gore and ending with Moorehead.

• In Alachua County, a Gore stronghold, 102 overvotes were recorded. Many of them came from voters who filled in ovals for every presidential candidate but Bush. Supervisor of Elections Beverly Hill said her employees created a nickname for those ballots. "That's an E-B-B," she said. "Everyone but Bush."

• In Sarasota County, a Bush stronghold, 826 overvotes were found. Voters punched every number, every even number, every odd number, or various combinations. Many voted for Bush and Gore. A few voted for Gore and Buchanan. On one ballot, a voter punched through the Gore and Bush selections. Then the voter wrote "yes" next to Gore's name and "no" next to Bush's. Even though the intent seemed clear, no one saw that until it was too late, so the vote was never included in certified results.

• In rural Wakulla County in Florida's Panhandle, punch-card ballot forms featured a hole next to every person's name. Bush and Cheney, two holes. Gore and Lieberman, two holes. The result: great confusion and 373 overvotes created by people who thought they had to vote for the candidate *and* the running mate. The phenomenon was most apparent in the poorest areas, places with names like Sopchoppy and Smith Creek, places more likely to have black residents, places euphemistically dubbed "more cultural" by some local politicians and election officials.

Residents of these places cast all kinds of combination votes, ballots for Gore and Browne, Gore and Nader, Cheney and Gore, Bush and Browne, Bush and Buchanan, Bush and Nader, Gore and Nader, Bush and many others, Gore and many others. You name it, they voted for it here. At Sopchoppy City Hall, someone voted for Gore and then marked two other holes in the presidential area that missed actual candidates. Several people also missed the proper hole, punching the hole next to the name of the party above the candidate instead of next to the candidate. In Panacea, a fishing town near the Gulf of Mexico, Browne was paired 13 times with either Bush or Gore. In Wakulla County, there may be a village called Panacea. But in Florida's election, it seems, there was no panacea.

Sometimes voters were sabotaged by circumstances completely out of their control. In Charlotte County, Bush lost at least 15 absentee votes and Gore lost at least 1 because of a bizarre turn of events. It happened when some absentee voters cleanly filled in their optical scan bubble for Bush or Gore and also, farther down the ballot and in a different contest, marked the bubble for the Republican candidate for state insurance commissioner, Tom Gallagher.

Because of the position of the two names on the ballot and because of the way Charlotte County's absentee ballots were folded when they were mailed, a tiny trace of pencil lead from Gallagher's bubble apparently rubbed off into the presidential write-in bubble. The tabulating computer, seeing both a filled-in Bush or Gore bubble and a smudge in the presidential write-in bubble, read that as two marks and disqualified the ballot. The absentee votes were not tabulated in the certified results.

A spokesman for Electronic Systems and Software, the Nebraska firm that manufactured the equipment used in Charlotte County, said the ballot reader is so sensitive it could pick up a smudge from another ballot. But "it's not very common," said Todd Urosevich, vice president for elections services at ES&S. He said the voters probably marked their ballots very heavily, allowing a buildup of lead from the pencil. Some smudges were so minute as to be visible only with the aid of a magnifying glass.

The shading on those 16 ballots usually began just above the write-in bubble and intruded ever so slightly into it. When the ballots were folded for mailing, the Gallagher bubble lined up precisely with the write-in bubble. The problem, when recognized, is easy to fix. Ion Sancho, Leon County's election supervisor, said he sends his ballots laid flat in an oversized envelope to avoid difficulties.

On the whole, election supervisors say they would embrace any responsible reform that would allow them to recover otherwise lost votes. "You want people's votes to count and count accurately," said Miami-Dade's Leahy. But tight deadlines imposed by Florida's election laws discourage him and most other election supervisors from attempting to salvage undervotes and overvotes.

If state law required a survey of uncounted votes, all ballots for all races would have to be examined, he said, and that could not be done in the seven days between Election Day and official state certification. "You're probably talking about weeks of work," Leahy said.

In addition, the policy would have to apply to all elections, including primaries. Florida squeezes its primary, its runoff primary, and the general election into nine weeks, one of the shortest periods in the nation. "We are literally running to the printer after the first primary so we can have ballots in time for the second primary," Leahy said. "With our election schedule, we have virtually no time to get much of anything done."

He and others recommend that Florida eliminate its runoff primary or move both primaries to the spring. Thus far, those recommendations have not been seriously considered, though a Florida legislative committee proposed lengthening the certification period to eleven days, which would probably still not be enough.

"We're not going to get the extra time," Leahy said, "so at this point, my recommendation would be a voting system that simply does not allow for errors." It is one of many solutions now being floated—and considered—at nearly every level of the nation's electoral system.

12

SOLUTIONS

Simply put, many voters in this nation need modernized election systems that offer enhanced accuracy and reliability, and many election officials in this nation need statewide standards to guide them through ballot recounts.

Florida's experience in the presidential election of 2000 exposed the state and its voters to ridicule, some of it justified. But it also cast a spotlight—no, a wide and powerful searchlight—on the nation's electoral system, and many Americans did not like what they saw.

Hanging chads, dangling chads, pregnant chads. Punch card, optical scanner, electronic touch screen. Voter intent and various standards to determine that intent. Election protest, election contest. Machine recount and manual recount and then no recount.

All of it aroused enduring questions about the accuracy and validity of election results. At the end of February, a poll conducted for the *Herald* found that a decreasing number of voters believed that the state's presidential election was accurate or fair—only 57 percent compared with 65 percent in November. "What happened in this election was an embarrassment," said

Miriam Oliphant, the new election supervisor in Florida's Broward County.

And it must have seemed inexplicable to many people overseas. In England, the entire nation uses a single, simple system—paper ballots. Candidates are listed alphabetically, and voters mark an X next to the candidate of their choice. (Scanning machines are just now being used experimentally.) In France, the entire nation uses a single, simple system—paper ballots. Voters place ballots with the names of their selections inside sealed envelopes. In Germany, the entire nation uses a single, simple system—paper ballots. Voters mark an X to indicate their choice.

But in the United States, citizens vote on equipment that varies from state to state and often from county to county. Only four states—Delaware, Hawaii, Oklahoma, and Rhode Island—use standardized voting machines, generally versions of the optical scan system. The other forty-six states, including Florida, employ a hodgepodge of systems that differ widely in reliability. "With respect to voting systems, the U.S. is . . . a bad case," said John Carey, associate professor of political science at Washington University in St. Louis. "Other countries do a better job of making it easy to vote."

In its final ruling on the election, the U.S. Supreme Court not only blocked further recounts in Florida and essentially endorsed—some would say mandated—the narrow victory of George W. Bush, it also illuminated electoral flaws that have gradually accumulated in many states. Now, the court seemed to say, these flaws have grown into problems so fundamental and profound that they call into question the very basis of our democracy: elections in which each citizen's vote has equal weight.

Item 1: Punch-card ballots. They are so unreliable that voters who use them stand a far greater chance than other voters of having their ballots discarded. Yet about one-third of all Americans still live in punch-card districts.

"This case has shown that punch-card balloting machines can

produce an unfortunate number of ballots which are not punched in a clean, complete way by the voter," the justices wrote in *Bush versus Gore.* "After the current counting, it is likely legislative bodies nationwide will examine ways to improve the mechanisms and machinery for voting."

That search is already underway. Florida and many other states seem certain to jettison punch-card ballots, in most cases before the next major election in 2002 and certainly by the next presidential election in 2004. "The case has been made that the punch-card system cannot be used in another election," said Pam Iorio, president of the Florida State Association of Supervisors of Elections and supervisor of elections in Tampa and the rest of Hillsborough County.

Said Ernest Hawkins, president of the National Association of County Recorders, Election Officials and Clerks, and registrar of voters in California's Sacramento County: "The other states that use punch cards have to go to a new voting system or develop stricter standards for recounts. Eventually no one is going to be in the punch-card business anymore."

Item 2: Varying standards—in Florida and many other states—were used during recounts to determine the intent of voters and thus the legitimacy of their ballots. These shifting standards raise serious constitutional issues of fairness. The standards "might vary not only from county to county but indeed within a single county from one recount team to another," the U.S. Supreme Court said. As a result, the justices said, voters' rights to equal protection under the law could be violated.

As a matter of fact, a dimpled chad accepted by Broward County inspectors in 2000 as a presidential vote cast by Mr. Jones of Deerfield Beach might have been rejected by inspectors in Palm Beach County if it were cast by Ms. Smith of Boca Raton, just across the county line.

Something must be done to correct this inequity. At the very least, states must modify their laws to standardize the definition of an acceptable vote, satisfy the U.S. Supreme Court, and avoid lower court challenges during future elections.

"When you go into that booth to vote, Donald Trump and that guy on the street corner are the same size," said Philip Lewis, a member of Florida's new election reform task force. "They have the same power."

At least they should.

The place to start is with voting systems themselves. Machines with improved accuracy and reliability will, by definition, require fewer recounts and fewer disputes over the legitimacy of disputed ballots. "If we want to avoid any equal protection challenge, we must have a uniform technology," said Jim Smith, cochairman of the Florida task force on electoral reform and a former secretary of state. "Once we eliminate the punch-card machines, we won't have to worry about standards for problems like hanging chads."

Within three months of the election, state legislators across the nation had filed 650 bills seeking to modernize electoral systems in their states, according to the National Conference of State Legislatures. Abolishing the punch-card ballot was often their chief goal. In addition, members of Congress sifted through twenty-seven bills demanding electoral reform at the national level.

Innumerable state and national agencies impaneled task forces and blue ribbon committees to examine electoral reform. Legislators, governors, secretaries of state, election officials at municipal, county, and state levels—all established electoral task forces. Former presidents Jimmy Carter and Gerald Ford sat on one panel. "In every legislature, there are members who are taking a look at voting machines and voting techniques that their state uses," said Tim Storey, an election expert at the National Conference of State Legislatures. "They're under the impression that there are a lot of antiquated machines out there and they need to be replaced."

Among the arguments: Punch-card balloting produces a higher error rate than optical scanning and other systems, largely because most punch-card systems cannot protect voters from overvotes and undervotes. Touch-screen systems offer that protection, as do optical scan systems that include ballot-reading machines at the precinct level. In these "fail-safe" systems, botched ballots are rejected immediately and voters are given another chance to get it right. A *Herald* analysis showed that discard rates for all categories of voters were minimal in precincts where electronic machines scan fill-in-the-oval ballots and immediately alert voters to spoiled ballots so they can correct them. Forty-one Florida counties used some form of optical scan system during the 2000 election, but only twenty-six of them employed precinct-based ballot-reading machines. Those precinct scanners are critically important, the analysis showed. Optical-scan systems in counties that lack the error-notification feature had discard rates higher than in punch-card counties. This is a major problem, as are punch cards. "I think [punch cards] should go sooner rather than later," said Robert Richie, executive director of the Center for Voting and Democracy, a watchdog group in Takoma Park, Maryland. "I'm hoping that message comes out of Washington, and I think it should come out of the White House."

In fact, companies that manufacture voting machines and balloting software are already planning for a future that does not include the punch card. "I'm adapting my business plan to provide for the chance that there will be an exodus [from punch-card balloting]," said Paul Nolte of Election Resources Corporation, which sells election preparation software to twelve Florida counties, including Miami-Dade, Broward, and Palm Beach.

Much of the reform effort is concentrated in the nation's big cities, which are more likely than suburbs or rural areas to use punch-card systems. Florida's five most populous counties, Miami-Dade, Broward, Palm Beach, Pinellas, and Hillsborough, are all punch-card counties. "Why do the big urban counties use punch cards?" asked Iorio, the Hillsborough County election supervisor. "Because we're big urban counties with big urban needs. Parks and roads and sidewalks and libraries and water and sewer systems and on and on. And where does a new voting system rank?"

As always, money is key. Experts estimate that $3 billion is needed to replace punch-card, lever-machine, and other antiquated systems around the country. That could rise to $4 billion if electronic touch screens are installed in all 191,000 U.S. precincts. In Florida alone, the cost of full modernization ranges from $40 million to $200 million, depending on the system selected.

Most of the bills filed in Congress create bipartisan commissions to overhaul election laws and, perhaps more to the point, sanction federal grants to help states and counties buy new voting equipment. One bill would create the Election Administration Commission, a four-member body to study voting procedures across the nation. As envisioned, the commission would release $500 million in matching funds to state and local governments buying voting systems. That's just for the first year. After that, $100 million would be allocated annually over the next several years.

Another bill, the Federal Election Modernization Act of 2001, would authorize $2.5 billion in matching funds over five years for state and local governments to buy voting equipment, train poll workers, and enact other reforms.

Still, electoral reform could degenerate into a battle between zealous federal lawmakers and local election supervisors, many of whom question the proper extent of federal oversight in this area. "The Constitution really does allow states to run elections, quite exclusively," said Storey, who represents the state legislatures. "Elections are the domain of the states, unless you've got obvious problems, like civil rights violations. The states are not going to be pleased if the federal government tries to provide a one-size-fits-all solution."

But some federal lawmakers see things differently. The U.S. Constitution empowers Congress to enact laws governing "the times, places, and manner" of congressional elections, though it also gives states broad authority to govern their own elections. "I think our authority is pretty clear," said Rep. Peter DeFazio, a Democrat from Oregon.

He points to that U.S. Supreme Court decision in *Bush versus Gore*. "Whether we do it with inducement from federal funds or whether we do it by mandate, we have to throw out the [punch-card] technology and either induce or compel counties to purchase technologies that can accurately count votes," DeFazio said. "The Supreme Court opened the door very wide."

Many states are not waiting for direction from the nation's capital, and Florida—humbled by its experience in November 2000—is leading the way. The state assembled one of the first state task forces on election reform. "There is a widespread concern that the Florida system, at least some of the system, didn't work very well last time," said Edward "Tad" Foote II, president of the University of Miami and cochairman of the task force, speaking with characteristic understatement.

Assembled by Gov. Jeb Bush, the task force held its first meetings in January and February, and it sent an immediate message: punch cards must go. Jim Smith, the task force cochairman: "If the best that we can do after what we've been through is to go back and say we ought to go through another election with punch cards, we ought to have our fannies kicked."

But when the time came to make decisions, the group turned cautious. In a report released at the end of February, the task force decided to lease, rather than buy, nearly 4,000 optical scanners to replace punch-card systems as a temporary fix for the 2002 elections. Many found the plan unambitious. It was relatively cheap—$20.4 million, somewhat practical, and immediately controversial. Many county leaders and election supervisors in Miami-Dade, Broward, and Palm Beach Counties said that they would rather use touch-screen voting. Among other things, they fear that optical scan equipment may not be suitable for a county such as Miami-Dade, which has ballots in three languages and hundreds of choices presented to voters in different parts of the county. "I've never been a fan of optical scan machines," said David Leahy, Miami-Dade's supervisor of elections. "With touch screens, you get the same count every time." Broward's Oliphant said in written testimony that "radical change is needed." She called a move to optical scanning machines "short-sighted."

Secretary of State Katherine Harris appeared to agree with that assessment. In late February, she announced support for a $200 million, three-year move to a statewide electronic voting system by 2004. That almost certainly means a form of touch-screen voting. "I want voting systems that will make the will of the voter self-evident," she said. "You want to design a system that can be counted mechanically, so you take the human error out of it."

She said she would recommend her plan as part of a budget request to the state legislature. While the precise technology would be identified as the plan is carried out, her agency would probably focus on touch-screen computer voting for the 2004 election. It might not be an easy sell, even after all that has happened in Florida. Harris was expected to encounter resistance to her plan from fellow Republicans who run the Legislature with tight fists and who were already skeptical of spending $20.4 million for the leased scanners. Touch-screen units cost from $3,000 to $4,000 each, and most precincts would need several. An optical scanner costs $5,000 to $6,000, but no precinct would need more than one.

Florida House Speaker Tom Feeney suggested a state loan or

matching grants for counties that want to use scanners (Gov. Jeb Bush set aside about $30 million in his proposed state budget to help counties upgrade voting systems), but Feeney insisted that no machinery could overcome the need for voter education in basic balloting. "We can go out and spend on my watch two hundred million dollars to buy the most updated machinery in the world, but are we really fixing the symptom and not the underlying problem?" he said. "It may be that we loan some money to counties that do not now meet standards we think are acceptable." On the other hand, he left his options open. "If people think there is a long-term solution that is affordable, we will look at that. This is one where we are really letting the thing play out. . . . It's all on the drawing board."

Still, Harris is pressing for something like the touch-screen system. Though scanners are more precise than punch-card ballots and will work as a temporary fix, they are not as accurate as touch screens, she said. Voters sometimes circle—rather than fill in—the bubbles on paper ballots, causing the scanners that read them to overlook votes. "The interim solution of leasing is good, so long as there is the commitment . . . to make certain that we purchase the kind of technology that will last a long time—that we feel sufficiently confident that the voter's intention is understood and every vote counts," she said.

Touch-screen voting is already in place in small communities and some larger cities around the country. Casting a ballot on that system is like withdrawing money from a bank's ATM. The selection is usually made by touching a screen. The name of the candidate is lighted when it's touched. Only one vote per race is permitted, and the system will alert a voter who has overlooked any race. As appealing as these machines are to big-city election supervisors, only about 10 percent of the nation used them in 2000, and no state deploys them statewide.

Thus far, however, Florida has not certified any touch screens for use, a state requirement. Three companies are now seeking state approval, but Harris and her staff need to resolve several issues, including security. One common concern: the safety of a computerized voting record. Florida's "standards require a complete audit trail and that images be maintained in multiple memories," said Paul Craft, manager of Harris's Voting Systems Section, who will be testing touch screens. "We will be simulating failure of a memory to make sure the other memory can be accessed."

So Harris's department recommended that $50 million be spent in 2001 for development of a "Florida Election System." This included the design and development of an electronic voting system. She also recommended a $100 million effort in 2002 to adapt computerized voter registration in each county to the new system, produce a prototype of the electronic voting machine that will be used, and start distributing the machines statewide. That would be followed by a $50 million campaign to complete distribution and installation of electronic voting machines by January 30, 2004.

Rep. Carlos Lacasa, R-Miami, chairman of the Florida House Appropriations Committee, said that the legislature will be compelled to approve some sort of plan. "I am very concerned about the lack of confidence that voters have in the system," Lacasa said. "I'm sure we can find some money to do things right. . . . I have to imagine we will make some kind of expenditure."

The task force reasoned that leasing scanners for one election cycle would help the state avoid getting stuck with obsolete equipment if better technology came along in a few years—or if touch-screen units dropped in price. "Given what's going on in the country, I think we're going to see some smart people develop some new voting processes," Smith said. "Rather than spend forty million dollars and lock us into something, I'd rather have some flexibility."

In fact, some of the top names in Silicon Valley and academia have jumped in with proposals to build a better ballot counter. A team of engineers from two top math and science universities, the

California Institute of Technology and the Massachusetts Institute of Technology, is working under a $250,000 grant from the Carnegie Corporation to size up existing voting systems and possibly develop new ones. And three top computer companies, Unisys Corporation, Microsoft Corporation, and Dell Computer Corporation, announced a partnership in January to develop new election equipment.

At any rate, the Florida legislature must make the final decision. Looming over the entire enterprise is the fear of lawsuits by voters who claim they are disenfranchised by an inferior and unequal voting system. After all, no longer can an election supervisor—or elected officer—in Florida or anywhere else deny knowledge of the problem. "We certainly don't want to be in a position where the equal protection clause is thrown at us," said Mark Pritchett, executive vice president of the Collins Center for Public Policy at Florida State University, which aided the state task force.

Some states are pursuing more far-reaching reforms. Georgia Secretary of State Cathy Cox hopes the Florida debacle will jumpstart full-scale reform in her state. Cox is proposing touch-screen systems for every Georgia county by 2004. "She is advocating dramatic, sweeping change. We're hoping there will be someone in the audience who claps," said Chris Riggall, a spokesman for Cox. "I'm sure Florida wants to be first in line, and we want to be right behind them."

As of 2000, about 17 percent of Georgia's residents were still using unwieldy lever-operated voting machines, which have not been manufactured in forty years. Many others used punch-card ballots. Georgia recorded undervotes and overvotes at a rate of 3.5 percent on Election Day, *a rate higher than Florida's* and well above the national average of 2 percent.

Like California and a handful of other cutting-edge states,

Georgia hopes to leapfrog past the optical scan voting system that some states are embracing as a solution to the electoral dilemma. Cox believes she can bring touch-screen voting to Georgia at a cost as low as $10 per registered voter, or about $50 million in all. "If you're going to make investments, don't invest in the technology of yesteryear, which is what Opti-Scan is," Riggall said. "We saw counties in Georgia that had undervote rates of more than 10 percent that used Opti-Scan. What that's telling us is, it's no panacea."

In Michigan, a fiscally conservative Republican is nudging the state toward a uniform voting system. Secretary of State Candice Miller disputes the notion that punch cards primarily disenfranchise minority voters. The predominantly black city of Detroit uses optical scan technology, while more affluent and largely white suburbs vote on punch cards. "I don't consider this to be a partisan issue or a racial issue or anything else," Miller said. "It's just good government."

Miller falls into a growing camp of state election officials who believe that the U.S. Supreme Court ruling amounted to a mandate for uniform voting systems. The equipment used in Michigan runs the gamut. Of 5,376 precincts, 3,006 use optical scan machines, 1,443 use punch cards, 693 use lever voting machines, 137 use paper ballots, and 97 use electronic touch screens. "When you have these different types of voting systems, and you have an error rate that's much higher in some than in others, a very strong argument could be made for disenfranchisement," Miller said.

She has impaneled a bipartisan Blue Ribbon Committee on Uniform Voting Systems to evaluate all voting systems and select one for the entire state. She projects a cost of $30 million to $60 million. Too expensive for a fiscal conservative? Not at all. "I consider it an investment in the future of our democracy," Miller said.

In California, generally at the edge of every new wave, consensus is building to move toward touch-screen voting. Riverside County recently unveiled one of the nation's first countywide electronic voting systems, and the $14 million touch-screen system worked flawlessly on Election Day 2000. Los Angeles, which has used a punch-card voting system for thirty-five years, installed touch screens in a few precincts last year and reported a successful trial run.

Four other counties allowed voters to test a cutting-edge Internet voting system during the November 2000 election. The experiment transmitted about 1,000 sample votes from Contra Costa, Sacramento, San Diego, and Santa Clara Counties directly to the secretary of state's office over a secure Internet line. Few problems were reported. "We don't ever want to hear the words *dangling chad* or anything like that again," said Robert Pacheco, a California Republican assemblyman from Walnut.

Equipping all of Los Angeles with touch screens would cost an estimated $100 million. Outfitting the rest of the state might cost another $400 million, Pacheco estimates. As of November, 71 percent of California voters were using punch-card ballots, 25 percent were using optical scan systems, and 4 percent were voting electronically, according to the California secretary of state's office.

"I think the time has come for new techniques in voting, and I think the touch screen would be the best thing," Pacheco said. He sponsored a bill to provide counties with $300 million for new voting systems and $100,000 to study how to streamline electoral hardware and software.

Political pressure is also mounting to banish the punch card from Illinois, which generated truckloads of spoiled ballots on Election Day 2000. "Illinois is not going to be a punch-card state anymore," said Robert Saar, executive director of the Election

Commission in DuPage County, Illinois. "I think that has been pretty well established."

The county, near Chicago, approved a $530,000 contract in January to test an optical scan voting system in half its precincts. Some industry officials believe DuPage was the first county in the nation to formally move away from punch-card voting systems in response to the problems identified by the 2000 election.

County leaders cite the political climate in Illinois: to many voters, any county that sticks with punch-card ballots is short-changing the electorate. "You have to answer to the citizens why they're not having made available to them the best system that's available in the state of Illinois," Saar said.

Cook County (Chicago) seeks a simpler solution for its residents. The county uses a new $25 million punch-card system that can tell voters instantly if they have failed to cast a valid vote. But state law requires legislative approval to switch on that feature, and the Illinois legislature has yet to approve it for Cook County despite two years of lobbying. Yet, several other counties employ optical scan systems that have the second-chance feature built in.

In February a Cook County judge said that officials there could activate the second-chance voting feature in a February 27 primary—with or without the approval of the legislature. So Cook County's chief election official is in no hurry to abandon the punch card. He said that the county would be hard-pressed to cram the full content of a Cook County ballot onto an optical scan sheet. "The big cities—L.A., Chicago, Houston—still go with punch cards because of the size and complexity of the ballot," said David Orr, Cook County clerk. "The bigger the jurisdiction, the more you've got to get on there."

Orr said he is willing to wait for electronic voting. "The punch card will take us until we have the Internet or a touch-screen system that is less expensive," he said.

Even in Oregon, a state that conducts its elections entirely by mail, the punch-card ballots have caused problems. Oregonians vote at home, though residents of seven counties must do so on punch cards, which can be a difficult, confusing exercise. "We hold them up in the air and we stab at them with safety pins and paper clips," said DeFazio, the congressman from Oregon. In the presidential contest, Oregon needed nine days to determine a winner.

Optical scan ballot sheets list candidate names next to every bubble; punch cards do not. A voter who makes a wrong punch must contact the nearest election office for a new ballot. Nancy Padberg, a nurse from Zigzag, Oregon, made a mistake on her punch-card ballot in the November election. Unsure what to do, she taped the chad back in and punched out the correct one. "I would have to go to Oregon City to get a new ballot," said Padberg, who lives thirty-five miles away, up the side of Mount Hood.

Democratic leaders in the Oregon legislature filed a bill in late January that would require all counties to use the optical scan system. With an optical scan ballot sheet, "you can look at the ballot and review what you did when you finish voting," said John Kauffman, clerk of Clackamas County, which still uses punch cards. "With a punch card, you're just looking at a bunch of holes."

Abolishing the punch-card ballot and creating a uniform statewide voting system is the first order of business. But other work must also be considered, from a standardized ballot design to state-sponsored voter education programs to poll worker training. That last one is crucial. Well-trained poll workers are the front line of defense against ballot errors, and Pam Iorio of Hillsborough County said that higher pay is just a minor issue. More important, people must be found who are committed to the task.

"What you want is people who are there for civic reasons," she said. "The person who is there for eighty-five dollars is not the person you want running your elections. One of the things that has come out of this election is that we need to have a call to arms in the business community." Like United Way, which calls on employers to enlist volunteers for social service projects, she said, "We need our corporations to allow a day off for employees to work the polls—particularly if we move to more sophisticated systems. If you're going to modem the [electronic] results at the end of the night, you need people who are comfortable with that technology."

What may be even more important, though, is the creation of a uniform standard for measuring voter intent. Even the best equipment and the best personnel will occasionally yield a result so close or so controversial that a recount is required, and it is now clear that statewide standards for such recounts are necessary. That issue dogged Florida election officials and judges throughout the post-election ordeal. At the county level, recounts often halted briefly over disputes concerning the legitimacy of a particular ballot. At top judicial levels, even more difficult and weighty issues were debated.

The four to three majority of the Florida Supreme Court that ordered the last-minute statewide recount of undervotes went out of its way to avoid creating a new, comprehensive voter intent standard. The justices feared they would be overruled by the U.S. Supreme Court because they were making new election laws—the domain of the state legislature. But in their caution, they boxed themselves in, because they failed to develop a common standard that might have passed constitutional muster on the basis of equal protection. "It was a catch-22," said David Cole, a constitutional scholar at Georgetown University Law Center. "Having failed to set a standard on voter intent, the Florida court loses either way."

In late January, the Florida trial judge who presided over the statewide recount said that he didn't understand the U.S. Supreme Court's point in halting it. "I could see the Supreme Court saying the statutory scheme in Florida was insufficient [for the recount] because of the lack of time," said Leon County Circuit Judge Terry Lewis. "But their equal protection argument didn't resonate well with me. If they were concerned with our different standards in counting the votes, then what about the different machines used throughout the state? Why wasn't the whole election thrown out?"

The legal task that lies ahead might not be as onerous as first thought. Most states simply need to modify existing election laws. As an example of what to do, many point to Oklahoma, a model of conformity. It has one voting system—optical scanners—and a strict standard for interpreting voter intent. Voters must mark an oval space in the arrow that points to a candidate's name on the ballot. If they mark outside that space, or circle the candidate's name, their vote doesn't count. "I don't want election officials to be able to exercise judgment," said Lance Ward, secretary of Oklahoma's State Election Board. "I want the laws and rules to be so clear and the standards to be so obvious that they don't have any decisions to make—that it's black or it's white. People sue you when it's gray."

Doug Lewis, executive director of the Election Center, a nonprofit, nonpartisan group in Houston that monitors election administration, said that most states simply need to modify existing election laws, and he offered three suggestions.

First, he said, states must define what constitutes a valid vote. Roughly half the states have no such definition, relying on subjective interpretations of voter intent as found on the ballots. That was the case in Florida, where local canvassing boards had the authority to determine whether dimpled, pregnant, or hanging chads on punch-card ballots constituted legal votes.

States should also allow comprehensive manual recounts, if requested, of undervotes, overvotes, and all other disputed ballots in an election, he said. The Florida Supreme Court restricted its recount order to undervotes, another point for which it was criticized by the U.S. Supreme Court.

Last, he said, states should certify results only after all recounts required by law are complete. That was the opposite of the way Florida handled its certification.

It also seems clear that legislatures should consider stretching the period between Election Day and the certification deadline and should require county election supervisors to sift through rejected ballots with an eye toward redeeming as many as possible. In addition, states must remain vigilant, ever ready to recognize new problems that might be created by new technologies, ever ready to solve those problems rapidly.

Like some other experts around the country, Lewis does not blame outdated punch-card technology for Florida's election woes. "What created the problem was Florida's lack of a definition of what constitutes a vote," he said. "If Florida had that, then it would not have had the thirty-six days of chaos that made everybody wonder whether its voting system was broken. Mistake number two was the lack of recount procedures for Florida's six million votes. That was nuts. That was insane."

With good reason, Florida was one of the first states to confront the constitutional issues raised by the U.S. Supreme Court. Ten days after the high Court's ruling, the Florida Supreme Court agreed that it was not authorized to rewrite state election laws. "Upon reflection," Florida justices wrote in their final December 22 opinion on the election, "we conclude that the development of a specific, uniform standard necessary to ensure equal application and to secure the fundamental right to vote . . . should be left to the body we believe best equipped to study and address it, the Legislature."

In a fifteen-page concurring opinion that quoted John Greenleaf Whittier's poem "The Poor Voter on Election Day" ("My palace is the people's hall, the ballot-box my throne"), Justice Barbara Pariente outlined several problems with state election laws.

Among them: whether it is fair to conduct manual recounts only in selected counties rather than the whole state. "What should concern all of us is not whether the uncounted votes were for President-elect Bush or for Vice President Gore, but that thousands of voters in Florida did not have their votes included," Pariente said.

She also took Secretary of State Katherine Harris to task for declaring that state law does not allow for the counting of undervotes. "The implication" of her decision "would be that voters who cast votes that were incapable of being read by the machine would not be counted . . . even if upon a manual review the voter's intent was clearly ascertainable," Pariente wrote.

Though modern and uniform voting technology certainly would reduce the number of spoiled ballots and the magnitude of recounts, Florida election experts point out that some disputes are inevitable. Kurt Browning, the supervisor of elections in Pasco County, said the state must ensure that every possible vote is counted, even if the voter does not cast a perfect ballot. With the optical scan system, for example, Browning said that Florida should count ballots on which the voter circles a candidate's name instead of marking the oval space, even though the scanner can only register the vote if the space is marked properly on the ballot. "If there is a very intentional mark on that card, we will count it," said Browning, who sits on the governor's task force. "We always want to give credit where credit is due."

The state's election supervisors also want the legislature to rewrite Florida's recount laws, which were embraced by Gore but challenged by Bush. In addition to the automatic machine recount now required when the margin between candidates is less than 0.5 percent, they also want an automatic *manual* recount if the difference falls below 0.25 percent. That manual recount would be mandated throughout the contested area—all of Florida in a statewide race like governor or U.S. senator or president—rather than just selected precincts. During the presidential election, Gore requested manual recounts only in four counties that were friendly to him.

Pam Iorio, president of the election supervisors' association, said that automatic machine and hand recounts might alleviate the need for Florida's canvassing boards to judge recount requests in close races. It might also eliminate court challenges.

"It would have taken a lot of the litigation out of the mix in the presidential election," Iorio said. "Instead of targeting specific counties, there would have been a statewide [manual] recount automatically."

Outside monitors are also becoming involved. The American Civil Liberties Union of Florida received a $300,000 grant from the Steven and Michele Kirsch Foundation of San Jose, California, to help prevent voting irregularities in Florida. The Florida Equal Voting Rights Project, a collaboration between the ACLU, the Florida Justice Institute, and Florida Legal Services, will be staffed by three attorneys and a coordinator. The project plans to lobby for translators and other forms of language assistance at the polls, speedier restoration of voting rights for felons, and easier access to registration rolls and voting booths for all citizens, particularly minorities.

And so, as always, a crisis was required before change was effected. But now, already, change is arriving.

During local elections in early 2001, Broward County tried some new techniques, all the result of the tarnished presidential election. Special workers roamed from precinct to precinct, inspecting machines throughout the day. Additional staffers at election headquarters responded to phoned-in questions from poll workers. Large signs titled "ATTENTION VOTERS" were posted at voter sign-in desks to remind voters that they could ask for machine operating demonstrations and replacement ballots if they made mistakes. And poll workers asked voters to check their punch cards for clean removals of chads. "It's probably a bit of overkill," said Peggy Breeschoten, a veteran poll worker, "but in view of what happened, it needs to be done."

No argument there. It was only a beginning, but at least it *was* a beginning. If nothing else, Florida's presidential election of 2000 demonstrated the need for a comprehensive overhaul of the machinery of our electoral system—and well beyond the borders of this single state.

"We've all looked at our voting systems and asked, 'Could this happen in our state?' " said Stewart Greenleaf, a state senator in Pennsylvania. "And, you know, it could. If we can spend money building buildings and roads, we can certainly spend money updating the very foundation of our democracy."

Appendix:
BDO Seidman Report

Mr. Martin Baron
The Miami Herald, Knight Ridder and USA Today
1 Herald Plaza
Miami, Florida 33132

Re: Tabulation of "Under Votes" for the State of Florida

We have performed the procedures enumerated below, which were agreed to by the Miami Herald, Knight Ridder and USA Today, solely to assist you in observing and tabulating certain information relating to ballots classified by each County Canvassing Board in the State of Florida as "under votes" (votes not tabulated by the machine or manual count as certified to the State of Florida) in connection with the presidential election on November 7, 2000. This agreed-upon procedures engagement was performed in accordance with standards established by the American Institute of Certified Public Accountants. The sufficiency of these procedures is solely the responsibility of the specified users of the report. Consequently, we make no representation regarding the sufficiency of the procedures described below either for the purpose for which this report has been requested or for any other purpose.

Our procedures and findings are as follows:

1. We met with representatives of The Miami Herald and Knight Ridder to discuss the nature and timing of the engagement.

2. We reviewed sample ballots with The Miami Herald and Knight Ridder personnel in order to have an understanding of the criteria to be documented.

3. A BDO representative, accompanied by a Miami Herald, Knight Ridder or USA Today representative observed the ballots displayed to us by each County Canvassing Board and noted their various characteristics in accordance with the specifications you provided us in Exhibits 1 and 2 of the engagement letter. We also did not make any determinations as to any other characteristics that may be possible in under vote ballots. We also did not make any determinations to the under vote population nor did we interpret voters intent. We did not make a determination as to which ballots were included in the tabulated machine or manual count as certified by the State of Florida; whether or not such ballots have been segregated by the supervisor of elections. In the event there were differences of observation between BDO and the Miami Herald, Knight Ridder or USA Today representative over the characteristics of a ballot, the observation of the BDO representative was recorded.

4. We tabulated the results of the ballot information gathered in procedure 3 of this letter based on the format of Exhibits 1 and 2 of the engagement letter. The tabulation was done by precinct and then summarized by county. The results of this tabulation are presented as Exhibits A and B to this report and further supported by county summaries as Exhibit A-1 for punch card counties and Exhibit B-1 for optical scan and manually counted counties. It should also be noted that 3,053 votes were not tabulated since they had markings for more than one presidential candidate and therefore, were considered by the Miami Herald, Knight Ridder and USA Today to be an over vote as presented (see Exhibit C).

We were not engaged to, and did not, perform an examination, the objective of which would be the expression of an opinion on the tabulated results of the under vote ballots. Accordingly, we do not express such an opinion. Had we performed additional procedures, other matters might have come to our attention that would have been reported to you.

This report is intended solely for the information and use of The Miami Herald, Knight Ridder and USA Today and is not intended to and should not be used by anyone other than The Miami Herald, Knight Ridder and USA Today, except that other media organizations may report on the results of our procedures, relying on articles published by the Miami Herald or USA Today. To the extent that such other media organizations request to see our report, such report would be considered as if it were a matter of public record and its distribution would not be limited. In that regard, if such other media request to see our report, the Miami Herald, Knight Ridder and USA Today may make it available for inspection, but will not provide copies without our prior express approval.

BDO Seidman, LLP
Certified Public Accountants
Miami, Florida
March 30, 2001

How To Read These Charts

These are statewide and county-by-county summaries of the *Miami Herald*'s survey of undervotes in all sixty-seven Florida counties. They are listed here in alphabetical order.

The charts reflect ballots that were not counted in the presidential race, either because they were unmarked or because the marks on them could not be read by machines that count votes. Over-votes—ballots that were not counted because voters marked more than one presidential candidate—are not recorded here.

The observation of 64,248 ballots was conducted by personnel from the public accounting firm BDO Seidman, LLP. The firm made no effort to determine voters' intent or whether a mark on a ballot was a legally valid vote. Instead, its accountants noted what kind of mark was present and its location, then totaled the marks of various kinds and reported them to the *Herald*.

In addition, BDO Seidman, LLP did not make a determination as to which ballots were included in the tabulated machine or manual counts certified by the State of Florida (whether or not such ballots were segregated by the supervisors of election).

There are two formats for these charts—one for the twenty-five counties that use punch-card ballots and machines, one for the forty-two counties that optically scan or manually count ballots. (Union County hand-counts its ballots but uses a form nearly identical to that used by optical scan counties; Martin County uses a mechanical voting machine that leaves no paper records, but absentee voters there use punch cards—and that is what is reflected in the Martin County chart.)

In both ballot formats, presidential candidates are listed by name. In punch-card counties, they are also listed by the ballot number assigned to them by each county. The "No Mark" field reflects ballots on which no marks of any kind were found for any presidential candidate—in other words, an unequivocal "No Vote," or undervote.

The "Other Races" section shows marks in races other than the presidential race. This is useful in assessing the consistency with which voters for a particular candidate mismarked other races on their ballots. In some cases, a consistently mismarked punch-card ballot could suggest faulty machinery; in others, it could indicate a failure by the voter to insert the punch-card ballot into the machine properly. In both punch-card and optical scan counties, a consistently mismarked ballot could indicate careless voting.

Punch-Card Counties

Voters in punch-card counties use a stylus or other sharp object to punch out numbered tabs, or chads, from a computer card. Punch cards generally have more numbered chads than are needed.

Election officials in each county match specific chads to specific candidates, and voters can erroneously punch leftover, unassigned chads. Blank fields are listed on these charts if voters in the indicated county punched chads that were not assigned to any candidate.

These are the definitions employed by the *Herald*'s reviewers to gauge each punch-card ballot:

- Dimple—A visible impression, best seen from the back of the ballot, that has pushed the chad up but has not detached it from the ballot. A dimpled chad might have been completely attached or partially detached from the ballot, but not at the corners.

- Pinprick—A mark in which the ballot has been punched through with a stylus or other device and light can be seen through the hole, but the chad has not been dislodged.
- Detached (one, two, or three corners)—The chad has been partially detached from the ballot by the number of corners indicated.
- Punched Cleanly—An unambiguous vote. Counting machines might have missed these ballots, or hanging chads might have fallen off after Election Day, or these ballots might have been challenged by partisan observers. In some cases, unassigned chads were also found to be punched cleanly, but these are lost votes and—though some patterns might be discerned—no definitive conclusions can be reached as to voter intent.

Optical Scan Counties

Voters in optical scan counties darken an oval or connect two parts of an arrow, generally with a special pen or pencil provided by election officials. Some voters, however, used other instruments, or they underlined, circled, or otherwise mismarked the ballot to indicate the candidate of their choice.

In a few counties, optical scan ballots contain more voting fields than are needed. Leftover, unassigned fields can be marked erroneously. Blank fields are listed on these charts if voters in the indicated county marked fields that were not assigned to any candidate.

Otherwise, the categories are self-explanatory, revealing the manner in which each voter mismarked the ballot.

ALACHUA:	optical scan, counted in each precinct
BAKER:	optical scan, counted in each precinct
BAY:	optical scan, counted in each precinct
BRADFORD:	optical scan, counted in central location
BREVARD:	optical scan, counted in each precinct
BROWARD:	punch card
CALHOUN:	optical scan, counted in each precinct
CHARLOTTE:	optical scan, counted in central location
CITRUS:	optical scan, counted in each precinct
CLAY:	optical scan, counted in each precinct
COLLIER:	punch card
COLUMBIA:	optical scan, counted in each precinct
DESOTO:	punch card
DIXIE:	punch card
DUVAL:	punch card
ESCAMBIA:	optical scan, counted in each precinct
FLAGLER:	optical scan, counted in each precinct
FRANKLIN:	optical scan, counted in central location
GADSDEN:	optical scan, counted in central location
GILCHRIST:	punch card
GLADES:	punch card

GULF:	optical scan, counted in central location
HAMILTON:	optical scan, counted in central location
HARDEE:	punch card
HENDRY:	optical scan, counted in central location
HERNANDO:	optical scan, counted in each precinct
HIGHLANDS:	punch card
HILLSBOROUGH:	punch card
HOLMES:	optical scan, counted in each precinct
INDIAN RIVER:	punch card
JACKSON:	optical scan, counted in central location
JEFFERSON:	punch card
LAFAYETTE:	optical scan, counted in central location
LAKE:	optical scan, counted in central location
LEE:	punch card
LEON:	optical scan, counted in each precinct
LEVY:	optical scan, counted in central location
LIBERTY:	optical scan, counted in central location
MADISON:	punch card
MANATEE:	optical scan, counted in each precinct
MARION:	punch card
MARTIN:	mechanical
MIAMI-DADE:	punch card
MONROE:	optical scan, counted in each precinct

NASSAU:	punch card
OKALOOSA:	optical scan, counted in each precinct
OKEECHOBEE:	optical scan, counted in central location
ORANGE:	optical scan, counted in each precinct
OSCEOLA:	punch card
PALM BEACH:	punch card
PASCO:	punch card
PINELLAS:	punch card
POLK:	optical scan, counted in each precinct
PUTNAM:	optical scan, counted in each precinct
SANTA ROSA:	optical scan, counted in each precinct
SARASOTA:	punch card
SEMINOLE:	optical scan, counted in each precinct
ST. JOHNS:	optical scan, counted in each precinct
ST. LUCIE:	optical scan, counted in each precinct
SUMTER:	punch card
SUWANEE:	optical scan, counted in central location
TAYLOR:	optical scan, counted in central location
UNION:	paper
VOLUSIA:	optical scan, counted in each precinct
WAKULLA:	punch card
WALTON:	optical scan, counted in each precinct
WASHINGTON:	optical scan, counted in each precinct

State of Florida Reporting of Undervotes for Punch Card Counties

Totals For All Counties And Precincts

CANDIDATE NAME**	PRESIDENTIAL RACE								OTHER RACES*		
	DIMPLE	PINPRICK	DETACHED 1 CORNER	DETACHED 2 CORNER	DETACHED 3 CORNER	PUNCHED CLEANLY	NO MARK	TOTAL BALLOTS	DIMPLED	HANGING CHADS	PUNCHED CLEANLY
Blank	322	115	66	66	60	3275	0	3854	706	666	3394
BROWNE/OLIVIER	140	26	1	2	0	6	0	175	114	26	99
BUCHANAN/FOSTER	190	30	0	2	1	6	0	229	121	33	173
BUSH/CHENEY	10004	750	132	304	512	456	0	12158	5305	3505	11300
GORE/LIEBERMAN	10745	807	79	255	297	970	0	13153	5962	3852	12118
HAGELIN/GOLDHABER	106	71	1	0	1	12	0	191	115	38	106
HARRIS/TROWE	69	51	1	1	0	2	0	123	93	34	50
McREYNOLDS/HOLLIS	29	7	1	0	0	2	0	39	31	3	17
MOOREHEAD/LARIVA	59	7	0	0	0	2	0	68	61	6	28
NADER/LADUKE	298	36	4	6	7	21	0	372	214	99	262
Nomark	0	0	0	0	0	0	23856	23856	2484	2519	15479
PHILLIPS/FRAZIER	100	2	0	0	0	30	0	132	80	9	61
Grand Totals:	22062	1902	234	635	878	4782	23856	54350	15286	10790	43087

* This tabulation is a compilation of markings with respect to other races on those ballots on which there were either markings for one presidential candidate or no markings for any presidential candidate.

** Blank consists of markings on a line where there was no presidential candidate.

Note (1): The number of ballots for Bush and Gore that had a dimple in the presidential race and a dimple in the other races were as follows:
Bush 4593
Gore 5240

Note (2): The number of ballots not included above that had a written candidate name in the presidential race were as follows:
Bush 37
Gore 46
Other 1

BDO Seidman, LLP

231

EXHIBIT B: *THE MIAMI HERALD*

State of Florida Reporting of Undervotes for Optical Scan and Manually Counted Counties

Totals For All Counties and Precincts

CANDIDATE NAME***	PRESIDENTIAL RACE								OTHERRACES*
	UNDERLINED CANDIDATE	CIRCLED OR MARKED CANDIDATE OR PARTY	CIRCLED OR PARTIALLY FILLED BUBBLE OR ARROW	MARKED X OR CHECKED	ERROR WITH WRITING INSTRUMENT	OTHER**	NO MARK	TOTAL BALLOTS	ERRORS IN OTHER RACES
Blank	0	0	0	1	0	7	0	8	3
BROWNE/OLIVIER	1	5	3	1	2	0	0	12	7
BUCHANAN/FOSTER	0	4	0	1	3	2	0	10	7
BUSH/CHENEY	32	198	105	274	216	35	0	860	631
GORE/LIEBERMAN	40	369	161	367	187	55	0	1179	902
HAGELIN/GOLDHABER	0	3	0	5	2	0	0	10	4
HARRIS/TROWE	0	1	0	0	0	0	0	1	1
MOOREHEAD/LARIVA	0	0	1	0	0	0	0	1	0
NADER/LADUKE	0	17	1	12	7	4	0	41	32
Nomark	0	0	0	0	0	0	4419	4419	384
Otherwrite-Ins	0	3	0	1	0	211	0	215	22
PHILLIPS/FRAZIER	0	0	0	3	0	2	0	5	1
GrandTotals:	73	600	271	665	417	316	4419	6761	1994

* This tabulation is a compilation of markings considered errors with respect to other races on ballots that had either markings for a presidential candidate or no markings for any presidential candidate.

** Other is comprised primarily of write-ins on the presidential candidate box.

*** Blank consists of markings on a line where there was no presidential candidate.

COUNTY-BY-COUNTY CHARTS

EXHIBIT B-1: THE MIAMI HERALD

State of Florida Precinct Reporting of Undervotes for Optical Scan and Manually Counted Counties

COUNTY : *Alachua County*

PRECINCT : Totals For All Precincts

PRESIDENTIAL RACE | **OTHER RACES***

CANDIDATE NAME	UNDERLINED CANDIDATE	CIRCLED OR MARKED CANDIDATE OR PARTY	CIRCLED OR PARTIALLY FILLED BUBBLE OR ARROW	MARKED X OR CHECKED	ERROR WITH WRITING INSTRUMENT	OTHER**	NO MARK	TOTAL BALLOTS	ERRORS IN OTHER RACES
BROWNE/OLIVIER	0	0	0	1	0	0	0	1	1
BUSH/CHENEY	0	1	2	8	0	0	0	11	11
GORE/LIEBERMAN	0	5	2	14	0	0	0	21	16
HAGELIN/GOLDHABER	0	0	0	1	0	0	0	1	1
NADER/LADUKE	0	0	0	2	0	0	0	2	2
Nomark	0	0	0	0	0	0	173	173	10
Otherwrite-ins	0	0	0	0	0	6	0	6	0
Grand Totals:	0	6	4	26	0	6	173	215	41

* This tabulation is a compilation of markings considered errors with respect to other races on ballots that had either markings for a presidential candidate or no markings for any presidential candidate.

** Other is comprised primarily of write-ins on the presidential candidate box.

BDO Seidman, LLP

EXHIBIT B-1: THE MIAMI HERALD

State of Florida Precinct Reporting of Undervotes for Optical Scan and Manually Counted Counties

COUNTY: **Baker County**

PRECINCT: **Totals For All Precincts**

CANDIDATE NAME	PRESIDENTIAL RACE								OTHER RACES*
	UNDERLINED CANDIDATE	CIRCLED OR MARKED CANDIDATE OR PARTY	CIRCLED OR PARTIALLY FILLED BUBBLE OR ARROW	MARKED X OR CHECKED	ERROR WITH WRITING INSTRUMENT	OTHER**	NO MARK	TOTAL BALLOTS	ERRORS IN OTHER RACES
BUSH/CHENEY	3	0	0	9	10	2	0	24	14
GORE/LIEBERMAN	4	0	1	2	12	2	0	21	15
No mark	0	0	0	0	0	0	46	46	3
Grand Totals:	7	0	1	11	22	4	46	91	32

* This tabulation is a compilation of markings considered errors with respect to other races on ballots that had either markings for a presidential candidate or no markings for any presidential candidate.

** Other is comprised primarily of write-ins on the presidential candidate box.

BDO Seidman, LLP

235

EXHIBIT B-1: THE MIAMI HERALD

State of Florida Precinct Reporting of Undervotes for Optical Scan and Manually Counted Counties

COUNTY: *BayCounty*

PRECINCT: **Totals For All Precincts**

CANDIDATE NAME	PRESIDENTIAL RACE								OTHER RACES*
	UNDERLINED CANDIDATE	CIRCLED OR MARKED CANDIDATE OR PARTY	CIRCLED OR PARTIALLY FILLED BUBBLE OR ARROW	MARKED X OR CHECKED	ERROR WITH WRITING INSTRUMENT	OTHER**	NO MARK	TOTAL BALLOTS	ERRORS IN OTHER RACES
Nomark	0	0	0	0	0	0	367	367	1
BUSH/CHENEY	13	2	0	12	0	9	0	36	15
GORE/LIEBERMAN	15	0	0	18	0	3	0	36	22
BROWNE/OLIVIER	1	0	0	0	0	0	0	1	0
NADER/LADUKE	0	0	0	0	0	1	0	1	0
Grand Totals:	29	2	0	30	0	13	367	441	38

* This tabulation is a compilation of markings considered errors with respect to other races on ballots that had either markings for a presidential candidate or no markings for any presidential candidate.

** Other is comprised primarily of write-ins on the presidential candidate box.

EXHIBIT B-1: *THE MIAMI HERALD*

State of Florida Precinct Reporting of Undervotes for Optical Scan and Manually Counted Counties

COUNTY : **Bradford County**

PRECINCT : **Totals For All Precincts**

CANDIDATE NAME	PRESIDENTIAL RACE							OTHERRACES*
	UNDERLINED CANDIDATE	CIRCLE OR MARKED CANDIDATE OR PARTY	CIRCLED OR PARTIALLY FILLED BUBBLE OR ARROW	MARKED X OR CHECKED	ERROR WITH WRITING INSTRUMENT	OTHER**	NO MARK	TOTAL BALLOTS	ERRORS IN OTHER RACES
BROWNE/OLIVIER	0	0	0	0	1	0	0	1	0
BUSH/CHENEY	0	5	0	3	0	0	0	8	4
GORE/LIEBERMAN	0	5	0	3	0	0	0	8	4
NADER/LADUKE	0	0	0	1	0	0	0	1	1
Nomark	0	0	0	0	0	0	18	18	4
Grand Totals:	0	10	0	7	1	0	18	36	13

* This tabulation is a compilation of markings considered errors with respect to other races on ballots that had either markings for a presidential candidate or no markings for any presidential candidate.

** Other is comprised primarily of write-ins on the presidential candidate box.

BDO Seidman, LLP

EXHIBIT B-1: THE MIAMI HERALD

State of Florida Precinct Reporting of Undervotes for Optical Scan and Manually Counted Counties

COUNTY: Brevard County

PRECINCT: Totals For All Precincts

PRESIDENTIAL RACE — OTHER RACES*

CANDIDATE NAME	UNDERLINED CANDIDATE	CIRCLED OR MARKED CANDIDATE OR PARTY	CIRCLED OR PARTIALLY FILLED BUBBLE OR ARROW	MARKED X OR CHECKED	ERROR WITH WRITING INSTRUMENT	OTHER**	NO MARK	TOTAL BALLOTS	ERRORS IN OTHER RACES
BUSH/CHENEY	0	0	4	5	0	0	0	9	5
GORE/LIEBERMAN	0	2	6	15	0	0	0	23	13
HAGELIN/GOLDHABER	0	0	0	1	0	0	0	1	1
NADER/LADUKE	0	0	0	2	0	0	0	2	1
Nomark	0	0	0	0	0	0	217	217	2
Otherwrite-ins	0	0	0	0	0	16	0	16	2
Grand Totals:	0	2	10	23	0	16	217	268	24

* This tabulation is a compilation of markings considered errors with respect to other races on ballots that had either markings for a presidential candidate or no markings for any presidential candidate.

** Other is comprised primarily of write-ins on the presidential candidate box.

BDO Seidman, LLP

EXHIBIT A-1: THE MIAMI HERALD

State of Florida Precinct Reporting of Undervotes for Punch Card Counties

COUNTY: BrowardCounty

PRECINCT: Totals For All Precincts

CANDIDATE NAME**	PRESIDENTIAL RACE								OTHER RACES*		
	DIMPLE	PINPRICK	DETACHED 1 CORNER	DETACHED 2 CORNER	DETACHED 3 CORNER	PUNCHED CLEANLY	NO MARK	TOTAL BALLOTS	DIMPLED	HANGING CHADS	PUNCHED CLEANLY
Blank	22	6	4	4	6	291	0	333	106	98	315
BROWNE/OLIVIER	15	4	0	0	0	4	0	23	11	2	15
BUCHANAN/FOSTER	16	8	0	0	0	1	0	25	20	0	9
BUSH/CHENEY	594	34	17	40	27	252	0	964	423	272	906
GORE/LIEBERMAN	1376	79	19	106	73	786	0	2439	962	565	2230
HAGELIN/GOLDHABER	11	9	0	0	0	0	0	20	17	0	10
HARRIS/TROWE	8	5	0	0	0	0	0	13	10	0	3
McREYNOLDS/HOLLIS	4	1	0	0	0	1	0	6	5	0	3
MOOREHEAD/LARIVA	1	1	0	0	0	0	0	2	1	0	0
NADER/LADUKE	12	2	0	0	0	4	0	18	10	8	16
Nomark	0	0	0	0	0	0	3185	3185	367	225	1908
PHILLIPS/FRAZIER	1	1	0	0	0	1	0	3	2	0	1
GrandTotals:	2060	150	40	150	106	1340	3185	7031	1934	1170	5416

* This tabulation is a compilation of markings with respect to other races on those ballots on which there were either markings for one presidential candidate or no markings for any presidential candidate.

** Blank consists of markings on a line where there was no presidential candidate.

Note: The number of ballots for Bush and Gore that had a dimple in the presidential race and a dimple in the other races were as follows:

Bush 336

Gore 744

BDO Seidman, LLP

239

State of Florida Precinct Reporting of Undervotes for Optical Scan and Manually Counted Counties

COUNTY : *Calhoun County*

PRECINCT : **Totals For All Precincts**

PRESIDENTIAL RACE

CANDIDATE NAME	UNDERLINED CANDIDATE	CIRCLED OR MARKED CANDIDATE OR PARTY	CIRCLED OR PARTIALLY FILLED BUBBLE OR ARROW	MARKED X OR CHECKED	ERROR WITH WRITING INSTRUMENT	OTHER**	NO MARK	TOTAL BALLOTS	ERRORS IN OTHER RACES
Nomark	0	0	0	0	0	0	77	77	1
Grand Totals:	0	0	0	0	0	0	77	77	1

OTHERRACES*

* This tabulation is a compilation of markings considered errors with respect to other races on ballots that had either markings for a presidential candidate or no markings for any presidential candidate.

** Other is comprised primarily of write-ins on the presidential candidate box.

EXHIBIT B-1: THE MIAMI HERALD

State of Florida Precinct Reporting of Undervotes for Optical Scan and Manually Counted Counties

COUNTY: Charlotte County

PRECINCT: Totals For All Precincts

| CANDIDATE NAME | PRESIDENTIAL RACE | | | | | | | | OTHER RACES* |
	UNDERLINED CANDIDATE	CIRCLED OR MARKED CANDIDATE OR PARTY	CIRCLED OR PARTIALLY FILLED BUBBLE OR ARROW	MARKED X OR CHECKED	ERROR WITH WRITING INSTRUMENT	OTHER**	NO MARK	TOTAL BALLOTS	ERRORS IN OTHER RACES
BUSH/CHENEY	0	8	0	0	22	4	0	34	22
GORE/LIEBERMAN	0	7	4	3	11	1	0	26	15
NADER/LADUKE	0	0	0	0	1	0	0	1	1
Nomark	0	0	0	0	0	0	93	93	2
Otherwrite-ins	0	0	0	0	0	7	0	7	0
Grand Totals:	0	15	4	3	34	12	93	161	40

* This tabulation is a compilation of markings considered errors with respect to other races on ballots that had either markings for a presidential candidate or no markings for any presidential candidate.

** Other is comprised primarily of write-ins on the presidential candidate box.

BDO Seidman, LLP

EXHIBIT B-1: *THE MIAMI HERALD*

State of Florida Precinct Reporting of Undervotes for Optical Scan and Manually Counted Counties

COUNTY: *Citrus County*

PRECINCT: Totals For All Precincts

| CANDIDATE NAME | PRESIDENTIAL RACE | | | | | | | | OTHERRACES* |
	UNDERLINED CANDIDATE	CIRCLED OR MARKED CANDIDATE OR PARTY	CIRCLED OR PARTIALLY FILLED BUBBLE OR ARROW	MARKED X OR CHECKED	ERROR WITH WRITING INSTRUMENT	OTHER**	NO MARK	TOTAL BALLOTS	ERRORS IN OTHER RACES
BUSH/CHENEY	0	6	0	6	16	0	0	28	16
GORE/LIEBERMAN	0	10	3	7	12	0	0	32	18
NADER/LADUKE	0	2	0	1	1	1	0	5	4
Nomark	0	0	0	0	0	0	115	115	0
Otherwrite-ins	0	0	0	0	0	6	0	6	0
Grand Totals:	0	18	3	14	29	7	115	186	38

* This tabulation is a compilation of markings considered errors with respect to other races on ballots that had either markings for a presidential candidate or no markings for any presidential candidate.

** Other is comprised primarily of write-ins on the presidential candidate box.

BDO Seidman, LLP

EXHIBIT B-1: THE MIAMI HERALD

State of Florida Precinct Reporting of Undervotes for Optical Scan and Manually Counted Counties

COUNTY: Clay County

PRECINCT: Totals For All Precincts

PRESIDENTIAL RACE / **OTHER RACES***

CANDIDATE NAME	UNDERLINED CANDIDATE	CIRCLED OR MARKED CANDIDATE OR PARTY	CIRCLED OR PARTALLY FILLED BUBBLE OR ARROW	MARKED X OR CHECKED	ERROR WITH WRITING INSTRUMENT	OTHER**	NO MARK	TOTAL BALLOTS	ERRORS IN OTHER RACES
BROWNE/OLIVIER	0	0	0	0	1	0	0	1	1
BUCHANAN/FOSTER	0	1	0	0	0	0	0	1	0
BUSH/CHENEY	0	4	4	3	63	0	0	74	70
GORE/LIEBERMAN	0	12	3	1	19	1	0	37	33
NADER/LADUKE	0	0	0	0	1	0	0	1	1
Nomark	0	0	0	0	0	0	63	63	1
Otherwrite-ins	0	1	1	0	0	1	0	2	0
Grand Totals:	0	20	6	4	84	2	63	179	106

* This tabulation is a compilation of markings considered errors with respect to other races on ballots that had either markings for a presidential candidate or no markings for any presidential candidate.

** Other is comprised primarily of write-ins on the presidential candidate box.

BDO Seidman, LLP

EXHIBIT A-1: THE MIAMI HERALD

State of Florida Precinct Reporting of Undervotes for Punch Card Counties

COUNTY: CollierCounty

PRECINCT: Totals For All Precincts

CANDIDATE NAME**	PRESIDENTIAL RACE								OTHER RACES*		
	DIMPLE	PINPRICK	DETACHED 1 CORNER	DETACHED 2 CORNER	DETACHED 3 CORNER	PUNCHED CLEANLY	NO MARK	TOTAL BALLOTS	DIMPLED	HANGING CHADS	PUNCHED CLEANLY
Blank	1	1	0	4	2	83	0	91	7	15	84
BROWNE/OLIVIER	6	1	0	0	0	0	0	7	3	0	6
BUCHANAN/FOSTER	1	2	0	0	0	0	0	3	2	0	1
BUSH/CHENEY	801	20	2	12	31	8	0	874	393	233	839
GORE/LIEBERMAN	563	10	1	4	10	0	0	588	264	135	563
HAGELIN/GOLDHABER	5	4	0	0	0	0	0	9	8	1	7
HARRIS/TROWE	1	2	0	0	0	0	0	3	3	0	0
NADER/LADUKE	8	1	0	0	0	1	0	10	1	0	10
Nomark	0	0	0	0	0	0	455	455	39	71	274
GrandTotals:	1386	41	3	20	43	92	455	2040	720	455	1784

* This tabulation is a compilation of markings with respect to other races on those ballots on which there were either markings for one presidential candidate or no markings for any presidential candidate.

** Blank consists of markings on a line where there was no presidential candidate.

Note: The number of ballots for Bush and Gore that had a dimple in the presidential race and a dimple in the other races were as follows:
Bush 371
Gore 255

BDO Seidman, LLP

244

EXHIBIT B-1: THE MIAMI HERALD

State of Florida Precinct Reporting of Undervotes for Optical Scan and Manually Counted Counties

COUNTY: ColumbiaCounty

PRECINCT: Totals For All Precincts

CANDIDATE NAME	PRESIDENTIAL RACE								OTHERRACES*
	UNDERLINED CANDIDATE	CIRCLED OR MARKED CANDIDATE OR PARTY	CIRCLED OR PARTIALLY FILLED BUBBLE OR ARROW	MARKED X OR CHECKED	ERROR WITH WRITING INSTRUMENT	OTHER**	NO MARK	TOTAL BALLOTS	ERRORS IN OTHER RACES
BUSH/CHENEY	0	4	2	2	0	0	0	8	8
GORE/LIEBERMAN	0	7	1	0	0	0	0	8	7
HAGELIN/GOLDHABER	0	0	0	1	0	0	0	1	1
Nomark	0	0	0	0	0	0	39	39	7
Otherwrite-ins	0	0	0	0	0	1	0	1	0
Grand Totals:	0	11	3	3	0	-	39	57	23

* This tabulation is a compilation of markings considered errors with respect to other races on ballots that had either markings for a presidential candidate or no markings for any presidential candidate.

** Other is comprised primarily of write-ins on the presidential candidate box.

BDO Seidman, LLP

245

EXHIBIT A-1: THE MIAMI HERALD

State of Florida Precinct Reporting of Undervotes for Punch Card Counties

COUNTY : **DesotoCounty**

PRECINCT : **Totals For All Precincts**

CANDIDATE NAME	PRESIDENTIAL RACE								OTHERRACES*		
	DIMPLE	PINPRICK	DETACHED 1 CORNER	DETACHED 2 CORNER	DETACHED 3 CORNER	PUNCHED CLEANLY	NO MARK	TOTAL BALLOTS	DIMPLED	HANGING CHADS	PUNCHED CLEANLY
BUSH/CHENEY	12	0	0	0	0	0	0	12	0	0	0
GORE/LIEBERMAN	12	0	0	0	0	0	0	12	0	1	0
NADER/LADUKE	1	0	0	0	0	0	0	1	0	0	0
Nomark	0	0	0	0	0	0	55	55	0	0	0
Grand Totals:	25	0	0	0	0	0	55	80	0	1	0

* This tabulation is a compilation of markings with respect to other races on those ballots on which there were either markings for one presidential candidate or no markings for any presidential candidate.

Note (1): The number of ballots for Bush and Gore that had a dimple in the presidential race and a dimple in the other races were as follows:
Bush 0
Gore 0

Note (2): The number of ballots not included above that had a written candidate name in the presidential race were as follows:
Bush 2
Gore 10
Other 0

BDO Seidman, LLP

246

EXHIBIT A-1: THE MIAMI HERALD

State of Florida Precinct Reporting of Undervotes for Punch Card Counties

COUNTY: DixieCounty

PRECINCT: Totals For All Precincts

CANDIDATE NAME	PRESIDENTIAL RACE								OTHER RACES*		
	DIMPLE	PINPRICK	DETACHED 1 CORNER	DETACHED 2 CORNER	DETACHED 3 CORNER	PUNCHED CLEANLY	NO MARK	TOTAL BALLOTS	DIMPLED	HANGING CHADS	PUNCHED CLEANLY
Nomark	0	0	0	0	0	0	14	14	0	0	10
Grand Totals:	0	0	0	0	0	0	14	14	0	0	10

* This tabulation is a compilation of markings with respect to other races on those ballots on which there were either markings for one presidential candidate or no markings for any presidential candidate.

Note (1): The number of ballots for Bush and Gore that had a dimple in the presidential race and a dimple in the other races were as follows:

Bush 0

Gore 0

Note (2): The number of ballots not included above that had a written candidate name in the presidential race were as follows:

Bush 3

Gore 4

Other 0

BDO Seidman, LLP

247

EXHIBIT B-1: *THE MIAMI HERALD*
State of Florida Precinct Reporting of Undervotes for Punch Card Counties

COUNTY: DuvalCounty

PRECINCT: Totals For All Precincts

CANDIDATE NAME**	PRESIDENTIAL RACE								OTHERRACES*		
	DIMPLE	PINPRICK	DETACHED 1 CORNER	DETACHED 2 CORNER	DETACHED 3 CORNER	PUNCHED CLEANLY	NO MARK	TOTAL BALLOTS	DIMPLED	HANGING CHADS	PUNCHED CLEANLY
Blank	53	4	0	16	16	114	0	203	66	48	165
BROWNE/OLIVIER	6	4	0	1	0	0	0	11	5	2	6
BUCHANAN/FOSTER	4	0	0	2	0	2	0	8	4	2	7
BUSH/CHENEY	1442	93	20	124	248	77	0	2004	906	429	1886
GORE/LIEBERMAN	840	50	3	60	77	44	0	1074	583	287	995
HAGELIN/GOLDHABER	2	0	0	0	1	1	0	4	2	2	4
MOOREHEAD/LARIVA	2	0	0	0	0	1	0	3	1	2	2
NADER/LADUKE	12	1	0	4	1	5	0	23	12	9	22
Nomark	0	0	0	0	0	0	1548	1548	299	252	925
PHILLIPS/FRAZIER	0	0	0	0	0	2	0	2	0	0	2
Grand Totals:	2361	152	23	207	343	246	1548	4880	1878	1033	4014

* This tabulation is a compilation of markings with respect to other races on those ballots on which there were either markings for one presidential candidate or no markings for any presidential candidate.

** Blank consists of markings on a line where there was no presidential candidate.

Note (1): The number of ballots for Bush and Gore that had a dimple in the presidential race and a dimple in the other races were as follows:

Bush 715

Gore 494

Note (2): The number of ballots not included above that had a written candidate name in the presidential race were as follows:

Bush 10

Gore 6

Other 0

BDO Seidman, LLP

248

EXHIBIT B-1: THE MIAMI HERALD

State of Florida Precinct Reporting of Undervotes for Optical Scan and Manually Counted Counties

COUNTY: Escambia County

PRECINCT: Totals For All Precincts

CANDIDATE NAME	PRESIDENTIAL RACE								OTHER RACES*
	UNDERLINED CANDIDATE	CIRCLED OR MARKED CANDIDATE OR PARTY	CIRCLED OR PARTIALLY FILLED BUBBLE OR ARROW	MARKED X OR CHECKED	ERROR WITH WRITING INSTRUMENT	OTHER**	NO MARK	TOTAL BALLOTS	ERRORS IN OTHER RACES
BROWNE/OLIVIER	0	1	0	0	0	0	0	1	0
BUCHANAN/FOSTER	0	1	0	0	0	0	0	1	0
BUSH/CHENEY	0	6	9	4	0	1	0	20	14
GORE/LIEBERMAN	0	22	17	5	0	1	0	45	38
Nomark	0	0	0	0	0	0	598	598	16
Grand Totals:	0	30	26	9	0	2	598	665	68

* This tabulation is a compilation of markings considered errors with respect to other races on ballots that had either markings for a presidential candidate or no markings for any presidential candidate.

** Other is comprised primarily of write-ins on the presidential candidate box.

EXHIBIT B-1: THE MIAMI HERALD

State of Florida Precinct Reporting of Undervotes for Optical Scan and Manually Counted Counties

COUNTY: *Flagler County*

PRECINCT: **Totals For All Precincts**

CANDIDATE NAME	PRESIDENTIAL RACE								OTHER RACES*
	UNDERLINED CANDIDATE	CIRCLED OR MARKED CANDIDATE OR PARTY	CIRCLED OR PARTIALLY FILLED BUBBLE OR ARROW	MARKED X OR CHECKED	ERROR WITH WRITING INSTRUMENT	OTHER**	NO MARK	TOTAL BALLOTS	ERRORS IN OTHER RACES
BROWNE/OLIVIER	0	1	0	0	0	0	0	1	1
BUSH/CHENEY	0	4	1	11	0	0	0	16	15
GORE/LIEBERMAN	0	4	8	10	0	0	0	22	16
Nomark	0	0	0	0	0	0	22	22	2
Otherwrite-ins	0	0	0	0	0	9	0	9	2
Grand Totals:	0	9	9	21	0	9	22	70	36

* This tabulation is a compilation of markings considered errors with respect to other races on ballots that had either markings for a presidential candidate or no markings for any presidential candidate.

** Other is comprised primarily of write-ins on the presidential candidate box.

BDO Seidman, LLP

State of Florida Precinct Reporting of Undervotes for Optical Scan and Manually Counted Counties

COUNTY: *Franklin County*

PRECINCT: Totals For All Precincts

PRESIDENTIAL RACE

CANDIDATE NAME	UNDERLINED CANDIDATE	CIRCLED OR MARKED CANDIDATE OR PART.	CIRCLED OR PARTIALLY FILLED BUBBLE OR ARROW	MARKED X OR CHECKED	ERROR WITH WRITING INSTRUMENT	OTHER**	NO MARK	TOTAL BALLOTS	ERRORS IN OTHER RACES
BUSH/CHENEY	6	0	0	0	0	0	0	6	2
GORE/LIEBERMAN	9	1	0	0	0	0	0	10	3
No mark	0	0	0	0	0	0	52	52	4
Grand Totals:	*15*	*1*	*0*	*0*	*0*	*0*	*52*	*68*	*9*

OTHER RACES*

* This tabulation is a compilation of markings considered errors with respect to other races on ballots that had either markings for a presidential candidate or no markings for any presidential candidate.

** Other is comprised primarily of write-ins on the presidential candidate box.

BDO Seidman, LLP

EXHIBIT B-1: THE MIAMI HERALD

State of Florida Precinct Reporting of Undervotes for Optical Scan and Manually Counted Counties

COUNTY: Gadsden County

PRECINCT: Totals For All Precincts

CANDIDATE NAME	PRESIDENTIAL RACE								OTHER RACES*
	UNDERLINED CANDIDATE	CIRCLED OR MARKED CANDIDATE OR PARTY	CIRCLED OR PARTIALLY FILLED BUBBLE OR ARROW	MARKED X OR CHECKED	ERROR WITH WRITING INSTRUMENT	OTHER**	NO MARK	TOTAL BALLOTS	ERRORS IN OTHER RACES
BUSH/CHENEY	0	1	0	3	10	0	0	14	12
GORE/LIEBERMAN	0	11	2	7	8	2	0	30	16
Nomark	0	0	0	0	0	0	56	56	9
Otherwrite-ins	0	0	0	0	0	2	0	2	0
Grand Totals:	0	12	2	10	18	4	56	102	37

* This tabulation is a compilation of markings considered errors with respect to other races on ballots that had either markings for a presidential candidate or no markings for any presidential candidate.

** Other is comprised primarily of write-ins on the presidential candidate box.

BDO Seidman, LLP

252

EXHIBIT A-1: THE MIAMI HERALD

State of Florida Precinct Reporting of Undervotes for Punch Card Counties

COUNTY: GilchristCounty

PRECINCT: **Totals For All Precincts**

CANDIDATE NAME	PRESIDENTIAL RACE								OTHER RACES*		
	DIMPLE	PINPRICK	DETACHED 1 CORNER	DETACHED 2 CORNER	DETACHED 3 CORNER	PUNCHED CLEANLY	NO MARK	TOTAL BALLOTS	DIMPLED	HANGING CHADS	PUNCHED CLEANLY
BUSH/CHENEY	2	0	0	0	0	0	0	2	0	0	1
GORE/LIEBERMAN	0	0	0	0	0	1	0	1	0	0	1
Nomark	0	0	0	0	0	0	44	44	0	0	39
Grand Totals:	2	0	0	0	0	1	44	47	0	0	41

* This tabulation is a compilation of markings with respect to other races on those ballots on which there were either markings for one presidential candidate or no markings for any presidential candidate.

Note: The number of ballots for Bush and Gore that had a dimple in the presidential race and a dimple in the other races were as follows:

   Bush 0

   Gore 0

BDO Seidman, LLP

EXHIBIT A-1: THE MIAMI HERALD

State of Florida Precinct Reporting of Undervotes for Punch Card Counties

COUNTY: GladesCounty

PRECINCT: Totals For All Precincts

CANDIDATE NAME	PRESIDENTIAL RACE								OTHERRACES*		
	DIMPLE	PINPRICK	DETACHED 1 CORNER	DETACHED 2 CORNER	DETACHED 3 CORNER	PUNCHED CLEANLY	NO MARK	TOTAL BALLOTS	DIMPLED	HANGING CHADS	PUNCHED CLEANLY
BUSH/CHENEY	0	15	0	0	0	0	0	15	0	0	14
GORE/LIEBERMAN	1	12	0	0	0	0	0	13	0	0	12
Nomark	0	0	0	0	0	0	34	34	0	0	26
Grand Totals:	1	27	0	0	0	0	34	62	0	0	52

* This tabulation is a compilation of markings with respect to other races on those ballots on which there were either markings for one presidential candidate or no markings for any presidential candidate.

Note (1): The number of ballots for Bush and Gore that had a dimple in the presidential race and a dimple in the other races were as follows:
Bush 0
Gore 0

Note (2): The number of ballots not included above that had a written candidate name in the presidential race were as follows:
Bush 1
Gore 3
Other 0

EXHIBIT B-1: THE MIAMI HERALD

State of Florida Precinct Reporting of Undervotes for Optical Scan and Manually Counted Counties

COUNTY: *GulfCounty*

PRECINCT: **Totals For All Precincts**

CANDIDATE NAME	PRESIDENTIAL RACE								OTHERRACES*
	UNDERLINED CANDIDATE	CIRCLED OR MARKED CANDIDATE OR PARTY*	CIRCLED OR PARTIALLY FILLED BUBBLE OR ARROW	MARKED X OR CHECKED	ERROR WITH WRITING INSTRUMENT	OTHER**	NO MARK	TOTAL BALLOTS	ERRORS IN OTHER RACES
BUSH/CHENEY	0	0	0	1	1	0	0	2	1
GORE/LIEBERMAN	0	1	0	2	2	1	0	6	1
No mark	0	0	0	0	0	0	39	39	0
Grand Totals:	0	1	0	3	3		39	47	2

* This tabulation is a compilation of markings considered errors with respect to other races on ballots that had either markings for a presidential candidate or no markings for any presidential candidate.

** Other is comprised primarily of write-ins on the presidential candidate box.

BDO Seidman, LLP

255

EXHIBIT B-1: THE MIAMI HERALD

State of Florida Precinct Reporting of Undervotes for Optical Scan and Manually Counted Counties

COUNTY : **Hamilton County**

PRECINCT : **Totals For All Precincts**

PRESIDENTIAL RACE

CANDIDATE NAME	UNDERLINED CANDIDATE	CIRCLED OR MARKED CANDIDATE OR PARTY	CIRCLED OR PARTIALLY FILLED BUBBLE OR ARROW	MARKED X OR CHECKED	ERROR WITH WRITING INSTRUMENT	OTHER**	NO MARK	TOTAL BALLOTS	ERRORS IN OTHER RACES
BUSH/CHENEY	0	2	0	0	0	0	0	2	0
GORE/LIEBERMAN	0	1	0	0	0	0	0	1	0
Nomark	0	0	0	0	0	0	22	22	1
Otherwrite-ins	0	0	0	0	0	2	0	2	0
Grand Totals:	0	3	0	0	0	2	22	27	1

OTHER RACES*

* This tabulation is a compilation of markings considered errors with respect to other races on ballots that had either markings for a presidential candidate or no markings for any presidential candidate.

** Other is comprised primarily of write-ins on the presidential candidate box.

BDO Seidman, LLP

EXHIBIT A-1: THE MIAMI HERALD
State of Florida Precinct Reporting of Undervotes for Punch Card Counties

COUNTY: HardeeCounty

PRECINCT: Totals For All Precincts

CANDIDATE NAME	PRESIDENTIAL RACE								OTHER RACES*		
	DIMPLE	PINPRICK	DETACHED 1 CORNER	DETACHED 2 CORNER	DETACHED 3 CORNER	PUNCHED CLEANLY	NO MARK	TOTAL BALLOTS	DIMPLED	HANGING CHADS	PUNCHED CLEANLY
BUSH/CHENEY	7	0	0	0	0	1	0	8	0	0	0
GORE/LIEBERMAN	7	0	1	0	0	0	0	8	0	0	0
Nomark	0	0	0	0	0	0	65	65	0	0	0
Grand Totals:	14	0	1	0	0	1	65	81	0	0	0

* This tabulation is a compilation of markings with respect to other races on those ballots on which there were either markings for one presidential candidate or no markings for any presidential candidate.

Note: The number of ballots for Bush and Gore that had a dimple in the presidential race and a dimple in the other races were as follows:
Bush 0
Gore 0

EXHIBIT B-1: THE MIAMI HERALD

State of Florida Precinct Reporting of Undervotes for Optical Scan and Manually Counted Counties

COUNTY: *Hendry County*

PRECINCT: **Totals For All Precincts**

| | | | | PRESIDENTIAL RACE | | | | | OTHER RACES* |
CANDIDATE NAME	UNDERLINED CANDIDATE	CIRCLED OR MARKED CANDIDATE OR PARTY	CIRCLED OR PARTIALLY FILLED BUBBLE OR ARROW	MARKED X OR CHECKED	ERROR WITH WRITING INSTRUMENT	OTHER**	NO MARK	TOTAL BALLOTS	ERRORS IN OTHER RACES
Nomark	0	0	0	0	0	0	39	39	6
Grand Totals:	0	0	0	0	0	0	39	39	6

* This tabulation is a compilation of markings considered errors with respect to other races on ballots that had either markings for a presidential candidate or no markings for any presidential candidate.

** Other is comprised primarily of write-ins on the presidential candidate box.

EXHIBIT B-1: THE MIAMI HERALD

State of Florida Precinct Reporting of Undervotes for Optical Scan and Manually Counted Counties

COUNTY: Hernando County

PRECINCT: Totals For All Precincts

CANDIDATE NAME	PRESIDENTIAL RACE								OTHERRACES*
	UNDERLINED CANDIDATE	CIRCLED OR MARKED CANDIDATE OR PARTY	CIRCLED OR PARTIALLY FILLED BUEBLE OR ARROW	MARKED X OR CHECKED	ERROR WITH WRITING INSTRUMENT	OTHER**	NO MARK	TOTAL BALLOTS	ERRORS IN OTHER RACES
BUSH/CHENEY	0	1	0	0	0	0	0	1	1
GORE/LIEBERMAN	1	3	0	0	0	0	0	4	3
HARRIS/TROWE	0	1	0	0	0	0	0	1	1
Nomark	0	0	0	0	0	0	67	67	3
Otherwrite-ins	0	1	0	0	0	8	0	9	1
Grand Totals:	1	6	0	0	0	8	67	82	9

* This tabulation is a compilation of markings considered errors with respect to other races on ballots that had either markings for a presidential candidate or no markings for any presidential candidate.

** Other is comprised primarily of write-ins on the presidential candidate box.

BDO Seidman, LLP

EXHIBIT A-1: *THE MIAMI HERALD*
State of Florida Precinct Reporting of Undervotes for Punch Card Counties

COUNTY: Highlands County

PRECINCT: Totals For All Precincts

CANDIDATE NAME**	PRESIDENTIAL RACE								OTHER RACES*		
	DIMPLE	PINPRICK	DETACHED 1 CORNER	DETACHED 2 CORNER	DETACHED 3 CORNER	PUNCHED CLEANLY	NO MARK	TOTAL BALLOTS	DIMPLED	HANGING CHADS	PUNCHED CLEANLY
Blank	4	0	0	1	0	16	0	21	5	7	15
BROWNE/OLIVIER	0	1	0	0	0	0	0	1	1	0	0
BUSH/CHENEY	71	15	0	3	3	4	0	96	16	12	91
GORE/LIEBERMAN	38	20	2	0	0	0	0	60	13	11	54
HAGELIN/GOLDHABER	2	3	0	0	0	0	0	5	4	0	3
HARRIS/TROWE	2	0	0	0	0	0	0	2	2	0	0
NADER/LADUKE	0	0	1	0	0	0	0	1	0	0	1
No mark	0	0	0	0	0	0	295	295	25	24	223
Grand Totals:	*117*	*39*	*3*	*4*	*3*	*20*	*295*	*481*	*66*	*54*	*387*

* This tabulation is a compilation of markings with respect to other races on those ballots on which there were either markings for one presidential candidate or no markings for any presidential candidate.

** Blank consists of markings on a line where there was no presidential candidate.

Note: The number of ballots for Bush and Gore that had a dimple in the presidential race and a dimple in the other races were as follows:

   Bush 9

   Gore 9

BDO Seidman, LLP

State of Florida Precinct Reporting of Undervotes for Punch Card Counties

COUNTY : HillsboroughCounty

PRECINCT : Totals For All Precincts

CANDIDATE NAME**	PRESIDENTIAL RACE								OTHERRACES*		
	DIMPLE	PINPRICK	DETACHED 1 CORNER	DETACHED 2 CORNER	DETACHED 3 CORNER	PUNCHED CLEANLY	NO MARK	TOTAL BALLOTS	DIMPLED	HANGING CHADS	PUNCHED CLEANLY
Blank	27	0		5	6	144	0	180	49	46	166
BROWNE/OLIVIER	15	3			0	0	0	18	10	4	15
BUCHANAN/FOSTER	14	0			1	1	0	16	13	4	11
BUSH/CHENEY	1450	14		21	59	45	0	1591	1023	707	1507
GORE/LIEBERMAN	1568	33	7	13	57	42	0	1723	1105	715	1634
HAGELIN/GOLDHABER	11	5			0	3	0	19	13	4	10
HARRIS/TROWE	1	2	1		0	0	0	4	3	1	3
McREYNOLDS/HOLLIS	0	1			0	0	0	1	1	0	0
MOOREHEAD/LARIVA	2	2			0	1	0	5	4	0	5
NADER/LADUKE	65	2			1	2	0	70	32	21	67
Nomark	0	0			0	0	1767	1767	237	205	1167
GrandTotals:	3153	62		47	124	238	1767	5394	2490	1707	4585

* This tabulation is a compilation of markings with respect to other races on those ballots on which there were either markings for one presidential candidate or no markings for any presidential candidate.

** Blank consists of markings on a line where there was no presidential candidate.

Note: The number of ballots for Bush and Gore that had a dimple in the presidential race and a dimple in the other races were as follows:
Bush 965
Gore 1035

BDO Seidman, LLP

State of Florida Precinct Reporting of Undervotes for Optical Scan and Manually Counted Counties

COUNTY : Holmes County

PRECINCT : Totals For All Precincts

CANDIDATE NAME	PRESIDENTIAL RACE								OTHER RACES*
	UNDERLINED CANDIDATE	CIRCLED OR MARKED CANDIDATE OR PARTY	CIRCLED OR PARTIALLY FILLED BUBBLE OR ARROW	MARKED X OR CHECKED	ERROR WITH WRITING INSTRUMENT	OTHER**	NO MARK	TOTAL BALLOTS	ERRORS IN OTHER RACES
BUCHANAN/FOSTER	0	0	0	0	0	1	0	1	1
BUSH/CHENEY	1	0	1	0	3	2	0	7	4
GORE/LIEBERMAN	1	2	1	0	4	1	0	9	6
No mark	0	0	0	0	0	0	77	77	0
Other write-ins	0	0	0	0	0	3	0	3	0
Grand Totals:	2	2	2	0	7	7	77	97	11

* This tabulation is a compilation of markings considered errors with respect to other races on ballots that had either markings for a presidential candidate or no markings for any presidential candidate.

** Other is comprised primarily of write-ins on the presidential candidate box.

BDO Seidman, LLP

EXHIBIT A-1: THE MIAMI HERALD

State of Florida Precinct Reporting of Undervotes for Punch Card Counties

COUNTY: IndianRiverCounty

PRECINCT: Totals For All Precincts

CANDIDATE NAME**	PRESIDENTIAL RACE								OTHERRACES*		
	DIMPLE	PINPRICK	DETACHED 1 CORNER	DETACHED 2 CORNER	DETACHED 3 CORNER	PUNCHED CLEANLY	NO MARK	TOTAL BALLOTS	DIMPLED	HANGING CHADS	PUNCHED CLEANLY
Blank	30	9	0	1	0	100	0	140	37	15	118
BROWNE/OLIVIER	3	1	0	0	0	0	0	4	2	0	2
BUSH/CHENEY	251	11	3	7	14	3	0	289	149	107	270
GORE/LIEBERMAN	157	5	0	4	1	2	0	169	76	61	155
HARRIS/TROWE	9	4	0	0	0	0	0	13	12	0	4
NADER/LADUKE	9	4	0	0	1	0	0	14	7	1	9
Nomark	0	0	0	0	0	0	334	334	33	22	241
Grand Totals:	459	34	11	12	16	105	334	963	316	206	799

* This tabulation is a compilation of markings with respect to other races on those ballots on which there were either markings for one presidential candidate or no markings for any presidential candidate.

** Blank consists of markings on a line where there was no presidential candidate.

Note: The number of ballots for Bush and Gore that had a dimple in the presidential race and a dimple in the other races were as follows:

Bush 137

Gore 75

BDO Seidman, LLP

EXHIBIT B-1: THE MIAMI HERALD

State of Florida Precinct Reporting of Undervotes for Optical Scan and Manually Counted Counties

COUNTY: Jackson County

PRECINCT: Totals For All Precincts

CANDIDATE NAME	PRESIDENTIAL RACE								OTHER RACES*
	UNDERLINED CANDIDATE	CIRCLED OR MARKED CANDIDATE OR PARTY	CIRCLED OR PARTIALLY FILLED BUBBLE OR ARROW	MARKED X OR CHECKED	ERROR WITH WRITING INSTRUMENT	OTHER**	NO MARK	TOTAL BALLOTS	ERRORS IN OTHER RACES
BUSH/CHENEY	1	3	0	7	0	0	0	11	3
GORE/LIEBERMAN	0	2	0	14	0	4	0	20	4
Nomark	0	0	0	0	0	0	54	54	10
Otherwrite-ins	0	0	0	0	0	5	0	5	0
PHILLIPS/FRAZIER	0	0	0	2	0	0	0	2	0
Grand Totals:	1	5	0	23	0	9	54	92	17

* This tabulation is a compilation of markings considered errors with respect to other races on ballots that had either markings for a presidential candidate or no markings for any presidential candidate.

** Other is comprised primarily of write-ins on the presidential candidate box.

BDO Seidman, LLP

264

EXHIBIT A-1: THE MIAMI HERALD

State of Florida Precinct Reporting of Undervotes for Punch Card Counties

COUNTY: JeffersonCounty

PRECINCT: Totals For All Precincts

CANDIDATE NAME	PRESIDENTIAL RACE								OTHER RACES*		
	DIMPLE	PINPRICK	DETACHED 1 CORNER	DETACHED 2 CORNER	DETACHED 3 CORNER	PUNCHED CLEANLY	NO MARK	TOTAL BALLOTS	DIMPLED	HANGING CHADS	PUNCHED CLEANLY
BUSH/CHENEY	0	3	0	0	0	0	0	3	0	3	0
GORE/LIEBERMAN	0	2	0	0	0	0	0	2	0	1	0
Nomark	0	0	0	0	0	0	24	24	0	0	19
Grand Totals:	0	5	0	0	0	0	24	29	0	4	19

* This tabulation is a compilation of markings with respect to other races on those ballots on which there were either markings for one presidential candidate or no markings for any presidential candidate.

Note (1): The number of ballots for Bush and Gore that had a dimple in the presidential race and a dimple in the other races were as follows:

    Bush 0

    Gore 0

Note (2): The number of ballots not included above that had a written candidate name in the presidential race were as follows:

    Bush 0

    Gore 1

    Other 0

BDO Seidman, LLP

State of Florida Precinct Reporting of Undervotes for Optical Scan and Manually Counted Counties

COUNTY: *LaFayette County*

PRECINCT: **Totals For All Precincts**

CANDIDATE NAME	PRESIDENTIAL RACE								OTHER RACES*
	UNDERLINED CANDIDATE	CIRCLED OR MARKED CANDIDATE OR PARTY	CIRCLED OR PARTIALLY FILLED BUBBLE OR ARROW	MARKED X OR CHECKED	ERROR WITH WRITING INSTRUMENT	OTHER**	NO MARK	TOTAL BALLOTS	ERRORS IN OTHER RACES
N/A***	0	0	0	0	0	0	0	0	0
Grand Totals:	0	0	0	0	0	0	0	0	0

* This tabulation is a compilation of markings considered errors with respect to other races on ballots that had either markings for a presidential candidate or no markings for any presidential candidate.

** Other is comprised primarily of write-ins on the presidential candidate box.

*** All 217 ballots observed in LaFayette County were overvotes.

BDO Seidman, LLP

EXHIBIT B-1: THE MIAMI HERALD

State of Florida Precinct Reporting of Undervotes for Optical Scan and Manually Counted Counties

COUNTY: **Lake County**

PRECINCT: **Totals For All Precincts**

CANDIDATE NAME		PRESIDENTIAL RACE							OTHER RACES*
	UNDERLINED CANDIDATE	CIRCLED OF MARKED CANDIDATE OR PARTY	CIRCLED OR PARTIALLY FILLED BUBBLE OR ARROW	MARKED X OR CHECKED	ERROR WITH WRITING INSTRUMENT	OTHER**	NO MARK	TOTAL BALLOTS	ERRORS IN OTHER RACES
BUSH/CHENEY	0	3	2	5	2	0	0	12	10
GORE/LIEBERMAN	2	1	4	3	1	6	0	17	10
NADER/LADUKE	0	1	0	0	0	0	0	1	1
No mark	0	0	0	0	0	0	138	138	13
Other write-ins	0	0	0	0	0	12	0	12	1
Grand Totals:	2	5	6	8	3	18	138	180	35

* This tabulation is a compilation of markings considered errors with respect to other races on ballots that had either markings for a presidential candidate or no markings for any presidential candidate.

** Other is comprised primarily of write-ins on the presidential candidate box.

BDO Seidman, LLP

EXHIBIT A-1: THE MIAMI HERALD

State of Florida Precinct Reporting of Undervotes for Punch Card Counties

COUNTY: LeeCounty

PRECINCT: Totals For All Precincts

CANDIDATE NAME**	PRESIDENTIAL RACE								OTHERRACES*		
	DIMPLE	PINPRICK	DETACHED 1 CORNER	DETACHED 2 CORNER	DETACHED 3 CORNER	PUNCHED CLEANLY	NO MARK	TOTAL BALLOTS	DIMPLED	HANGING CHADS	PUNCHED CLEANLY
Blank	1	0	0	0	0	1	0	2	1	0	1
BROWNE/OLIVIER	3	0	0	0	0	0	0	3	2	1	2
BUCHANAN/FOSTER	6	2	0	0	0	1	0	9	7	1	7
BUSH/CHENEY	187	5	1	6	13	1	0	213	120	93	187
GORE/LIEBERMAN	100	12	1	1	2	1	0	117	67	39	98
HAGELIN/GOLDHABER	11	4	0	0	0	0	0	15	13	1	9
HARRIS/TROWE	6	1	0	0	0	0	0	7	5	0	3
McREYNOLDS/HOLLIS	1	1	0	0	0	0	0	2	2	0	0
MOOREHEAD/LARIVA	1	0	0	0	0	0	0	1	0	0	1
NADER/LADUKE	4	1	0	0	0	0	0	5	3	1	4
Nomark	0	0	0	0	0	0	1600	1600	202	229	1188
Grand Totals:	320	26	2	7	15	4	1600	1974	422	365	1500

* This tabulation is a compilation of markings with respect to other races on those ballots on which there were either markings for one presidential candidate or no markings for any presidential candidate.

** Blank consists of markings on a line where there was no presidential candidate.

Note: The number of ballots for Bush and Gore that had a dimple in the presidential race and a dimple in the other races were as follows:

Bush 109

Gore 55

BDO Seidman, LLP

EXHIBIT B-1: THE MIAMI HERALD

State of Florida Precinct Reporting of Undervotes for Optical Scan and Manually Counted Counties

COUNTY: Leon County

PRECINCT: Totals For All Precincts

CANDIDATE NAME	UNDERLINED CANDIDATE	CIRCLED OR MARKED CANDIDATE OR PART	CIRCLED OR PARTIALLY FILLED BUBBLE OR ARROW	MARKED X OR CHECKED	ERROR WITH WRITING INSTRUMENT	OTHER**	NO MARK	TOTAL BALLOTS	ERRORS IN OTHER RACES
			PRESIDENTIAL RACE						OTHER RACES*
BUSH/CHENEY	0	5	0	4	0	1	0	10	8
GORE/LIEBERMAN	0	7	0	2	0	0	0	9	5
No mark	0	0	0	0	0	0	153	153	3
Other write-ins	0	0	0	0	0	3	0	3	0
Grand Totals:	0	12	0	6	0	4	153	175	16

* This tabulation is a compilation of markings considered errors with respect to other races on ballots that had either markings for a presidential candidate or no markings for any presidential candidate.

** Other is comprised primarily of write-ins on the presidential candidate box.

BDO Seidman, LLP

269

EXHIBIT B-1: THE MIAMI HERALD

State of Florida Precinct Reporting of Undervotes for Optical Scan and Manually Counted Counties

COUNTY: *LevyCounty*

PRECINCT: **Totals For All Precincts**

CANDIDATE NAME	PRESIDENTIAL RACE								OTHER RACES*
	UNDERLINED CANDIDATE	CIRCLED OR MARKED CANDIDATE OR PARTY	CIRCLED OR PARTIALLY FILLED BUBBLE OR ARROW	MARKED X OR CHECKED	ERROR WITH WRITING INSTRUMENT	OTHER**	NO MARK	TOTAL BALLOTS	ERRORS IN OTHER RACES
BUSH/CHENEY	0	0	0	2	3	3	0	8	5
GORE/LIEBERMAN	0	0	0	5	3	1	0	9	6
Nomark	0	0	0	0	0	0	33	33	3
Otherwrite-ins	0	0	0	0	0	1	0	1	0
Grand Totals:	0	0	0	7	6	5	33	51	14

* This tabulation is a compilation of markings considered errors with respect to other races on ballots that had either markings for a presidential candidate or no markings for any presidential candidate.

** Other is comprised primarily of write-ins on the presidential candidate box.

BDO Seidman, LLP

EXHIBIT B-1: THE MIAMI HERALD

State of Florida Precinct Reporting of Undervotes for Optical Scan and Manually Counted Counties

COUNTY: Liberty County

PRECINCT: Totals For All Precincts

CANDIDATE NAME	PRESIDENTIAL RACE								OTHER RACES*
	UNDERLINED CANDIDATE	CIRCLED OR MARKED CANDIDATE OR PARTY	CIRCLED OR PARTIALLY FILLED BUBBLE OR ARROW	MARKED X OR CHECKED	ERROR WITH WRITING INSTRUMENT	OTHER**	NO MARK	TOTAL BALLOTS	ERRORS IN OTHER RACES
BUSH/CHENEY	0	0	0	0	0	2	0	2	1
GORE/LIEBERMAN	0	1	0	1	0	1	0	3	1
Nomark	0	0	0	0	0	0	20	20	2
Grand Totals:	0	1	0	1	0	3	20	25	4

* This tabulation is a compilation of markings considered errors with respect to other races on ballots that had either markings for a presidential candidate or no markings for any presidential candidate.

** Other is comprised primarily of write-ins on the presidential candidate box

BDO Seidman, LLP

State of Florida Precinct Reporting of Undervotes for Punch Card Counties

COUNTY : MadisonCounty

PRECINCT : Totals For All Precincts

CANDIDATE NAME	PRESIDENTIAL RACE								OTHER RACES*		
	DIMPLE	PINPRICK	DETACHED 1 CORNER	DETACHED 2 CORNER	DETACHED 3 CORNER	PUNCHED CLEANLY	NO MARK	TOTAL BALLOTS	DIMPLED	HANGING CHADS	PUNCHED CLEANLY
BUSH/CHENEY	0	0	0	0	2	0	0	2	0	0	2
Nomark	0	0	0	0	0	0	25	25	0	0	18
Grand Totals:	0	0	0	0	2	0	25	27	0	0	20

* This tabulation is a compilation of markings with respect to other races on those ballots on which there were either markings for one presidential candidate or no markings for any presidential candidate.

Note (1): The number of ballots for Bush and Gore that had a dimple in the presidential race and a dimple in the other races were as follows:

    Bush 0
    Gore 0

Note (2): The number of ballots not included above that had a written candidate name in the presidential race were as follows:

    Bush 0
    Gore 4
    Other 0

BDO Seidman, LLP

EXHIBIT B-1: THE MIAMI HERALD

State of Florida Precinct Reporting of Undervotes for Optical Scan and Manually Counted Counties

COUNTY: Manatee County

PRECINCT: Totals For All Precincts

CANDIDATE NAME***	PRESIDENTIAL RACE								OTHER RACES*
	UNDERLINED CANDIDATE	CIRCLED OR MARKED CANDIDATE OR PARTY	CIRCLED OR PARTIALLY FILLED BUBBLE OR ARROW	MARKED X OR CHECKED	ERROR WITH WRITING INSTRUMENT	OTHER**	NO MARK	TOTAL BALLOTS	ERRORS IN OTHER RACES
Blank	0	0	0	0	0	2	0	2	0
BUSH/CHENEY	0	5	0	7	0	1	0	13	11
GORE/LIEBERMAN	0	6	3	4	0	1	0	14	10
NADER/LADUKE	0	1	0	0	0	1	0	2	1
Nomark	0	0	0	0	0	0	74	74	12
Otherwrite-ins	0	0	0	0	0	6	0	6	1
Grand Totals:	0	12	3	11	0	11	74	111	35

* This tabulation is a compilation of markings considered errors with respect to other races on ballots that had either markings for a presidential candidate or no markings for any presidential candidate.

** Other is comprised primarily of write-ins on the presidential candidate box.

*** Blank consists of markings on a line where there was no presidential candidate.

BDO Seidman, LLP

273

EXHIBIT A-1: THE MIAMI HERALD

State of Florida Precinct Reporting of Undervotes for Punch Card Counties

COUNTY: Marion County

PRECINCT: Totals For All Precincts

CANDIDATE NAME**	PRESIDENTIAL RACE								OTHER RACES*		
	DIMPLE	PINPRICK	DETACHED 1 CORNER	DETACHED 2 CORNER	DETACHED 3 CORNER	PUNCHED CLEANLY	NO MARK	TOTAL BALLOTS	DIMPLED	HANGING CHADS	PUNCHED CLEANLY
Blank	4	0	3	6	4	79	0	96	4	25	96
BROWNE/OLIVIER	1	0	0	0	0	0	0	1	1	1	1
BUCHANAN/FOSTER	3	1	0	0	0	0	0	4	2	1	4
BUSH/CHENEY	549	10	8	8	15	3	0	593	62	64	588
GORE/LIEBERMAN	383	8	5	7	1?	1	0	421	58	44	411
HAGELIN/GOLDHABER	11	3	0	0	0	1	0	15	3	4	12
HARRIS/TROWE	4	4	0	0	0	0	0	8	3	3	5
MOOREHEAD/LARIVA	1	0	0	0	0	0	0	1	1	0	0
NADER/LADUKE	4	0	0	0	1	0	0	5	2	0	5
No mark	0	0	0	0	0	0	1249	1249	77	274	1036
GrandTotals:	960	26	16	21	37	84	1249	2393	213	416	2158

* This tabulation is a compilation of markings with respect to other races on those ballots on which there were either markings for one presidential candidate or no markings for any presidential candidate.

** Blank consists of markings on a line where there was no presidential candidate.

Note (1): The number of ballots for Bush and Gore that had a dimple in the presidential race and a dimple in the other races were as follows:

Bush 61

Gore 51

Note (2): The number of ballots not included above that had a written candidate name in the presidential race were as follows:

Bush 0

Gore 1

BDO Seidman, LLP

274

EXHIBIT A-1: THE MIAMI HERALD

State of Florida Precinct Reporting of Undervotes for Punch Card Counties

COUNTY: , MartinCounty

PRECINCT: Totals For All Precincts

CANDIDATE NAME	PRESIDENTIAL RACE								OTHER RACES*		
	DIMPLE	PINPRICK	DETACHED 1 CORNER	DETACHED 2 CORNER	DETACHED 3 CORNER	PUNCHED CLEANLY	NO MARK	TOTAL BALLOTS	DIMPLED	HANGING CHADS	PUNCHED CLEANLY
BROWNE/OLIVIER	1	0	0	0	0	0	0	1	0	0	0
BUSH/CHENEY	38	1	6	4	0	2	0	51	6	2	34
GORE/LIEBERMAN	21	2	11	4	0	0	0	38	12	6	30
NADER/LADUKE	0	0	1	1	0	0	0	2	0	0	1
Nomark	0	0	0	0	0	0	41	41	0	2	38
Grand Totals:	60	3	18	9	0	2	41	133	18	10	103

* This tabulation is a compilation of markings with respect to other races on those ballots on which there were either markings for one presidential candidate or no markings for any presidential candidate.

Note (1): The number of ballots for Bush and Gore that had a dimple in the presidential race and a dimple in the other races were as follows:

Bush 6

Gore 9

Note (2): The number of ballots not included above that had a written candidate name in the presidential race were as follows:

Bush 21

Gore 17

Other 1

BDO Seidman, LLP

EXHIBIT A-1: THE MIAMI HERALD
State of Florida Precinct Reporting of Undervotes for Punch Card Counties

COUNTY: Miami-DadeCounty

PRECINCT: Totals For All Precincts

CANDIDATE NAME**	PRESIDENTIAL RACE								OTHERRACES*		
	DIMPLE	PINPRICK	DETACHED 1 CORNER	DETACHED 2 CORNER	DETACHED 3 CORNER	PUNCHED CLEANLY	NO MARK	TOTAL BALLOTS	DIMPLED	HANGING CHADS	PUNCHED CLEANLY
Blank	102	84	2	15	14	1840	0	2057	257	272	1805
BROWNE/OLIVIER	8	6	1	0	0	0	0	15	7	8	6
BUSH/CHENEY	1092	323	14	20	25	33	0	1507	872	854	1283
GORE/LIEBERMAN	1203	291	0	10	15	37	0	1556	898	891	1343
HAGELIN/GOLDHABER	3	3	0	0	0	1	0	7	2	2	4
HARRIS/TROWE	17	13	0	0	0	1	0	31	22	26	11
McREYNOLDS/HOLLIS	2	0	0	0	0	0	0	2	1	0	0
NADER/LADUKE	30	20	0	0	1	0	0	51	25	31	21
Nomark	0	0	0	0	0	0	4892	4892	541	561	3096
PHILLIPS/FRAZIER	0	0	0	0	0	1	0	1	0	0	1
Grand Totals:	2457	740	17	45	55	1913	4892	10119	2625	2645	7570

* This tabulation is a compilation of markings with respect to other races on those ballots on which there were either markings for one presidential candidate or no markings for any presidential candidate.

** Blank consists of markings on a line where there was no presidential candidate.

Note: The number of ballots for Bush and Gore that had a dimple in the presidential race and a dimple in the other races were as follows:

Bush 684

Gore 749

BDO Seidman, LLP

EXHIBIT B-1: THE MIAMI HERALD

State of Florida Precinct Reporting of Undervotes for Optical Scan and Manually Counted Counties

COUNTY: *MonroeCounty*

PRECINCT: **Totals For All Precincts**

CANDIDATE NAME***	PRESIDENTIAL RACE								OTHERRACES*
	UNDERLINED CANDIDATE	CIRCLED OR MARKED CANDIDATE OR PARTY	CIRCLED OR PARTIALLY FILLED BUBBLE OR ARROW	MARKED X OR CHECKED	ERROR WITH WRITING INSTRUMENT	OTHER**	NO MARK	TOTAL BALLOTS	ERRORS IN OTHER RACES
Blank	0	0	0	0	0	1	0	1	1
BUSH/CHENEY	0	0	0	4	0	0	0	4	4
GORE/LIEBERMAN	0	0	0	6	0	0	0	6	6
Nomark	0	0	0	0	0	0	58	58	7
Otherwrite-ins	0	0	0	0	0	12	0	12	2
Grand Totals:	0	0	0	10	0	13	58	81	20

* This tabulation is a compilation of markings considered errors with respect to other races on ballots that had either markings for a presidentia candidate or no markings for any presidential candidate.

** Other is comprised primarily of write-ins on the presidential candidate box.

*** Blank consists of markings on a line where there was no presidential candidate.

BDO Seidman, LLP

EXHIBIT A-1: THE MIAMI HERALD

State of Florida Precinct Reporting of Undervotes for Punch Card Counties

COUNTY: NassauCounty

PRECINCT: Totals For All Precincts

	PRESIDENTIAL RACE								OTHER RACES*		
CANDIDATE NAME	DIMPLE	PINPRICK	DETACHED 1 CORNER	DETACHED 2 CORNER	DETACHED 3 CORNER	PUNCHED CLEANLY	NO MARK	TOTAL BALLOTS	DIMPLED	HANGING CHADS	PUNCHED CLEANLY
BUSH/CHENEY	7	0	4	6	14	4	0	35	9	6	25
GORE/LIEBERMAN	1	0	1	2	2	1	0	7	0	1	4
HARRIS/TROWE	0	0	0	0	0	1	0	1	0	0	0
McREYNOLDS/HOLLIS	0	0	1	0	0	0	0	1	0	0	1
No mark	0	0	0	0	0	0	104	104	5	7	59
Grand Totals:	8	0	6	8	16	6	104	148	14	14	89

* This tabulation is a compilation of markings with respect to other races on those ballots on which there were either markings for one presidential candidate or no markings for any presidential candidate.

Note: The number of ballots for Bush and Gore that had a dimple in the presidential race and a dimple in the other races were as follows:

Bush 3

Gore 0

BDO Seidman, LLP

278

EXHIBIT B-1: THE MIAMI HERALD

State of Florida Precinct Reporting of Undervotes for Optical Scan and Manually Counted Counties

COUNTY: **Okaloosa County**

PRECINCT: **Totals For All Precincts**

CANDIDATE NAME	PRESIDENTIAL RACE								OTHER RACES*
	UNDERLINED CANDIDATE	CIRCLED OR MARKED CANDIDATE OF PARTY	CIRCLED OR PARTIALLY FILLED BUBBLE OR ARROW	MARKED X OR CHECKED	ERROR WITH WRITING INSTRUMENT	OTHER**	NO MARK	TOTAL BALLOTS	ERRORS IN OTHER RACES
BUSH/CHENEY	0	1	4	0	0	1	0	6	2
GORE/LIEBERMAN	0	3	0	1	0	1	0	5	3
Nomark	0	0	0	0	0	0	60	60	8
Otherwrite-ins	0	1	0	0	0	8	0	9	2
Grand Totals:	0	5	4	1	0	10	60	80	15

* This tabulation is a compilation of markings considered errors with respect to other races on ballots that had either markings for a presidential candidate or no markings for any presidential candidate.

** Other is comprised primarily of write-ins on the presidential candidate box.

BDO Seidman, LLP

EXHIBIT B-1: THE MIAMI HERALD

State of Florida Precinct Reporting of Undervotes for Optical Scan and Manually Counted Counties

COUNTY: *Okeechobee County*

PRECINCT: Totals For All Precincts

CANDIDATE NAME	PRESIDENTIAL RACE								OTHER RACES*
	UNDERLINED CANDIDATE	CIRCLED OR MARKED CANDIDATE OR PARTY	CIRCLED OR PARTIALLY FILLED BUBBLE OR ARROW	MARKED X OR CHECKED	ERROR WITH WRITING INSTRUMENT	OTHER**	NO MARK	TOTAL BALLOTS	ERRORS IN OTHER RACES
BROWNE/OLIVIER	0	0	1	0	0	0	0	1	1
BUSH/CHENEY	0	1	1	4	9	0	0	15	13
GORE/LIEBERMAN	0	1	3	6	16	6	0	32	28
HAGELIN/GOLDHABER	0	0	0	1	0	0	0	1	0
NADER/LADUKE	0	0	0	0	2	0	0	2	2
Nomark	0	0	0	0	0	0	50	50	6
Otherwrite-ins	0	0	0	0	0	3	0	3	0
GrandTotals:	0	2	5	11	27	9	50	104	50

* This tabulation is a compilation of markings considered errors with respect to other races on ballots that had either markings for a presidential candidate or no markings for any presidential candidate.

** Other is comprised primarily of write-ins on the presidential candidate box.

BDO Seidman, LLP

EXHIBIT B-1: *THE MIAMI HERALD*

State of Florida Precinct Reporting of Undervotes for Optical Scan and Manually Counted Counties

COUNTY: *OrangeCounty*

PRECINCT: **Totals For All Precincts**

CANDIDATE NAME***	UNDERLINED CANDIDATE	CIRCLED OR MARKED CANDIDATE OR PARTY	CIRCLED OR PARTIALLY FILLED EUBBLE OR ARROW	MARKED X OR CHECKED	ERROR WITH WRITING INSTRUMENT	OTHER**	NO MARK	TOTAL BALLOTS	ERRORS IN OTHER RACES
				PRESIDENTIAL RACE					OTHERRACES*
Blank	0	0	0	0	0	2	0	2	1
BROWNE/OLIVIER	0	0	1	0	0	0	0	1	1
BUSH/CHENEY	6	11	50	42	3	1	0	113	89
GORE/LIEBERMAN	4	51	79	108	3	5	0	250	214
HAGELIN/GOLDHABER	0	0	0	1	0	0	0	1	1
NADER/LADUKE	0	0	1	4	0	0	0	5	4
Nomark	0	0	0	0	0	0	247	247	8
Otherwrite-ins	0	0	0	0	0	20	0	20	2
GrandTotals:	10	62	131	155	6	28	247	639	320

* This tabulation is a compilation of markings considered errors with respect to other races on ballots that had either markings for a presidential candidate or no markings for any presidential candidate.

** Other is comprised primarily of write-ins on the presidential candidate box.

*** Blank consists of markings on a line where there was no presidential candidate.

BDO Seidman, LLP

EXHIBIT A-1: THE MIAMI HERALD

State of Florida Precinct Reporting of Undervotes for Punch Card Counties

COUNTY: OsceolaCounty

PRECINCT: Totals For All Precincts

CANDIDATE NAME**	PRESIDENTIAL RACE								OTHER RACES*		
	DIMPLE	PINPRICK	DETACHED 1 CORNER	DETACHED 2 CORNER	DETACHED 3 CORNER	PUNCHED CLEANLY	NO MARK	TOTAL BALLOTS	DIMPLED	HANGING CHADS	PUNCHED CLEANLY
Blank	2	0	0	0	1	31	0	34	5	4	33
BROWNE/OLIVIER	2	0	0	0	0	0	0	2	2	0	1
BUCHANAN/FOSTER	2	0	0	0	0	0	0	2	2	0	1
BUSH/CHENEY	50	0	1	1	3	1	0	56	27	10	55
GORE/LIEBERMAN	75	0	1	3	3	1	0	83	32	7	79
HAGELIN/GOLDHABER	3	0	0	0	0	0	0	3	3	1	2
NADER/LADUKE	1	0	0	0	0	0	0	1	0	0	1
Nomark	0	0	0	0	0	0	437	437	41	22	255
PHILLIPS/FRAZIER	1	0	0	0	0	0	0	1	1	0	0
Grand Totals:	136	0	2	4	7	33	437	619	113	44	427

* This tabulation is a compilation of markings with respect to other races on those ballots on which there were either markings for one presidential candidate or no markings for any presidential candidate.

** Blank consists of markings on a line where there was no presidential candidate.

Note: The number of ballots for Bush and Gore that had a dimple in the presidential race and a dimple in the other races were as follows:

Bush 24

Gore 29

BDO Seidman, LLP

EXHIBIT A-1: THE MIAMI HERALD

State of Florida Precinct Reporting of Undervotes for Punch Card Counties

COUNTY: PalmBeachCounty

PRECINCT: Totals For All Precincts

CANDIDATE NAME**	PRESIDENTIAL RACE								OTHER RACES*		
	DIMPLE	PINPRICK	DETACHED 1 CORNER	DETACHED 2 CORNER	DETACHED 3 CORNER	PUNCHED CLEANLY	NO MARK	TOTAL BALLOTS	DIMPLED	HANGING CHADS	PUNCHED CLEANLY
Blank	51	5	1	11	5	127	0	200	88	48	163
BROWNE/OLIVIER	72	3	0	1	0	2	0	78	65	6	37
BUCHANAN/FOSTER	133	4	0	0	0	1	0	138	54	25	124
BUSH/CHENEY	2599	103	12	14	3	8	0	2769	799	429	2701
GORE/LIEBERMAN	3613	168	10	8	5	46	0	3850	1413	844	3706
HAGELIN/GOLDHABER	11	0	0	0	0	6	0	17	10	0	16
HARRIS/TROWE	17	0	0	0	0	0	0	17	16	2	13
McREYNOLDS/HOLLIS	21	1	0	0	0	1	0	23	19	3	12
MOOREHEAD/LARIVA	52	1	0	0	0	0	0	53	51	4	18
NADER/LADUKE	124	0	2	0	0	8	0	134	104	18	73
Nomark	0	0	0	0	0	0	2236	2236	202	118	1426
PHILLIPS/FRAZIER	96	1	1	0	0	26	0	123	77	9	56
GrandTotals:	6789	286	55	34	13	225	2236	9638	2898	1506	8345

* This tabulation is a compilation of markings with respect to other races on those ballots on which there were either markings for one presidential candidate or no markings for any presidential candidate.

** Blank consists of markings on a line where there was no presidential candidate.

Note: The number of ballots for Bush and Gore that had a dimple in the presidential race and a dimple in the other races were as follows:

Bush 753

Gore 1341

BDO Seidman, LLP

EXHIBIT A-1: THE MIAMI HERALD

State of Florida Precinct Reporting of Undervotes for Punch Card Counties

COUNTY: PascoCounty

PRECINCT: Totals For All Precincts

CANDIDATE NAME**	PRESIDENTIAL RACE								OTHERRACES*		
	DIMPLE	PINPRICK	DETACHED 1 CORNER	DETACHED 2 CORNER	DETACHED 3 CORNER	PUNCHED CLEANLY	NO MARK	TOTAL BALLOTS	DIMPLED	HANGING CHADS	PUNCHED CLEANLY
Blank	11	0	1	0	1	107	0	120	35	40	64
BROWNE/OLIVIER	3	0	0	0	0	0	0	3	1	0	2
BUCHANAN/FOSTER	6	0	0	0	0	0	0	6	3	0	3
BUSH/CHENEY	165	15	1	3	10	8	0	202	94	54	86
GORE/LIEBERMAN	180	9	2	2	4	5	0	202	100	39	90
HAGELIN/GOLDHABER	3	1	0	0	0	0	0	4	4	1	0
HARRIS/TROWE	2	0	0	0	0	0	0	2	2	0	0
McREYNOLDS/HOLLIS	0	1	0	0	0	0	0	1	1	0	0
NADER/LADUKE	10	0	0	0	0	1	0	11	2	0	9
Nomark	0	0	0	0	0	0	1118	1118	84	90	570
GrandTotals:	380	26	4	5	15	121	1118	1669	326	224	824

* This tabulation is a compilation of markings with respect to other races on those ballots on which there were either markings for one presidential candidate or no markings for any presidential candidate.

** Blank consists of markings on a line where there was no presidential candidate.

Note: The number of ballots for Bush and Gore that had a dimple in the presidential race and a dimple in the other races were as follows:

Bush 83

Gore 93

BDO Seidman, LLP

EXHIBIT A-1: THE MIAMI HERALD

State of Florida Precinct Reporting of Undervotes for Punch Card Counties

COUNTY: PinellasCounty

PRECINCT: Totals For All Precincts

CANDIDATE NAME**	PRESIDENTIAL RACE								OTHER RACES*		
	DIMPLE	PINPRICK	DETACHED 1 CORNER	DETACHED 2 CORNER	DETACHED 3 CORNER	PUNCHED CLEANLY	NO MARK	TOTAL BALLOTS	DIMPLED	HANGING CHADS	PUNCHED CLEANLY
Blank	7	2	6	4	3	255	0	281	38	36	277
BROWNE/OLIVIER	3	1	0	0	0	0	0	4	2	2	3
BUCHANAN/FOSTER	3	10	0	0	0	0	0	13	11	0	3
BUSH/CHENEY	464	48	3	17	28	2	0	562	332	194	541
GORE/LIEBERMAN	422	63	8	15	13	3	0	524	294	164	471
HAGELIN/GOLDHABER	22	34	0	0	0	0	0	56	24	16	19
HARRIS/TROWE	1	7	0	0	0	0	0	8	3	0	3
McREYNOLDS/HOLLIS	1	2	0	0	0	0	0	3	2	0	1
MOOREHEAD/LARIVA	0	2	0	0	0	0	0	2	2	0	2
NADER/LADUKE	14	4	0	0	0	0	0	18	16	7	16
Nomark	0	0	0	0	0	0	2687	2687	253	317	1822
PHILLIPS/FRAZIER	1	0	0	0	0	0	0	1	0	0	1
GrandTotals:	938	173	11	36	44	270	2687	4159	977	736	3159

* This tabulation is a compilation of markings with respect to other races on those ballots on which there were either markings for one presidential candidate or no markings for any presidential candidate.

** Blank consists of markings on a line where there was no presidential candidate.

Note: The number of ballots for Bush and Gore that had a dimple in the presidential race and a dimple in the other races were as follows:

Bush 282

Gore 244

BDO Seidman, LLP

EXHIBIT B-1: THE MIAMI HERALD

State of Florida Precinct Reporting of Undervotes for Optical Scan and Manually Counted Counties

COUNTY: Polk County

PRECINCT: Totals For All Precincts

CANDIDATE NAME***	PRESIDENTIAL RACE								OTHER RACES*
	UNDERLINED CANDIDATE	CIRCLED OR MARKED CANDIDATE OR PARTY	CIRCLED OR PARTIALLY FILLED BUBBLE OR ARROW	MARKED X OR CHECKED	ERROR WITH WRITING INSTRUMENT	OTHER**	NO MARK	TOTAL BALLOTS	ERRORS IN OTHER RACES
Blank	0	0	0	0	0	1	0	1	0
BUCHANAN/FOSTER	0	0	0	1	0	1	0	2	1
BUSH/CHENEY	0	1	0	5	3	1	0	10	8
GORE/LIEBERMAN	0	0	2	7	4	2	0	15	10
HAGELIN/GOLDHABER	0	3	0	0	2	0	0	5	0
Nomark	0	0	0	0	0	0	168	168	10
Otherwrite-ins	0	0	0	0	0	12	0	12	0
PHILLIPS/FRAZIER	0	0	0	0	0	1	0	1	0
Grand Totals:	0	4	2	13	9	18	168	214	29

* This tabulation is a compilation of markings considered errors with respect to other races on ballots that had either markings for a presidential candidate or no markings for any presidential candidate.

** Other is comprised primarily of write-ins on the presidential candidate box.

*** Blank consists of markings on a line where there was no presidential candidate.

BDO Seidman, LLP

EXHIBIT B-1: THE MIAMI HERALD

State of Florida Precinct Reporting of Undervotes for Optical Scan and Manually Counted Counties

COUNTY: *Putnam County*

PRECINCT: ' Totals For All Precincts

CANDIDATE NAME	PRESIDENTIAL RACE								OTHER RACES*
	UNDERLINED CANDIDATE	CIRCLED OR MARKED CANDIDATE OF PARTY	CIRCLED OR PARTIALLY FILLED BUBBLE OR ARROW	MARKED X OR CHECKED	ERROR WITH WRITING INSTRUMENT	OTHER**	NO MARK	TOTAL BALLOTS	ERRORS IN OTHER RACES
BUSH/CHENEY	0	0	0	12	2	0	0	14	13
GORE/LIEBERMAN	0	0	1	17	0	1	0	19	18
Nomark	0	0	0	0	0	0	32	32	0
Otherwrite-ins	0	0	0	0	0	2	0	2	0
PHILLIPS/FRAZIER	0	0	0	0	0	1	0	1	0
Grand Totals:	0	0	1	29	2	4	32	68	31

* This tabulation is a compilation of markings considered errors with respect to other races on ballots that had either markings for a presidential candidate or no markings for any presidential candidate.

** Other is comprised primarily of write-ins on the presidential candidate box.

BDO Seidman, LLP

EXHIBIT B-1: THE MIAMI HERALD

State of Florida Precinct Reporting of Undervotes for Optical Scan and Manually Counted Counties

COUNTY: *Santa Rosa County*

PRECINCT: **Totals For All Precincts**

CANDIDATE NAME	PRESIDENTIAL RACE								OTHER RACES*
	UNDERLINED CANDIDATE	CIRCLED OR MARKED CANDIDATE OR PARTY	CIRCLED OR PARTIALLY FILLED BUBBLE OR ARROW	MARKED X OR CHECKED	ERROR WITH WRITING INSTRUMENT	OTHER**	NO MARK	TOTAL BALLOTS	ERRORS IN OTHER RACES
BROWNE/OLIVIER	0	1	0	0	0	0	0	1	0
BUSH/CHENEY	0	6	8	0	3	2	0	19	13
GORE/LIEBERMAN	0	2	3	0	2	1	0	8	7
Nomark	0	0	0	0	0	0	119	119	1
Otherwrite-ins	0	0	0	0	0	6	0	6	1
Grand Totals:	0	9	11	0	5	9	119	153	22

* This tabulation is a compilation of markings considered errors with respect to other races on ballots that had either markings for a presidential candidate or no markings for any presidential candidate.

** Other is comprised primarily of write-ins on the presidential candidate box.

BDO Seidman, LLP

288

EXHIBIT A-1: THE MIAMI HERALD

State of Florida Precinct Reporting of Undervotes for Punch Card Counties

COUNTY: Sarasota County

PRECINCT: Totals For All Precincts

CANDIDATE NAME**	PRESIDENTIAL RACE								OTHER RACES*		
	DIMPLE	PINPRICK	DETACHED 1 CORNER	DETACHED 2 CORNER	DETACHED 3 CORNER	PUNCHED CLEANLY	NO MARK	TOTAL BALLOTS	DIMPLED	HANGING CHADS	PUNCHED CLEANLY
Blank	4	4	5	1	2	65	0	81	5	11	77
BROWNE/OLIVIER	0	2	0	0	0	0	0	2	1	0	1
BUCHANAN/FOSTER	1	3	0	0	0	0	0	4	3	0	2
BUSH/CHENEY	98	39	2	13	11	2	0	165	23	21	141
GORE/LIEBERMAN	78	42	1	7	11	0	0	139	41	23	118
HAGELIN/GOLDHABER	6	5	0	0	0	0	0	11	7	3	7
HARRIS/TROWE	1	13	0	0	0	0	0	14	12	2	5
MOOREHEAD/LARIVA	0	1	0	0	0	0	0	1	1	0	0
NADER/LADUKE	3	1	0	1	2	0	0	7	0	3	6
Nomark	0	0	0	0	0	0	1309	1309	51	87	860
Grand Totals:	191	110	8	22	26	67	1309	1733	144	150	1217

* This tabulation is a compilation of markings with respect to other races on those ballots on which there were either markings for one presidential candidate or no markings for any presidential candidate.

** Blank consists of markings on a line where there was no presidential candidate.

Note: The number of ballots for Bush and Gore that had a dimple in the presidential race and a dimple in the other races were as follows:

Bush 8
Gore 15

BDO Seidman, LLP

289

EXHIBIT B-1: THE MIAMI HERALD

State of Florida Precinct Reporting of Undervotes for Optical Scan and Manually Counted Counties

COUNTY : *Seminole County*

PRECINCT : **Totals For All Precincts**

| CANDIDATE NAME | PRESIDENTIAL RACE | | | | | | | OTHER RACES* |
	UNDERLINED CANDIDATE	CIRCLED OR MARKED CANDIDATE OR PARTY	CIRCLED OR PARTIALLY FILLED BUBBLE OR ARROW	MARKED X OR CHECKED	ERROR WITH WRITING INSTRUMENT	OTHER**	NO MARK	TOTAL BALLOTS	ERRORS IN OTHER RACES
BUSH/CHENEY	0	8	0	15	12	0	0	35	35
GORE/LIEBERMAN	0	13	1	18	17	0	0	49	45
Nomark	0	0	0	0	0	0	131	131	14
Otherwrite-ins	0	0	0	0	0	3	0	3	1
Grand Totals:	0	21	1	33	29	3	131	218	95

* This tabulation is a compilation of markings considered errors with respect to other races on ballots that had either markings for a presidential candidate or no markings for any presidential candidate.

** Other is comprised primarily of write-ins on the presidential candidate box.

BDO Seidman, LLP

EXHIBIT B-1: THE MIAMI HERALD

State of Florida Precinct Reporting of Undervotes for Optical Scan and Manually Counted Counties

COUNTY: **St. Johns County**

PRECINCT: **Totals For All Precincts**

CANDIDATE NAME***	PRESIDENTIAL RACE								OTHER RACES*
	UNDERLINED CANDIDATE	CIRCLED OF MARKED CANDIDATE OR PARTY	CIRCLED OR PARTIALLY FILLED BUBBLE OR ARROW	MARKED X OR CHECKED	ERROR WITH WRITING INSTRUMENT	OTHER**	NO MARK	TOTAL BALLOTS	ERRORS IN OTHER RACES
Blank	0	0	0	1	0	1	0	2	1
BUSH/CHENEY	0	3	7	4	12	1	0	27	21
GORE/LIEBERMAN	0	5	1	13	5	9	0	33	25
NADER/LADUKE	0	3	0	0	0	0	0	3	3
Nomark	0	0	0	0	0	0	265	265	4
Otherwrite-ins	0	0	0	0	0	16	0	16	0
Grand Totals:	0	11	8	18	17	27	265	346	54

* This tabulation is a compilation of markings considered errors with respect to other races on ballots that had either markings for a presidential candidate or no markings for any presidential candidate.

** Other is comprised primarily of write-ins on the presidential candidate box.

*** Blank consists of markings on a line where there was no presidential candidate.

BDO Seidman, LLP

EXHIBIT B-1: *THE MIAMI HERALD*

State of Florida Precinct Reporting of Undervotes for Optical Scan and Manually Counted Counties

COUNTY : *St.LucieCounty*

PRECINCT : **Totals For All Precincts**

CANDIDATE NAME	PRESIDENTIAL RACE								OTHERRACES*
	UNDERLINED CANDIDATE	CIRCLED OR MARKED CANDIDATE OR PARTY	CIRCLED OR PARTIALLY FILLED BUBBLE OR ARROW	MARKED X OR CHECKED	ERROR WITH WRITING INSTRUMENT	OTHER**	NO MARK	TOTAL BALLOTS	ERRORS IN OTHER RACES
BROWNE/OLIVIER	0	2	0	0	0	0	0	2	2
BUCHANAN/FOSTER	0	2	0	0	1	0	0	3	3
BUSH/CHENEY	1	91	2	17	7	1	0	119	111
GORE/LIEBERMAN	0	162	2	18	9	1	0	192	182
NADER/LADUKE	0	8	0	0	1	0	0	9	8
Nomark	0	0	0	0	0	0	193	193	94
Otherwrite-ins	0	0	0	0	0	6	0	6	1
Grand Totals:	*1*	*265*	*4*	*35*	*18*	*8*	*193*	*524*	*401*

* **This tabulation is a compilation of markings considered errors with respect to other races on ballots that had either markings for a presidential candidate or no markings for any presidential candidate.**

** **Other Is comprised primarily of write-ins on the presidential candidate box.**

BDO Seidman, LLP

EXHIBIT A-1: THE MIAMI HERALD

State of Florida Precinct Reporting of Undervotes for Punch Card Counties

COUNTY: SumterCounty

PRECINCT: Totals For All Precincts

CANDIDATE NAME**	PRESIDENTIAL RACE								OTHERRACES*		
	DIMPLE	PIN/PRICK	DETACHED 1 CORNER	DETACHED 2 CORNER	DETACHED 3 CORNER	PUNCHED CLEANLY	NO MARK	TOTAL BALLOTS	DIMPLED	HANGING CHADS	PUNCHED CLEANLY
Blank	3	0	0	0	0	12	0	15	3	1	15
BROWNE/OLIVIER	2	0	0	0	0	0	0	2	1	0	2
BUCHANAN/FOSTER	1	0	0	0	0	0	0	1	0	0	1
BUSH/CHENEY	125	1	6	5	6	0	0	143	51	15	142
GORE/LIEBERMAN	106	1	6	6	7	0	0	126	43	18	124
HAGELIN/GOLDHABER	5	0	1	0	0	0	0	6	5	3	3
NADER/LADUKE	1	0	0	0	0	0	0	1	0	0	1
Nomark	0	0	0	0	0	0	292	292	28	13	239
PHILLIPS/FRAZIER	1	0	0	0	0	0	0	1	0	0	0
Grand Totals:	244	2	13	11	13	12	292	587	131	50	527

* This tabulation is a compilation of markings with respect to other races on those ballots on which there were either markings for one presidential candidate or no markings for any presidential candidate.

** Blank consists of markings on a line where there was no presidential candidate.

Note: The number of ballots for Bush and Gore that had a dimple in the presidential race and a dimple in the other races were as follows:

     Bush 47

     Gore 41

BDO Seldman, LLP

293

State of Florida Precinct Reporting of Undervotes for Optical Scan and Manually Counted Counties

COUNTY: *SuwanneeCounty*

PRECINCT: **Totals For All Precincts**

PRESIDENTIAL RACE

OTHERRACES*

CANDIDATE NAME	UNDERLINED CANDIDATE	CIRCLED OR MARKED CANDIDATE OR PARTY	CIRCLED OR PARTIALLY FILLED BUBBLE OR ARROW	MARKED X OR CHECKED	ERROR WITH WRITING INSTRUMENT	OTHER**	NO MARK	TOTAL BALLOTS	ERRORS IN OTHER RACES
BUSH/CHENEY	0	5	0	0	0	1	0	6	2
GORE/LIEBERMAN	0	3	0	2	1	0	0	6	2
No mark	0	0	0	0	0	0	21	21	1
Other write-ins	0	0	0	0	0	5	0	5	1
Grand Totals:	0	8	0	2	1	6	21	38	6

* This tabulation is a compilation of markings considered errors with respect to other races on ballots that had either markings for a presidential candidate or no markings for any presidential candidate.

** Other is comprised primarily of write-ins on the presidential candidate box.

EXHIBIT B-1: THE MIAMI HERALD

State of Florida Precinct Reporting of Undervotes for Optical Scan and Manually Counted Counties

COUNTY: Taylor County

PRECINCT: Totals For All Precincts

CANDIDATE NAME	PRESIDENTIAL RACE								OTHER RACES*
	UNDERLINED CANDIDATE	CIRCLED OR MARKED CANDIDATE OR PART*	CIRCLED OR PARTIALLY FILLED BUBBLE OR ARROW	MARKED X OR CHECKED	ERROR WITH WRITING INSTRUMENT	OTHER**	NO MARK	TOTAL BALLOTS	ERRORS IN OTHER RACES
BUSH/CHENEY	0	7	1	8	7	1	0	24	14
GORE/LIEBERMAN	0	7	8	9	9	1	0	34	25
Nomark	0	0	0	0	0	0	16	16	5
Otherwrite-ins	0	0	0	0	0	5	0	5	0
PHILLIPS/FRAZIER	0	0	0	1	0	0	0	1	1
Grand Totals:	0	14	9	18	16	7	16	80	45

* This tabulation is a compilation of markings considered errors with respect to other races on ballots that had either markings for a presidential candidate or no markings for any presidential candidate.

** Other is comprised primarily of write-ins on the presidential candidate box.

BDO Seidman, LLP

EXHIBIT B-1: THE MIAMI HERALD

State of Florida Precinct Reporting of Undervotes for Optical Scan and Manually Counted Counties

COUNTY: *Union County*

PRECINCT: Totals For All Precincts

| CANDIDATE NAME | PRESIDENTIAL RACE | | | | | | | | OTHER RACES* |
	UNDERLINED CANDIDATE	CIRCLED OR MARKED CANDIDATE OR PARTY	CIRCLED OR PARTIALLY FILLED BUBBLE OR ARROW	MARKED X OR CHECKED	ERROR WITH WRITING INSTRUMENT	OTHER**	NO MARK	TOTAL BALLOTS	ERRORS IN OTHER RACES
Nomark	0	0	0	0	0	0	21	21	20
Otherwrite-ins	0	0	0	0	0	4	0	4	4
Grand Totals:	0	0	0	0	0	4	21	25	24

* This tabulation is a compilation of markings considered errors with respect to other races on ballots that had either markings for a presidential candidate or no markings for any presidential candidate.

** Other is comprised primarily of write-ins on the presidential candidate box.

BDO Seidman, LLP

296

EXHIBIT B-1: THE MIAMI HERALD

State of Florida Precinct Reporting of Undervotes for Optical Scan and Manually Counted Counties

COUNTY : *Volusia County*

PRECINCT : **Totals For All Precincts**

| CANDIDATE NAME | PRESIDENTIAL RACE | | | | | | | OTHERRACES* |
	UNDERLINED CANDIDATE	CIRCLED OR MARKED CANDIDATE OR PARTY	CIRCLED OR PARTIALLY FILLED BUBBLE OR ARROW	MARKED X OR CHECKED	ERROR WITH WRITING INSTRUMENT	OTHER**	NO MARK	TOTAL BALLOTS	ERRORS IN OTHER RACES
BUCHANAN/FOSTER	0	0	0	0	2	0	0	2	2
BUSH/CHENEY	0	3	2	17	27	1	0	50	46
GORE/LIEBERMAN	0	10	5	17	48	3	0	83	70
NADER/LADUKE	0	1	0	1	1	1	0	4	2
No mark	0	0	0	0	0	0	176	176	3
Otherwrite-ins	0	0	0	1	0	19	0	20	1
Grand Totals:	0	14	7	36	78	24	176	335	124

* This tabulation is a compilation of markings considered errors with respect to other races on ballots that had either markings for a presidential candidate or no markings for any presidential candidate.

** Other is comprised primarily of write-ins on the presidential candidate box.

BDO Seidman, LLP

EXHIBIT A-1: *THE MIAMI HERALD*

State of Florida Precinct Reporting of Undervotes for Punch Card Counties

COUNTY: WakullaCounty

PRECINCT: Totals For All Precincts

| | PRESIDENTIAL RACE | | | | | | | | OTHER RACES* | | |
CANDIDATE NAME	DIMPLE	PINPRICK	DETACHED 1 CORNER	DETACHED 2 CORNER	DETACHED 3 CORNER	PUNCHED CLEANLY	NO MARK	TOTAL BALLOTS	DIMPLED	HANGING CHADS	PUNCHED CLEANLY
BUSH/CHENEY	0	0	0	0	0	2	0	2	0	0	1
GORE/LIEBERMAN	1	0	0	0	0	0	0	1	1	0	0
Nomark	0	0	0	0	0	0	46	46	0	0	40
Grand Totals:	*1*	*0*	*0*	*0*	*0*	*2*	*46*	*49*	*1*	*0*	*41*

* This tabulation is a compilation of markings with respect to other races on those ballots on which there were either markings for one presidential candidate or no markings for any presidential candidate.

Note: The number of ballots for Bush and Gore that had a dimple in the presidential race and a dimple in the other races were as follows:

Bush 0

Gore 1

BDO Seidman, LLP

EXHIBIT B-1: THE MIAMI HERALD

State of Florida Precinct Reporting of Undervotes for Optical Scan and Manually Counted Counties

COUNTY: *Walton County*

PRECINCT: 'Totals For All Precincts

	PRESIDENTIAL RACE							OTHERRACES*
CANDIDATE NAME	UNDERLINED CANDIDATE	CIRCLED OR MARKED CANDIDATE OR PARTY	CIRCLED OR PARTIALLY FILLED BUBBLE OR ARROW	MARKED X OR CHECKED	ERROR WITH WRITING INSTRUMENT	OTHER**	NO MARK	TOTAL BALLOTS	ERRORS IN OTHER RACES
BUSH/CHENEY	0	1	3	4	0	0	0	8	8
GORE/LIEBERMAN	0	0	0	1	1	0	0	2	2
NADER/LADUKE	0	1	0	0	0	0	0	1	1
No mark	0	0	0	0	0	0	94	94	85
Otherwrite-ins	0	0	0	0	0	1	0	1	0
Grand Totals:	0	2	3	5	1	1	94	106	96

* This tabulation is a compilation of markings considered errors with respect to other races on ballots that had either markings for a presidential candidate or no markings for any presidential candidate.

** Other is comprised primarily of write-ins on the presidential candidate box.

EXHIBIT B-1: *THE MIAMI HERALD*

State of Florida Precinct Reporting of Undervotes for Optical Scan and Manually Counted Counties

COUNTY: *Washington County*

PRECINCT: Totals For All Precincts

CANDIDATE NAME	PRESIDENTIAL RACE								OTHER RACES*
	UNDERLINED CANDIDATE	CIRCLED OR MARKED CANDIDATE OR PARTY	CIRCLED OR PARTIALLY FILLED BUBBLE OR ARROW	MARKED X OR CHECKED	ERROR WITH WRITING INSTRUMENT	OTHER**	NO MARK	TOTAL BALLOTS	ERRORS IN OTHER RACES
BROWNE/OLIVIER	0	0	1	0	0	0	0	1	0
BUSH/CHENEY	1	0	2	50	1	0	0	54	0
GORE/LIEBERMAN	4	0	2	28	0	0	0	34	3
MOOREHEAD/LARIVA	0	0	1	0	0	0	0	1	0
NADER/LADUKE	0	0	0	1	0	0	0	1	0
Nomark	0	0	0	0	0	0	116	116	3
Otherwrite-Ins	0	0	0	0	0	1	0	1	0
GrandTotals:	5	0	6	79	1	1	116	208	6

* This tabulation is a compilation of markings considered errors with respect to other races on ballots that had either markings for a presidential candidate or no markings for any presidential candidate.

** Other is comprised primarily of write-ins on the presidential candidate box.

BDO Seldman, LLP

300

EXHIBIT C
The Miami Herald, Knight Ridder and USA Today State of Florida Under Votes with Multiple Markings in the Presidential Race

County		County	
Alachua County	82	Lee County	11
Baker County	3	Liberty County	4
Bradford County	5	Marlon County	15
Brevard County	1	Martin County	2
Broward County	434	Miami-Dade County	523
Charlotte County	6	Monroe County	2
Citrus County	3	Nassau County	3
Clay County	2	Okaloosa County	2
Collier County	40	Oksachobee County	5
Columbia County	4	Orange County	52
Dixie County	1	Osccola County	17
Duval County	226	Palm Beach County	796
Escambia County	12	Pasco County	43
Flagler County	1	Pinellas County	52
Franklin County	2	Polk County	5
Gadaden County	19	Putnam County	2
Hamilton County	4	Santa Rosa County	4
Hardee County	1	Sarasota County	9
Hernando County	1	Seminole County	1
Highlands County	5	St Lucia County	12
Hillsborough County	106	Sumter County	9
Holmes County	40	Sewanee County	1
Indian River County	84	Taylor County	6
Jackson County	1	Volmais County	172
Lafayette County	217	Walton County	1
Lake County	3	Washington County	1
		Total	3,053

A Note from the Publisher

MAY 2001

As THE MIAMI HERALD REPORT goes to press, the *Herald*, Knight Ridder, and *USA Today* are completing a survey of all overvotes in Florida. Many will never reveal the true intent of voters who cast those ballots, but the survey is expected to shed more light on what went wrong during the election.

The results will be available by late spring or early summer 2001. When they are, expanded information on this survey will be available free of charge on a Web site maintained by the publisher, www.overvote.net. Please check it regularly for details.